CONTENTS

INTRODUCTION

What is a festival, anyway? Depending on who you ask, the word might conjure several different images. Dancing till dawn in a muddy field. Gathering with like-minded people in celebration of a shared hobby or interest. Sitting with family and friends for a period of quiet religious reflection. Explore more deeply, and many more expressions of the festival phenomenon reveal themselves: debauched costumed carnivals, mass annual pilgrimages, jingoistic national parades. We even find funerary festivals: howls of collective grief. I have long been fascinated by festivals, and during my career as a travel writer, I've been privileged to attend many of them, close to home and in distant corners of the earth. What I've come to believe is that festivals represent human culture in its most distilled form. They are special times in the calendar when a culture expresses itself more explicitly and deliberately than at any other time of year. As such, they are potent – not only physically, in their sounds and smells, colours and costumes, but symbolically, as illustrations of the motivating forces which underpin human culture.

A Journey Through Festivity

DANIEL STABLES

ICON

Published in 2025 by
Icon Books Ltd, Omnibus Business Centre,
39–41 North Road, London N7 9DP
email: info@iconbooks.com
www.iconbooks.com

ISBN: 978-183773-251-7
ebook: 978-183773-253-1

Typesetting by SJmagic DESIGN SERVICES, India

Printed and bound in the UK

Appointed GPSR EU Representative: Easy Access System Europe Oü, 16879218
Address: Mustamäe tee 50, 10621, Tallinn, Estonia
Contact Details: gpsr.requests@easproject.com, +358 40 500 3575

For my father, Andy Stables

Luminescent, effervescent and life-affirming, festivals represent humanity in all its absurdity, its cracked beauty and its gorgeous variety. They are the birds-of-paradise of human cultural expression.

I chose the title *Fiesta* for this book because in its various meanings – a saint's day, a secular festival, a feast, a party – it is the word I could best think of which comes closest to embodying the many different facets of the festival phenomenon. There is only one Spanish *fiesta* featured in depth in this book, but the many meanings of the word map on to the many types of festival that we find across languages, cultures and borders.

Festivals vary wildly, but most of them centre on collective acts of transcendent ritual, aimed at achieving some kind of union: with history, nation, nature, society at large, something divine. The means by which festivals achieve these ends are as varied, as kaleidoscopic, as human culture itself. In the course of researching this book, I watched the Taoists of Phuket mutilate their faces with skewers and knives, waded through pig blood at an animist funeral in the highlands of Sulawesi, and met the Dark Lord of the Underworld in a Lancashire garden shed. The experience of festivals allows us to celebrate and immerse ourselves in cultural difference and variety, at home and far away – but by examining that variety, in all its diverse madness and with all its apparent contradictions, we can end up perceiving more clearly the similarities and motivations which we all share, across cultures and throughout history.

I wanted to take a journey through festivity in all its forms, so did not limit myself to festivals with huge crowds – although these feature, too – but included smaller-scale rituals and cultural traditions, all rooted in some way in community, rather than just the individual. This is the thing which all festivals share, and which distinguishes them from other kinds of ritual: their communal nature. Festivals are not solitary experiences, but shared ones – what the sociologist Émile Durkheim described as events of 'collective effervescence', in which participants forgo their individual identity for a stronger sense of kinship with that which is greater than themselves.

As I delved more deeply into the festival world, themes emerged: instincts and patterns in cultural behaviour which run through human festivity like golden threads. Some of these – the desire to transcend mortality, the confusion as to why there is something rather than nothing and the need to explain it, the capacity to enter trance states and travel in identity, our enormous facility for tribalism – are part of our human hardware. The festivals themselves, and the cultural worlds which give rise to them, are the software, the operating systems: hugely diverse, always evolving, often indecipherable and infuriating; prone to be corrupted, and, sometimes, to crash and burn.

Certain themes seem to be particularly potent, cropping up in festivals time and time again. One of these is the relationship between humans and the wider natural world, often marked at equinoxes and solstices – festivals which root us in the earth, allowing us to experience the changing seasons and live, as Icelandic Neopagan chieftain Hilmar Örn Hilmarsson put it, 'like a farmer'.

Another recurrent theme is the dissolution of the ego, an objective of many festivals which is achieved through various means: costumery, quiet meditation, chemical transportation into altered states of consciousness. At Turkey's Şeb-i Arûs, pious Sufi dervishes whirl themselves into a state of ecstatic bliss, obliterating the ego in pursuit of union with the divine. Meanwhile, at contemporary music festivals, another kind of ego sacrifice is taking place: communal, deliberate derangement of the senses at the altar of the sound system.

This desertion of the individual ego leads naturally to a lurch towards the collective, which is another characteristic of festivals. From national days to ceremonial team sports, fancy dress parades to acts of collective ritual violence, festivals are vehicles for the creation and consolidation of cultural identity – but always in communal, not individual, ways.

Festivals are best understood through experience, and so this is a travel book, based on first-person narrative accounts. The travel writer is doomed to dilettantism, but I was not just interested in providing superficial accounts of *how* people engage in festivity around the world; I wanted to try and understand *why* we do it in those different ways, too. That's why, throughout the book, I've looked to experts in various fields – psychologists, anthropologists, archaeologists, historians – in the hope that their insight can further illuminate some of the more enigmatic and indecipherable extremes of human behaviour which we encounter as we travel through the twilight of the festival world.

Of these expert insights, the one that feels the most potent is the concept of liminality, the state of being on a threshold. Coined by the folklorist Arnold van Gennep in 1909, and later greatly developed by the anthropologist Victor Turner, liminality is an in-between state, when the normal rules and structures of life are suspended – 'life drawn out of its usual rut', as the Russian philosopher Mikhail Bakhtin described the carnivalesque. Festivals make permissible those extreme reaches of human behaviour which may usually be considered transgressive or downright strange: ecstatic trances, wanton sexuality, mask wearing and criminal damage, dipsomania and ritual mutilation. During which, we become stripped down: our inhibitions dissolve, and something raw and unaffected is revealed.

The anthropologist and folklorist James Frazer saw festivals 'as acts which reproduce the great systems of beliefs and mythologies',[1] and it's true that when we are in their midst, festivals can make life feel mythic and folkloric. We recognise tropes and archetypes in ourselves and each other – even as they are being subverted – and can feel like we are taking part in some primal theatre play, connected by a behavioural wormhole to the distant past, to our ancestors themselves.

But for all their elevated grandiosity, the real beauty of festivals lies in their universality. Every culture has produced them, and everybody has taken part in them. Throughout the year, proceeding alongside our humdrum lives on a parallel track, there is another place, a mirror-world of symbolism and meaning: the festival world. It is always there for us to dip into when we feel the want or the need, which, judging by the packed festival calendars of societies across the world, is often. Our festival selves are unseen dancers, shadow shapes which twirl with our everyday forms, pulling their strings throughout the year; but it is only on those special days, those festival days, that they reveal their true forms, awesome and terrifying and many-eyed, pulsating in vivid technicolour, there to lead us in a tango, hold us close and throw us high, garland us with *mundamalas* and festoon us with streamers; make us remember and forget ourselves all at once.

---

1. https://www.jstor.org/stable/43861801?read-now=1&seq= 2#page_scan_tab_contents

I

BEGIN AGAIN
Rituals of Renewal

SHETLAND, Scotland

'I'm not sure I can do this anymore,' sighed an ashen-faced man as he passed a hip flask to his friend, both shivering against the bone-rattling morning breeze. 'I've been in the boozer for four days. But I'm useless with it in my old age.' He was about 30, but it's a hard life up here in Shetland. On his head was a crocheted Viking helmet, complete with knitted horns, and his open jacket revealed a woolly jumper that said, *Where do old Vikings go? The Norsing home!*

'I know, mate,' his friend said in sympathy. 'But it's only once a year, isn't it? That's how I think about it, anyway.' I recognised this sentiment. It's hard sometimes, but you do it anyway. You suffer for your art. The boozehound's lament.

Many a hard-drinking Viking will have lived and died by just this credo, and their Shetlandic descendants fly the flag of their legacy proudly, not to mention literally – a vermillion banner, printed with the black raven silhouette of the Old Norse kings, flapped above our heads in the cold wind. It was barely eight o'clock in the morning, but the sunrise had yet to announce the new day, and high in the raw January sky the wolf moon shone bright as a coin. A couple of fireworks thundered above. An old man standing next to me jumped out of his skin. 'Ye bastard!' he exclaimed, holding a hand to his heart.

I was standing in a modest crowd of spectators who had dragged themselves out of bed to witness the opening procession of Up Helly Aa, the fire festival which marks the end of winter in the Shetland Islands. The object of our attention – a set of corrugated iron doors on the front of a large shed – clanked and screeched open, revealing a great beast with eyes of fire and a belly of iceberg blue; it groaned forwards on tractor tracks, its vast weight heaved on ropes by a team of struggling young men, looking Lilliputian next to their towering cargo. This was the big reveal of the galley, a Viking longship which is built each year by a team of volunteers only to be ritualistically burnt in the ceremony which would form the festival's centrepiece later that evening.

As the galley creaked into the cold dawn, I got talking to Lyall Gair, a big man with long hair tied back in a black headband and a brown, bushy beard, patched with white. 'The Scandinavian spirit is strong here – I feel Scottish by birth, but Viking by blood,' he said. 'Up Helly Aa is massive for the community of Lerwick. It's the biggest event of our year.' Hogmanay, Christmas and New Year's Eve, he said, pale in comparison. 'We'll have a dram, but that's about it.' Far more than a dram, I was about to discover, heralds the passing of Up Helly Aa, the Shetlandic ritual of renewal.

The galley building starts each October, Lyall said, and is carried out by volunteers who give up their evenings and weekends to lay down blueprints, gather materials, cut wood, and carry out the assembly and painting. All that monumental effort, only to see it all go up in flames at the end of January. Similar ritual sacrifices are carried out at festivals across the world: the Zozobra of Santa Fe, New Mexico, which culminates with an effigy of Zozobra, a personification of distress and anxiety, being set ablaze; and the Festa della Bruna in Matera, Italy, in which an elaborate and expensive festival float is ripped to shreds by frenzied townsfolk. It reminded me of the sand mandala, the Tibetan Buddhist practice of painstakingly creating cosmological artworks from coloured sand only to ritualistically destroy them as a symbol of transience and rebirth. I suggested that the burning of the galley represents renewal for the year ahead, and Lyall agreed – but a listening local suggested another, more prosaic motivation. 'There's fuck all else to do around here all winter,' he said, chuckling and blowing some warmth into his cold, cupped hands.

The galley was dragged up to the road, which bore the name Saint Sunniva Street – Sunniva being the patron saint of Western Norway. Many of the street names in Lerwick have a similarly Scandinavian ring; 96% of all the place names in Shetland, in fact, are derived from Old Norse. From around the corner, along King Haakon Street, came the rattling and jabbering of a marauding Viking mob. This was the Jarl Squad, the chosen few who would lead today's festivities. There were four dozen of them, wearing grey tunics and studded leather breastplates, pinned at the shoulder with turquoise cloaks. Their heads were crowned with round helmets. They carried painted wooden shields in one hand, and in the other they brandished axes inlaid with tendrilled, foliate patterns, which they thrust to the heavens with throaty cries of 'Eh!' and 'Oggy Oggy Oggy!'

At the head of the procession was this year's chief Viking (known as the Guizer Jarl), Richard Moar, a man whose beard alone was enough to qualify him for the role: down to his sternum, almost as wide as it was long; mostly white with a coal-black heart. His outfit differentiated him from the rest: he wore a helmet crowned with large black wings, a cloak of rich burgundy, and fish-like scale armour which glinted in the nascent dawn. Each year, the Guizer Jarl chooses to represent a different historical Viking. Richard Moar chose Haraldr Óláfsson, thirteenth-century King of Mann and the Isles, who died in a shipwreck in the Sumburgh Roost south of Shetland on the way home from his wedding in Norway. When Lyall himself served as Guizer Jarl in 2017, his outfit was modelled after Sweyn Forkbeard Haraldsson, who ruled (for five weeks) as the first Viking King of England in 1014 AD. It's fair to say that the Guizer Jarl's whole life leads up to this moment – they are elected fifteen years in advance by the Up Helly Aa Committee, a revolving board of seventeen volunteers, and spend the intervening years working their way up through a ladder of supporting roles within the Up Helly Aa structure. This year's new electee, a 33-year-old photographer called Scott Goudie, will be taking the reins in 2039.

Most of the procession, physically speaking, were in a similar mould to their leader – large men with fearsome beards. But there was a handful of fairer faces among their number this year, too. For the first time in history, women and girls were being allowed to join the Jarl Squad. Viking culture was taking its first baby steps into the twenty-first century.

In reality, there is nothing authentically Viking about Up Helly Aa. Historians believe that it originated in the mid-1800s, after Shetland's soldiering and seafaring men returned home from the wreckage of the Napoleonic Wars with wild, staring eyes, a newfound aptitude for pyrotechnics, and an appetite to party. They initially channelled this energy into tar barrelling, celebrating each 'Old Christmas' (Twelfth Night – traditionally celebrated on 1 January in Scotland) by lashing wooden barrels together, soaking them in tar, and setting them ablaze.[2] They would then parade them through town all night and the following day, while indulging in what a visiting missionary – who can always be relied upon to provide timorous, goggle-eyed accounts of native festivities – described as 'the blowing of horns, beating of drums, tinkling of old tin kettles, firing of guns, shouting, bawling, fiddling, fifeing, drinking, fighting ... the whole town was in an uproar.'

Lerwick's chattering classes found all this boisterousness distinctly unsavoury, so around the year 1870 a group of intellectuals got together and proposed remodelling the festival as a celebration of Shetland's Nordic heritage. These islands were part of the Kingdom of Denmark until 1472, when they were gifted by King Christian I as part of a dowry for the marriage of his daughter, Margaret, to King James III of Scotland. The Nordic influence abides not only in the place names, but in the wider Shaetlan language – *filsket*, meaning high-spirited or frisky, is one Norse-sounding local word which could appropriately be applied to Up Helly Aa. Then there's the folk music, which is dominated by the Norwegian-style fiddle rather than the Scottish bagpipes, and the folklore, which tells tales of sprites called *trows*, equivalent to Scandinavian trolls,

---

2. This tradition still abides elsewhere, most famously in the Devon town of Ottery St. Mary each Guy Fawkes Night.

who are said to have taught the islanders their tunes by whispering into their ears. Finally, and most verifiably, the Nordic influence on Shetlanders is evident in their DNA, with a 2019 study finding the population to be around 20% Scandinavian in their genetic makeup.[3]

The reformers could not have completely removed the pyromaniac element from Up Helly Aa – that would have been unthinkable – so they refocused it into a torchlit procession, and later the burning of a Viking longship, which would be built and set ablaze every winter as a symbol of renewal for the year ahead and of the driving away of the winter darkness by the return of warmth and light. The masks, which provided opportunities for anonymous violence and other troublemaking, were replaced by Viking costumes, and the rival 'squads' of tar barrellers who once brawled in the streets eventually evolved into the entertainment squads of the modern festival, who tour venues across town throughout the night's celebrations, staging comedy and dance routines and generally making mischief.

The Lerwick event was the original Up Helly Aa, but nowadays it is just the biggest in a series of twelve fire festivals which take place across the towns and islands of the Shetlands between January and mid-March. 'If you get really into it and go to all twelve festivals, you can get a bit swept away by it all,' Lyall had told me, with the air of lived experience. At some of them, the galleys are pushed out to sea once they have been set alight, but at the Lerwick event the inferno is raised in the centre of town, in a children's playpark – a concession to marine

---

3. https://www.pnas.org/doi/10.1073/pnas.1904761116

conservation, perhaps, or, in a rare sign of the influence of mainland Scotland, a blazing expression of Calvinist rage towards the very concept of children having fun.[4]

As a general rule, however, Up Helly Aa is anything but puritanical. I followed the procession as it joined up with the galley and made its merry march through the streets of the town, which had been closed off to traffic for the day. I and the rest of the watching crowd followed the procession into the Toll Clock shopping centre, where this horde of lusty Vikings was suddenly surrounded by shopfronts selling postcards and mugs, and decorative wooden boards saying things like 'Coffee is my morning wine!' and 'I don't need a man, I need a bikini and a tan!'

The Jarl Squad stood marching on the spot, their armour clanking a metallic rhythm, and broke into song:

In distant lands, their raven-flag flew like a blazing star;
And foreign foemen, trembling, heard their battle-cry afar;
And they thundered o'er the quaking earth, those mighty
   men of war;
The waves are rolling on.[5]

They finished the song to rapturous applause and came down like wolves upon rows of makeshift tables which were heaving with the weight of bottles of beer, wine and whisky; they helped themselves greedily, as did any stewards and spectators within arm's reach. A large black dog, which had

---

4. Religion is one area of Shetland life where the Scandinavian influence is less prominent. In fact, even more Shetlanders than mainlanders, as a proportion of the population, are members of the Calvinist Church of Scotland.
5. J.J. Haldane Burgess, *The Up Helly Aa Song.*

been barking madly throughout the singing, tore from its owner's grasp and knocked out the leg of one of the tables, sending bottles crashing to the ground in a roiling wave of foam and green glass. It was quarter to nine in the morning.

An appetite for chaos is characteristic of the festival world, and the turning of the year seems as good a time as any to descend into madness. Thailand celebrates Songkran (held on 13 April) with nationwide water fights to represent ritual cleansing ahead of the turning of the lunar year. The party lasts a week, and during this heightened time, arrests for public indecency skyrocket, traffic accidents soar on the slick roads, and many participants find themselves beginning the new year by getting well acquainted with the toilet bowl, the cumulative effect of gallons of alcohol curdling with accidentally imbibed Bangkok *khlong* water. The Danes, for their part, come over all Greek on New Year's Eve, smashing unwanted plates and mugs against their neighbours' front doors. Neapolitans, meanwhile, let go of the cares of the old year by hurling unwanted crockery, furniture and even household appliances off their balconies into the street below.

This kind of thing has a long and distinguished history. In medieval Europe, members of the clergy, no less, would engage each 1 January in a bacchanalian rite known as the Feast of Fools, which saw the Church hierarchy subverted as a peasant or minor cleric assumed the title of Lord of Misrule (known in Scotland, rather brilliantly, as the Abbot of Unreason). They would oversee a series of festivities described, in a condemnatory letter from the Theological Faculty of Paris in 1445, as follows:

Priests and clerks may be seen wearing masks and monstrous visages at the hours of office. They dance in the choir dressed as women, panders or minstrels. They sing wanton songs. They eat black puddings at the horn of the altar while the celebrant is saying mass. They play at dice there. They cense with stinking smoke from the soles of old shoes. They run and leap through the church, without a blush at their own shame. Finally they drive about the town and its theatres in shabby traps and carts; and rouse the laughter of their fellows and the bystanders in infamous performances with indecent gestures and verses scurrilous and unchaste.[6]

The British are particularly good at marking the turn of the year in eccentric and eye-catching ways. A few weeks before my trip to Shetland, I had travelled to the Welsh border town of Chepstow, which was marking the new year with its annual Mari Lwyd celebration. This strange ritual exhibits the very best qualities of British cultural tradition: obscure origins, baffling practices, and a healthy dose of folk horror. It goes like this. A horse's skull is decorated: festooned with ribbons, crowned with a mane of flowers and ivy, its eye sockets stuffed with baubles, bike lights, or something similarly round and colourful. It is then affixed to a pole, covered by a bedsheet, and worn as a costume by an individual who, traditionally, would go from door to door at sundown, accompanied by a group of men, begging for food and drink. This would play out in the form of a kind of prototypical rap battle, with the horse demanding entry to the house through the medium of poetry; the householder would then respond with a verse of their own, explaining why they couldn't let them

---

6. *Carnival in Religion: The Feast of Fools in France* by Ingvild Salid Gilhus.

in. This would continue until one of the parties could think of no further riposte. If that was the horse, they would move on to the next house; but if it was the householder left speechless, that was the horse's cue to charge inside the premises, eat and drink everything in sight, terrorise children and the elderly, and generally cause chaos.

'They tend not to go door-to-door anymore, though,' a woman called Yvette told me in Chepstow's Three Tuns pub on the morning of the event. 'They'd probably get thumped.' Instead, she said, Mari Lwyds make a ceremonial visit to the door of Chepstow Castle, before facing off in a ritualised Welsh–English border ceremony on the town bridge. Each Mari is accompanied by a squad of Morris dancers, who give performances at locations across town throughout the day while their associated horse-demon torments the gathered crowd.

Yvette was a member of one such Morris squad, known as the Widders. She was wearing a black outfit covered in rags of purple, crowned with a black top hat, and had a large purple handprint painted on her face, obscuring her features. Her fellow Widders, who had packed out the pub on this weekday morning, were dressed similarly, some having chosen to accessorise with steampunk goggles or gothic capes; one man wore a T-shirt emblazoned with an inverted cross. They looked halfway between Morris dancers and Hells Angels, which is no surprise, considering they were formed by a biker gang at the GuilFest music festival in 2001.

The Widders' rags are a common element in costumes related to traditions of guising, the practice of going door-to-door asking for food – a kind of ritualised begging also seen at Halloween and Día de los Muertos. 'Begging was illegal in the past, so the costumes originated as a way of people hiding their identity,' Yvette said. The origins of the Mari Lwyd itself, though, are far harder to pinpoint. Although its chaotic atmosphere, skeletal equine aspect, and history of being suppressed by the Christian authorities give it a decidedly paganistic feel, the earliest mention of it dates to as recently as 1800.

'The Mari Lwyd is just weird,' Yvette said, with some understatement. 'I think it means Grey Mare – like the pale horse from Celtic mythology. But it was probably just drunk Welsh people who found it hilarious; a rapping horse coming into your house and drinking your beer.' The association with Morris dancing is even more recent, probably arising in the Victorian era, and equally difficult to ascribe. 'Morris dancers tend to just go where the beer is,' Yvette explained cheerfully.

A poster in the pub window depicted the head of a Mari Lwyd, grinning broadly, with the slightly threatening exhortation: *You're cold. She's cold. LET HER IN.* There is something vaguely lascivious about the Mari Lwyd. They are physically imposing, for one thing – usually commandeered by men, who hold the huge horse's skull above their own head height, swooping and snapping its jaws in the faces of innocent bystanders – and with their white lacy veils, their hideous decomposed grins, their tinsel and their baubles and their ivy, they resemble an equine corpse bride reanimated for one night only to barrel through Wales in pursuit of a partner, willing or otherwise, for their weird wedding night. Or maybe that's just my imagination.

After their chaotic procession through the Toll Clock shopping centre, the Jarl Squad were diverted for the next few hours – first by a civic reception in the Town

Hall, then by an afternoon spent touring local schools and hospitals. With some time to explore, I walked through the streets of Lerwick, where it was clear that the Scandinavian influence on Shetland extends to the architecture. Sitting brightly amid the buildings of grubby, darkened limestone were colourful, Nordic-looking houses, built from timber or corrugated iron and painted fire-engine red or ultramarine blue. The whole scene brought to mind a cross between Reykjavík and Glossop.

The wind had picked up significantly. I collected my rental car and embarked on a wobbling, weatherbeaten drive to my hotel in the village of Veensgarth ('Old Norse: Vikingsgarðr, Viking's Farm', the road sign informed me). The wind was blowing so hard there were waves on the loch at Tingwall, the site of Shetland's first parliament. On the road, the gale was pushing puddles uphill; in the fields, Shetland ponies hid behind hay bales, bracing their stocky frames against the wind, their manes whipped into gravity-defying mohicans.

That afternoon, I had arranged a meeting with Jolene Garriock, a tour guide originally from the west side of Shetland who now lives in the Tingwall Valley, not far from where I was staying. I met Jolene in a seafront café called Fjarå, the name itself a nod to the Nordics – 'fjara' is Icelandic for beach.

'People come to Shetland expecting to find tartan and kilts, but what they find is Fair Isle knitwear and Vikings,' Jolene said. She herself was wearing a dark blue Fair Isle jumper, a style named for the southernmost Shetland island. Around its neck was a band of geometric patterns – zig-zags, crosses and diamonds in red, white and green – virtually identical, to my untrained eye at least, to the traditional knitwear of Iceland or Norway. 'We've only belonged to Scotland for just over 500 years; clan culture never made it here, and we weren't involved with the Jacobite Rising,' Jolene said. 'To this day, in Shetland you're more likely to put your flag up on the 17th of May for Norwegian national day than you are for St. Andrew's.'

Much of this is down to geography; Shetland has long served as a crossroads for the culture and trade of northern Europe, sitting in between Britain, Norway, Denmark, America, Iceland, Greenland, and the Faroe Islands. Certainly, it feels far away from Scotland – Jolene told me that when she was studying at university in Edinburgh, she met many mainlanders who couldn't place Shetland on a map or even seemed unaware that it was an offshore archipelago. 'One girl asked me if my boyfriend had seen me off at the train station when I came down for the new term,' she said, with a roll of her eyes. 'Ultimately, though, Shetland has a mixed culture. We don't identify with Scotland, but we don't quite identify as Scandinavian, either. We're our own thing.'

Jolene echoed Lyall's comments to me from earlier that morning, that Up Helly Aa was the biggest event in Shetland's calendar. 'Hogmanay's dying in Shetland; nobody makes an effort for that anymore. Christmas is still big, although religion's on the decline. But it's the same across most of the UK – Christmas has grown arms and legs and become its own thing. Most kids start off celebrating it without knowing why or where it came from.'

The most prominent festivals in the calendar are often so entrenched that most of us take them for granted; they come and go without us stopping to consider their origins, or why we celebrate them. In its celebration of the return of light and warmth amid the darkness of winter, Up Helly Aa reflects some of the same perennial festival themes as Christmas, and the pre-Christian celebrations of Yule which preceded it. But these motivations seem more explicit in modern festivals like Up Helly Aa, which allow us to see more clearly that although their manifestations may change, there are underlying motivations running through human festivity, across cultures and throughout the ages, like veins of ore.

Evening drew a veil over the short day. Crowds had begun to pack out the roads – around 5,000 people, according to official estimates – and all around me was a cosmopolitan chorus, with accents from England, Italy, America, even Australia interspersing the lilting Shetlandic chatter which emanated from most of the crowd. The streetlights had all been extinguished, to better allow the procession's torchlight and the blazing galley to illuminate the dark night. A flare blazed a molten trail through the evening sky, heralding the start of the procession down King Harald Street. Just like the Vikings of old, you smelt them before you saw them – but this time it was not the odour of rotten seal blubber and mead breath, but the bittersweet smell of kerosene, blown from their torches on the northern wind. There were some 900 torchbearers in the procession; at the front were the Jarl Squad, still in full voice, still crying 'Eeeehhh!' and 'Oggy Oggy Oggy!', the cumulative effect of the day's libations beginning to show itself in red eyes, slurred words, and sloppy grins. Behind them, making up most of the procession, were members of the 47 other squads who would be providing the evening's entertainments. They were already bringing an atmosphere of misrule to proceedings, many of them in drag, wearing French maids' or nuns'

outfits complete with huge fake breasts. One man was dressed as a can of Tennent's lager; everyone around him was drinking it, too, holding beers in one hand while their torches hung, often a little laxly, in the other, sparks flying off them into the faces of the assembled crowd, who were arrayed right up along the side of the road without any barriers to keep them out of harm's way. One torchbearer started flapping about – his red, bushy beard had caught light from a wandering spark. His neighbour pointed and laughed, poured a full can of beer over him, and the march went on without missing a step.

At the centre of it all was the galley, being pulled along on a truck bed like a carnival float. After a lap of the town centre, the procession entered the playpark, pulling the galley in their wake. It was manoeuvred into the centre of the field and doused in paraffin. The sound of bagpipes, fiddles and drums rose as a band struck up a tune, and the 900 torchbearers of the procession, beginning with the Jarl Squad, approached the galley in turn and hurled their torches into its belly. A small fire flared in the centre of the boat around the heap of criss-crossed torches, which grew and grew until after fifteen minutes or so the blaze reached some kind of terminal velocity, eliciting gasps of excitement from the watching crowd as the dragon's head and tail were swallowed by flames.

The wind was bitterly cold, but it was a double-edged sword – on its icy back were carried currents of warm bonfire air, as well as showers of sparks, which we in the crowd turned our faces away from in unison. Parents stood with young children on their shoulders, asking them, 'Can you see it? Has the head gone yet? What about the flag?' – and right on cue, the flames climbed higher up the mainmast, and the flapping flag, whose raven markings had been silhouetted against the background of smoke and firelight, was gathered into the blaze; at the same time there was a great crack as the dragon's neck gave way, and the head and the mast collapsed inwards together into the belly of the beast. The crowd applauded and began to dissipate – it was growing colder, and they had places to be, with the promise of drink and dancing, soup and sandwiches, and long hours of revelry.

After the burning of the galley is complete, Up Helly Aa moves into twelve venues across town, known as halls, for an all-night jamboree. Shetlanders like a party, or a *foy*, to use the Shaetlan word, which originated as a term for a feast held by a boat's crew when the fishing season was over. The halls are organised and paid for by the community, and take place mainly in repurposed community venues, like primary schools and leisure centres. Tickets are like gold dust, particularly those which grant entry to the most hallowed and glamorous of the events, which is held in Lerwick's stately Town Hall. I had been badgering every local I met to try and find me a ticket, and had been directed through several different channels to an enigmatic woman named Deborah who was involved with the Town Hall event. She was very responsive to my enquiries, and kindly offered to help me find a ticket, although her messages, infused with Shaetlan words, betrayed a consistent and curious fixation.

'Will ask Dave about ticket da night … plenty sandwiches to make today' read one; 'Think av got dee a ticket … 60 sandwiches made this morning already!' read another. She seemed to be a woman overcome by a mania for making sandwiches, but she still found the time to do me a favour, and before I had taken my place in the crowd to watch the galley burning, I had followed Deborah's instructions to visit Harry's Department Store, down on Lerwick's waterfront, where a hall ticket – a Town Hall ticket, no less – had been reserved in my name for the princely sum of £40 (cash).

Clutching my ticket, I hurried through the chill towards the Town Hall, where a warm, glowing halo-light shrouded the heavy wooden door. I checked in my coat and bag of cans (the halls are a bring-your-own-booze affair) and climbed the stone stairs into the main hall, where rows of chairs had been lined up on either side of the room. It felt like being inside an upturned galley; the ceiling was huge and vaulted, panelled in wood, and the oak floor was so well-polished that it cast back blurred impressions of everything above it. Reflected most prominently were the Town Hall's glorious stained-glass windows, which told in vibrant technicolour of Shetland's Nordic past: there was Magnus Erlendsson, ruler of the islands in the twelfth century, and Harald Hardrada, who a hundred years before had invaded England and died in spurious glory at the Battle of Stamford Bridge, an arrow in his throat, apparently armour-less and consumed by the sound and fury of the *berserkergang*, the frantic rage-trance which propelled the most potent Norse warriors.

There were more than a few berserkers in attendance tonight, too, forged in the crucible of the day's long hours of festivity. I saw a scuffle break out in the queue for the cloakroom, where two behelmeted warriors almost came to blows as they wrestled for ownership of a box of cheap wine. Lots of people were engaging in the kind of enthusiastic slanging match which is ostensibly banterous, but unmistakably pregnant with the potential for violence. Most of the energy, though, was channelled into cheerful shouting, full-throated singing, and, in particular, the dancing of spirited jigs on the polished floor. The alcoholic sloppiness which was blurring everybody's speech and movements seemed to vanish as soon as they stepped onto the dancefloor, where they exhibited the nimble grace of penguins entering the water; they spun in pairs and then in a wider figure-of-eight as they swapped partners, elegantly playing out moves which Shetlanders learn from their first years of primary school.

Setting the tempo, on a stage at the end of the room, was the band: two fiddlers, a drummer, and a tiny, perfectly round accordionist, who seemed engaged in a Sisyphean struggle against his huge-looking instrument, crushed beneath it like an overzealous bench-presser – but his fingers never stopped playing, as he rocked back and forth in the blue, sacral glow being cast from the stained-glass window above his head.

The whole ensemble seemed themselves to be seized by the berserker spirit, fingers moving at a million miles an hour, jerking in an epileptic dance, propelled by the fear of it all coming to an end. 'This one's a sleep-fighter!' roared one of the fiddlers as he introduced a new reel to howls of approval from the baying crowd. At one point a guest accordionist was welcomed onto the stage, with the introduction, 'Please welcome, all the way from Arbroath, Wayne Robertson!' An elderly woman in the seat behind me turned to her neighbour and said, 'Arbroath! Fancy that.'

For the most part it was wholesome, but people-watching revealed glimpses of lechery – young men were asking girls to dance and then, after repeated rejections, trying to drag them by their arms to the dancefloor; others, who had found a partner, were leaning in, mid-jig, for uninvited kisses. This year's festival had been the first in which women and girls were allowed to be members of the Jarl Squad, while the previous year had been the first in which they were allowed to participate as members of the other squads, which take part in the procession and tour the halls at night giving performances. Prior to that, women had been limited to contributing as organisers and hostesses, stitching uniforms, and preparing and serving Himalayan mountains of sandwiches. In 2019, then-Member of the Scottish Parliament for the Highlands and Islands, Maree Todd, claimed that the exclusion of girls and women from the proccedings was 'harmful' and 'indefensible'. Even now that women were allowed to be involved, I saw hardly any in the squads apart from the daughter and three nieces of Guizer Jarl Richard Moar, who had been accompanying him in the main procession.

Far more common were men in drag, a team of whom entered the hall now, to widespread applause – the French maids I had seen in the torchlit procession earlier. This was the first of the evening's entertainment squads, 47 of which would be gracing us with their presence over the next twelve hours or so, as they made their merry way around all twelve of the halls across town. There were around a dozen maids in this squad, and just as many others who were dressed as insects, in horrible beige skinsuits with fabric feelers wobbling out of their heads. The dancefloor cleared, and a stage set was hurriedly assembled: a couple of camp beds, and a whiteboard hung with a picture of the Eiffel Tower. The squads go round the halls performing skits, some of which are satirical in nature – this one was a send-up of the bedbug epidemic which was then ravaging the hotel rooms of Paris. The bugs lay down on skateboards and pushed themselves at speed around the dancefloor, grasping at the legs of spectators in the front row, while the maids followed them in hot pursuit, cackling wildly and pushing at them with brooms, like a deranged match of hurling imagined by William Burroughs. The crowd roared with laughter.

References to death and disease fly particularly well with festival crowds. The plague doctor mask has been a fixture of Venice Carnival for centuries, Halloween revels in imagery of skeletons, zombies, and rotting flesh, and the ghost festivals of East Asia have turned folk tales about the afterlife into a whole genre of festivity. A general state of frenzied hedonism has permeated nearly every festival I have attended in the years after the Covid-19 pandemic, since which festivity has returned with a fresh urgency, here to restore vitality in the face of pestilence and death. The festival spirit is half memento mori, half wild celebration of life – which, after all, are two sides of the same coin.

As I was pondering this fact, minding my own business, I felt someone's gaze burning a hole into me. A large Viking had taken up residence in the seat next to mine, and, in between grunts and dribbles, had asked me that simple question which, in circumstances such as these, can feel spiked with threat: 'Where you from?'

I told him.

'Hmm,' he grunted, and nodded, as if this was a piece of information which explained everything. 'You look English.' He meant this as an insult. His breath smelled of mutton and onions, and the legacy of an egg and cress sandwich bobbed on the hairs of his beard like dewdrops on wild grass.

This did not stoke my appetite, but I needed a reason to leave, so I left the boor raving to himself and headed downstairs to the dining hall, where I realised for the first time why Deborah had been so preoccupied by her task of food preparation. Tables groaned under the weight of sandwiches, rolls, baps and barms – hundreds, if not thousands, of them – while great vats bubbled and popped with gallons of steaming tatty soup, a hearty pottage made with onions, potatoes, and swede. To accompany the soup were servings of Shetland's national dish, reestit mutton – the meat of older sheep which is salted for several weeks and hung up to dry until it's so impenetrably stiff you'd need a diamond drill to bore through it. I took a portion and gnawed on a corner, almost cracking a tooth in the process. 'That's how you know it's the good stuff,' said a proud local standing next to me. 'So hard you could hammer a nail into it.'

I stopped by the cloakroom to pick up another can from my bag before heading back upstairs to watch some more of the squad performances. They weren't all as searingly political as the Parisian bedbug satire; some of the squads phoned it in a bit and just danced to an ABBA medley in light-up shoes or did a jig to Darude's 'Sandstorm' while dressed in Braveheart costumes. Other skits lampooned local current affairs in ways which went over my head – one of them, featuring men dressed as trees who fell to the earth to be replaced by tall, white figures with spinning propellers on their hats, seemed to be protesting the Viking Wind Farm, a huge onshore energy project which was currently under construction on Shetland's main island.

The Jarl Squad swung in around 4am, holding it together with varying degrees of success, although it was admirable they were still standing at all. Some were basically non-verbal by this point; others were vaguely vocalising the same tunes they had been singing earlier, but the lyrics had by now degenerated into wordless syllables which dribbled spittle onto their Viking beards. The flesh was willing, but the spirit had deserted them; the energy levels were as high as ever, but with red eyes and frothing mouths, feet marching on autopilot, and winged helmets all skew-whiff, they resembled a crew of lobotomy patients set loose in a fancy dress shop. The torches were lit, but no one was home. They would be continuing in this vein until 9am.

One of the squads was a group of men dressed as Wombles, who bowled in wearing expensive-looking costumes to the tune of 'The Wombling Song'. All very wholesome, you might think, except that by this time the long day and night were beginning to take their toll, and the Wombles, alcoholically incapable of sticking to their rehearsed dance moves, were careening about the hall like Mr Blobby-style agents of chaos, stumbling into seats and knocking plates of sandwiches out of people's hands, slipping arse over tit on spilt drinks on the polished floor. The soundtrack assumed a horrific quality – lyrical snippets about litter-picking and wombling free, crackling through the PA amid the screams of disturbed spectators. A Womble bowled past me; through the costume's mesh face covering, I caught a glimpse of its wearer's eyes, rolling back in his head.

The party had hours left to run, but I sensed that it was time for me to leave. I took my coat from the cloakroom and nodded a goodnight to the doorman, who could scarcely conceal his disgust that someone would want to leave the party after barely eleven hours. I walked back to my hotel. Sunrise was still hours off; my breath blew fluffy clouds into the dark morning air. The streets were mostly deserted, but I saw the odd wandering soul, lost on their way home or in vain pursuit of something to eat – a woman was slapping on the darkened window of the Happy Haddock fish and chip shop, screaming, 'Let me in! Or I'll shove a catfish up your arse!'

I walked along the waterfront. Just ahead of me, amid the blackness, moved a large shape, struggling to support itself against a lamppost. I walked a little closer, squinted, and realised it was a Womble – was that their wise old patriarch, Uncle Bulgaria, grappling with his costume's front zip? I wasn't sure; I looked away. There are certain events which signal the unequivocal death of childhood, and the irredeemable loss of innocence; seeing Uncle Bulgaria with sick in his beard, relieving himself against a lamppost, would doubtless be one of them.

In its symbolism of fire and ash, its marking of the end of winter and the return of warmth and light, and its frenzied, hedonistic desire to rip things up and start again, Up Helly Aa is an exemplar of a genre: the festivals of rebirth. In the western world, we resolve to be fitter, stronger, and kinder each 1 January, telling ourselves that the turning over of the year is a moment potent enough to kickstart in our bodies and souls some profound process of insect metamorphosis. The bars are quiet, and the gyms are packed – for a week or two, anyway.

There is no rebirth without death, no renewal without destruction – and the burning of the galley at Up Helly Aa has parallels with festivals of fire and fury across the world. Long before the Gunpowder Plot of 1605 made it socially acceptable – actively encouraged, in fact – for British schoolchildren to fashion and burn effigies of Catholics each 5 November, bonfires had been burning across Britain at this time of year to mark Samhain, the pre-Christian autumn festival. Pagans often mark Samhain by writing down on paper things they wish to release – worries or the names of lost loved ones – and casting them into the cleansing fire. In Iran, people mark the beginning of each Nowruz (New Year) with the Zoroastrian practice of Charshanbeh Suri (Scarlet Wednesday), in which bonfires are raised, and people jump over the flames as an act of purification.

Together with bonfires go fireworks. Invented in ancient China, they have long been associated with the power to scare away evil spirits and continue to fulfil this symbolic role in Lunar New Year celebrations. In Japan, fire festivals are similarly believed to banish evil spirits. The Oniyo Fire Festival, held each January in the Fukuoka city of Kurume, sees hundreds of men dressed only in loincloths carry vast flaming bamboo torches around Daizenji Tamatergu shrine, showering the crowd with sparks. It is considered highly auspicious for one to singe a hole through your clothes – or, even better, to burn a hole in your skin. The Yasothon Rocket Festival, meanwhile, marks the start of the wet season in Thailand and Laos by heralding the coming rains with thousands of bamboo bottle rockets, turning the skies into an ocean of smoke which swirls above cross-dressing parades, folk dances and the ingestion of inadvisable quantities of Laotian rice whisky.

The hangover, indeed, is a typical feature of the festival of rebirth. Many of us can relate to beginning a new year in this way, and while it often seems regrettable in the moment, there is something fitting about it – the act of bodily destruction followed by blessed renewal; the return of invigorated appetites; perhaps, even, a resolution never to drink again. But even if the new year does not provide such a moment of profound personal awakening, it can still be a time of symbolic rebirth, a chance to shake off the snow from your shoulders and travel a little lighter into a brave new dawn. A time to begin again.

2

MASQUERADE
Travels in Identity

VENICE, Italy

Jan Morris memorably described Venice in the summertime as 'one great itchy palm'. Venice during Carnival is another affliction entirely: a full-blown case of delirium tremens, quivering adrift in the back of a gondola, wearing nothing but 'I Heart Venice' boxer shorts and a plague doctor mask. What day is it? It doesn't matter – it's Carnival time. And as an old saying goes around these parts, '*A Carnevale, ogni scherzo vale*.' At Carnival, anything goes.

Venice Carnival can trace its roots back to 1162, when residents gathered in Piazza San Marco to dance in celebration of a Venetian military victory over the nearby city of Aquileia. It was not until the seventeenth and eighteenth-century heyday of the Venetian Republic, however, that Carnival reached its apogee: a Dionysian riot of gambling, theatre, and sexual freedom in the weeks leading up to Lent. Then as now, the festival wore an expressionless face: the city became a gallery of blank masks, used to disguise the wearers in their licentiousness.

'In the days of the Venetian Republic, society was very strictly divided into social classes,' tour guide Luisella Romeo explained as we fought through the crowds of the Castello district, my arteries bristling at the thick smell of *fritelle* – Carnival doughnut balls, fried in pork fat and filled with raisins and pine nuts. 'The aristocratic families only wanted to preserve their wealth, which meant having as few marriages and children as possible. Many were sent to be monks or nuns; those who married were not marrying the ones they loved. It was an economic choice.' The masked soirées of Carnival provided momentary opportunities for escape from this social straitjacket. 'Carnival was a time of rebellion and transgression,' Luisella said, 'but this came at a risk to your reputation. That's why everybody wore the same outfit: a long black wool mantle, a beaver-felt tricorn hat, and a plain white mask, called a *bauta*. Underneath could be anyone: a married man or woman, a cardinal, a nun.'

Costumery, to one degree or another, was all around us, illustrating in vivid technicolour the extent to which Carnival wear has evolved beyond its homogenous origins. Many people had opted for nothing more than a token eye mask, purchased on the cheap from one of the many stalls which dot the city's *campi* at this time of year, the rest of their bodies cloistered from the February chill in puffer jackets and woollen coats. Others, though, had gone for it hammer and tongs. With every few steps we passed another denizen of the *commedia dell'arte*, filtered through a psychedelic prism: Harlequins wearing frozen grins and patchwork doublets, arms sprouting from their hats like the petals of a corpse flower; Innamorati decked out in feathers and fans like mad masked peacocks, posing patiently for photographs with little crowds of admirers.

Where once the purpose of a Venetian mask was to look the same as everybody else, the opposite is now true; there is even a 'Most Beautiful Mask' competition held each year by the Carnival authorities. The essential motivation for wearing a mask remains the same, however: put one on and you become somebody else.

Our eyes are often drawn to meet the gaze of masks, staring out through shop windows, down from longhouse walls, or up from neatly arrayed market stalls. Apart from anything else, they make fantastic souvenirs: generations of artistry, festivity and ritual, all wrapped up in a little piece of wood which fits neatly in your hand luggage. But there is something deeper there than the merely decorative. The same human tendency to see faces where they are not – in Martian mountains and Rorschach splodges, in charred toast and frosted windows – makes it impossible not to ascribe a certain consciousness to anything face-shaped, with human eyes, nose and mouth, or holes where those things would be. Masks imply the existence of the masked, of some kind of consciousness or agency; even a never-worn one can seem to assume a personality of its own. More than anything else, the very existence of masks suggests something tantalising: that we can be transported, for a short time at least, into another identity.

Ceremonial mask wearing seems to have arisen in every known human society, and far pre-dates the evolution of written language. In the vanishingly unlikely event that you should ever be accused of a crime among the Tolai people of Papua New Guinea, you may be amused to find yourself before members of the Duk-Duk secret society, elaborately costumed in a leafy outfit and a conical mask, resembling an emu wearing a dunce's hat. That smirk would soon be wiped off your face, however, once the wearers had, via a frenzied dance, invoked the essence of the *duk-duk* or the *tubuan* (male and female spirits respectively, although the mask wearers are always men), aggressive spirits whose job is to serve as judge, jury, and executioner – with a licence to kill, should such a punishment fit the crime. Burning down the perpetrator's house is another tool within the remit of the Duk-Duk (or was; the practice has been on the decline since the early twentieth century). Once they have taken off their costume and returned to normal life, no trace of their actions haunts the mask wearers. It wasn't them, after all – they were wearing a mask. They were somebody else.

War is another realm which has laid bare the potent transformative power of the mask, far beyond the merely defensive functions of a helmet. The cosplaying berserkers I had seen at Up Helly Aa had taken their cues from the warriors of the Old Norse tradition – from where we get the English word 'berserk' – who are often depicted wearing bear or wolf masks, the animals from which they were said to derive their ferocious power. The sagas depict these warriors as if possessed by wild beasts, fighting savagely, howling at the heavens, even biting chunks out of their shields. The verb form for 'going berserk' was 'hamask' – literally, to 'change form'.

Masks have also veiled the horrific effects of war. The trenches of the First World War protected soldiers' bodies but left their heads exposed to the whims of bullets, mortars, and flying shrapnel. Almost unbelievably, it was only in 1915, after Latvian inventor John Leopold Brodie invented the steel Brodie helmet, that soldiers from most armies were given protective headgear; they had fought the first year of the most destructive war in history wearing hats of leather, cloth, or felt (the German *Pickelhaube*, a leather helmet with steel inserts, was the only thing close to an exception). Brodie's innovations saved many lives, but this also meant that there were many more people left disfigured by head injuries which previously would have killed them. In post-war France, facially disfigured servicemen were known as *gueules cassées* – 'broken faces' – and, in an age before plastic surgery, were equipped with prosthetic masks, designed individually to fill in the parts missing or disfigured – false eyes, noses, lips, and moustaches.

The medicinal power of masks has been keenly felt in societies throughout history and across the world. The Haudenosaunee First Nations people in North America include among their number a group of medicinal healers called the First Face Society, who drive away pestilence and disease while wearing masks made of basswood, carved with bent, broken noses. The mask makers move through the forest until they feel the call of a certain tree, in which they will carve their mask while the wood is still alive; only when the carving is complete is the tree cut down and the mask freed from the wood. Recent years have seen an effort by the Haudenosaunee to repatriate masks from museums, including Harvard University's Peabody Museum of Archaeology and Ethnology and the Smithsonian's National Museum of the American Indian. First Face Society masks should not be exhibited as objects or artefacts, the Haudenosaunee argue, because they are not merely symbolic but are living things – carved from living wood and imbued with the essence of a living spirit.

For many of us in the modern Western world, there may be only one day of the year on which we might be tempted to don a ceremonial mask: Halloween. Although followers of various pagan traditions celebrate

Samhain the following day (1 November), for most people Halloween itself is an occasion of fun rather than religious significance. The costumes associated with the holiday have occasionally been used to much darker ends, however. Beyond simply being used as a convenient cover in the committing of countless crimes, the transporting quality of Halloween masks appears to have been a contributing factor in some particularly chilling cases. In 2012, a German teenager named Fabian Kramer murdered his 82-year-old landlady while wearing a Halloween mask depicting a man with stitched-together skin; Kramer had apparently been inspired by the horror movie *Saw*. Another creepily masked ghoul was Edward Paisnel, the so-called 'Beast of Jersey', who terrorised the British Channel Island between 1956 and 1971 with a series of violent sexual assaults. Paisnel wore a hideous rubber mask of his own creation – imagine Michael Myers if he fell asleep against a radiator – and worshipped at an occult altar in a hidden room in his family home.

I hoped that no such villains were lying in wait for me at Venice Carnival, where mask-wearing has long had a similarly transporting, if less sinister, effect. Traditionally, mask-wearing at Carnival was an enabling factor in the creation of an atmosphere where the usual rules of society were suspended – something with far more ancient origins than the festival itself, drawing on the rites of classical antiquity.

The Bacchanalia of ancient Rome were expressions of the cult of the god Liber, chiefly concerned with wine, fertility and freedom – a holy trinity celebrated with just as much gusto at many modern, secular festivals, and values so timeless that the word 'bacchanalian' has come to describe all manner of dissolute merrymaking.

Rome's Bacchanalia drew heavily on the Dionysia of ancient Athens, dedicated to wine, fertility, and their corresponding deity, Dionysus – also the god of music, dance, ritual madness and ecstasy.

Dionysus is known as the 'masked god' for his many aliases,[7] and, like the later Venice Carnival, the Dionysia was dominated by masked theatre. Like the drinking of wine and the act of performance itself, the wearing of a mask, as the Greeks saw it, was a portal to another identity.

Two millennia later, in the Venetian Republic, this same principle was nowhere more vividly expressed than in the story of the *gnaga,* or cat mask – one of the few variations on the plain white *bauta* which were developed during Carnival's heyday. Although Venetians themselves were famed for their sexual freedom – among the city's most famous sons was one Giacomo Casanova, after all – the authorities were staunchly conservative, and homosexuality was illegal in the sixteenth-century Venetian Republic, punishable by hanging or burning in the Piazza San Marco. During Carnival, however, the usual strictures and conventions of society were suspended, and that extended to the law – anyone wearing a mask would not be arrested, because they were deemed to have become the character of the mask they were wearing; they were playing a role.

The mask that became associated with homosexuality (and remains so to this day) was the *gnaga,* the cat mask, worn with skirts and a crinoline; wearers would complete the feline look by walking around with a basket full of

---

7. Brown University's Joukowsky Institue, Dionysus.

kittens, and would make the most of their temporary legal immunity by delivering insults to passers-by in a high-pitched mew – the origin of the onomatopoeic *gnaga*. The story of the *gnaga* has become embedded as one of the most fascinating pieces of Venice Carnival lore. As it was deemed to be a female character, it allowed male wearers not only to dress as women, but to engage in 'heterosexual' relationships with men. So emboldening was this loophole, the legend goes, that it led to a boom in business for Venice's male prostitutes, to the extent that the city's female prostitutes began to go out of business. In 1511, they decided enough was enough and appealed for help to – who else? – the Bishop of Venice, Antonio Contarini. He responded by allowing female sex workers to stand topless in the streets, flaunting their wares to counteract the perceived corrupting influence of homosexuality. A pleasing legacy of this story can be found today in the name of an unassuming-looking bridge in the former red-light district of San Polo: Ponte delle Tette – the Bridge of Tits.

Perhaps the most potent ancient antecessor of Venice Carnival was the Saturnalia, the Roman festival celebrating the agricultural god Saturn. Proceedings saw social norms turned on their heads, as masters served their slaves at the table and gambling became temporarily permitted. The latter found a direct echo in the Venetian Carnival when, in 1638, the Venetian authorities issued a decree converting Il Ridotto, a room in the Palazzo Dandolo, into a gambling house for the duration of Carnival only – the first legal public casino in the Western world. This suspension of the normal rules of society is characteristic of carnivals, to the extent that the twentieth-century Russian philosopher Mikhail Bakhtin coined the term 'carnivalesque' to describe literature which reflected these same qualities. The 'carnival sense of the world', as Bakhtin described it (understanding 'carnival' to encompass 'the sum total of all diverse festivities, rituals and forms of a carnival type'), has four main characteristics:

Social levelling: 'All *distance* between people is suspended, and a special carnival category goes into effect: *free and familiar contact among people* ... People who in life are separated by impenetrable hierarchical barriers enter into free familiar contact on the carnival square.' – viz. the wearing of a mask to hide one's identity.

Eccentricity: Behaviour which is usually unacceptable is permitted in the mode of the carnival, which frees 'the latent sides of human nature to reveal and express themselves' – the ordinarily forbidden homosexuality allowed by wearing of the *gnaga* mask, for example. *A Carnevale, ogni scherzo vale.*

Carnivalistic mésalliances: The marriage of concepts usually thought to be incompatible. 'Carnival brings together, unifies, weds, and combines the sacred with the profane, the lofty with the low, the great with the insignificant, the wise with the stupid.' Heathens and bishops, paupers and kings rub shoulders at Venice Carnival, a festival of great indulgence to mark the start of Lent; an event with a religious framework and a decidedly unholy reputation.

Profanation: 'Carnivalistic blasphemies, a whole system of carnivalistic debasings and bringings down to earth, carnivalistic obscenities linked with the reproductive power of the earth and the body, carnivalistic parodies on sacred texts and sayings, etc.' Such as the proliferation in carnivals of imagery related to death and disease – the ever-present plague doctor mask at Venice Carnival, for example.

Aye, + Kernac's fine rub.

Bakhtin insisted that carnival was lived, not performed. 'Carnival is not contemplated and, strictly speaking, not even performed; its participants live in it, they live by its laws as long as those laws are in effect; that is, they live a carnivalistic life. Because carnivalistic life is life drawn out of its usual rut, it is to some extent "life turned inside out," "the reverse side of the world."'[8]

Venice Carnival, then, is, like the Saturnalia of ancient Rome, the reverse side of the world: a time when the status quo is turned upside down and social boundaries are erased by the anonymity of mask-wearing and the suspension of social rules. This is what anthropologists describe as a liminal state: an in-between quality, generated by transformative experiences or events, which is characteristic of ceremonies, rituals and festivals in societies across the world. The German-French folklorist Arnold van Gennep originated the concept of liminality in his 1909 book *Les rites de passage* – itself the origin of the term 'rite of passage'. Examining what he referred to as 'the rites of the doorway and the threshold',[9] van Gennep wrote that a human life can be thought of as a series of rites of transition – not only individual life events such as birth, marriage, pregnancy and death, but also shared

---

8. Mikhail Bakhtin, *Problems of Dostoevsky's Poetics*
9. Arnold van Gennep, *The Rites of Passage.*

experiences, both natural and cultural, such as the passage of the moon, the passing from one year into the next, and the celebration of festivals.[10]

Van Gennep addressed the issue of covering the face in a ceremonial context, quoting Plutarch: 'With reference to the veil, Plutarch inquired, "Why do people veil their heads when worshiping the gods?" The answer is simple: to separate themselves from the profane and to live only in the sacred world.' He also spoke of festivals being times of sexual license, citing Russian sects 'which allow men and women to unite according to their pleasure or to chance' following initiation ceremonies; these are also moments when ideas of social status and personal property are forgotten, with everybody eating the food brought by the others to communal meals. He cites a Chinese practice, whereby 'on the last day of the year, a meal brings all members of the family together, even those ordinarily separated by differences ... It is a preparatory rite whose object is to make the whole group cohesive.'

This final point was seized upon and greatly developed later by the British anthropologist Victor Turner, who wrote extensively on festivals and liminality. By casting off the normal strictures of society, he said, festivals allow people from all walks of life to enter a liminal state, which ends up bringing people together and strengthening society once the usual order has been reimposed. Turner gave the name 'communitas' to the unstructured, egalitarian state which emerges during a mass experience of liminality, and saw it as crucial to the functioning of society. 'Liminality

---

10. Arnold van Gennep, *The Rites of Passage*.

implies that the high could not be high unless the low existed, and he who is high must experience what it is like to be low,' he wrote in 1969's *The Ritual Process.*

We can all recognise examples of liminality from our own lives. The hazy, dateless week between Christmas and New Year. The permission for a nearly married man or woman to receive a lap dance on their stag or hen do. The strange night of the soul engendered by the drinking of ayahuasca, during which the participant travels to another place, is granted new perspectives and revelatory visions, and emerges forever changed. The stages of Joseph Campbell's monomyth, also known as The Hero's Journey and outlined in 1949's *The Hero with a Thousand Faces,* follow the same process: the hero travels to a faraway, marginal place, undergoes a transformation, and returns home a different person. This arc has been the basis of many famous works of literature and mythology, from Osiris and the Odyssey to *Star Wars* and *Lord of the Rings.*

For many of the heroes of the modern Venice Carnival, of course, the suspension of societal norms finds its expression in one thing above all else: a good old, gutter-spewing piss-up. It was not ever thus. In times past, the Carnival tipples of choice were non-alcoholic, with revellers finding coffee and hot chocolate – introduced to Italy in the late sixteenth and seventeenth centuries respectively – more conducive to staying up all night gambling and practising the art of seduction. Nowadays, however, Carnival is a strongly pickled affair. As Luisella led me through the streets, the putrid legacies of the night before lay all around in gutters and in the gathering foam of the canals, bobbing here and there with bottles of Moretti and plastic cups bearing the logo of Select, the key ingredient in the Venetian spritz. Rounding a corner into a darkened *sotoportego*, I hovered my leg mid-stride to avoid a discarded mask, its delicate filigree enmeshed in a pile of vomit.

'Drinking in Venice is becoming a problem,' said Luisella, as we paused for a rest in the Campo San Bartolomeo. 'Tourists and people from the mainland come deliberately to drink a lot, because you don't need a car here.' I shrank slightly, recalling my own profligate booze consumption of the night before. Arriving late in Venice, I had checked into an ageing Rialto hotel to find myself in a small single room with only a paper-thin wall between me and a terrace bar, rowdy with the strains of carousing Americans. I ran through the usual stages: telling myself they soon would tire, and I could go to sleep; fantasies of homicidal violence, ending with bodyless baseball caps drifting down the Grand Canal; and finally, a bargaining stage – perhaps if I joined them for one, I reasoned, they would acquiesce to calling it a night at around midnight. I eventually stumbled back to bed around 3 after several rounds of 'Negroni pong', full of sore throat and self-loathing after shamefully raucous group renditions of 'Take Me Home, Country Roads', howled en masse into the Venetian night.

The excesses of Carnival are just one example of the damaging effects that tourism is having on Venice, its bridges sighing under the weight of millions of footsteps, small businesses shovelled out of grand palazzos to make way for yet more hotels, locals shunted to the suburbs by the soaring cost of living. On the front of a pharmacy in the corner of the square, Luisella showed me a rather sad LED ticker which recorded Venice's permanent population in ever-declining digits. It read 49,708, down from over

174,000 in the 1950s. Meanwhile, tourist numbers surge: on a busy day, the city sees 120,000 visitors. Through the pharmacy window, a corpulent man in a Las Vegas sweatshirt and a Harlequin mask grabbed fistfuls of Alka-Seltzer from a shelf.

At its zenith during the days of the Venetian Republic, Carnival may well have met Turner's criteria as a generator of communitas – a time when, hidden by a mask, concepts of gender and sexuality dissolved, inhibitions were shed, and monks and nuns were emboldened to forget their vows. Everyone met on a level plane, and when normal business was resumed, society was the stronger for it. In its modern incarnation, however, Carnival is not exactly a local community event. When I asked Luisella how she would be spending Carnival's climactic weekend – the Doge's Ball in the Palazzo Pisani Moretta, perhaps, or a booze cruise on the lagoon – she looked confused. 'I'm going skiing,' she said. 'Venetians tend to escape during Carnival.'

There is a difference, of course, between the small-scale societies often studied by anthropologists and the international crowds found at major festivals. There were always a lot of tourists at Carnival – by the eighteenth century, aristocrats from across Europe were flocking to the event, which was one of the biggest tourist draws on the continent. The letters of Lord Byron indicate that Carnival was still going strong decades after it was officially outlawed. It probably won't surprise you to learn he was a regular attendee, writing in poems and letters to his friends of the charms he encountered there – and the hangovers he endured. In an 1817 letter to the Irish writer Thomas Moore, Byron wrote, 'At present, I am on the invalid regimen myself. The Carnival – that

is, the latter part of it, and sitting up late o' nights –
had knocked me up a little.' He then enclosed his poem
'So, we'll go no more a roving', inspired by his fragile,
overindulged state:

So we'll go no more a roving
  So late into the night,
Though the heart be still as loving,
  And the moon be still as bright.

For the sword outwears its sheath,
  And the soul wears out the breast,
And the heart must pause to breathe,
  And Love itself have rest.

Though the night was made for loving,
  And the day returns too soon,
Yet we'll go no more a roving
  By the light of the moon.

He was back the next year, by all accounts.

Two centuries later, Carnival remains the city's biggest
tourist draw. Venice is an open wound, never left alone
for long enough to heal; tourism is both the blade and
the balm. This is never more evident than during
Carnival, which may not engender much in the way of
communitas for modern Venetians, but as the busiest time
of year in a city dependent on tourism, it plays a crucial
role in preserving the identity of Venice itself – which in
all likelihood would probably not exist at all anymore
without the tourist trade. Around half of the population is
directly employed in the tourism industry, and many more
are almost entirely reliant on it, including paragons of

Venetian tradition and authenticity such as mask-makers and ateliers, for whom Carnival is the most important time of year. I was in the market for a mask myself, having been invited to an event that evening, so Luisella took me to Papier-Mâché, the oldest mask workshop in Venice.

Manuela Gottardo, who runs the shop with her brother, Stefano, showed us the workshop's selection of traditional facewear: the original, ghost-white *bauta*; the feline *gnaga*; and the eerie plague doctor mask, its beaked nose pinched by painted eyeglasses, which was enjoying a resurgence in post-pandemic popularity. Its appeal today is probably much the same as in the Renaissance era. It entered Carnival culture partly as a memento mori, and partly as a symbol of human adversity in the face of pestilence and death – another convention boldly upturned during Carnival time. In 2022, when Carnival returned after a two-year absence due to coronavirus pandemic restrictions, a topical costumed double act provided some comic relief as they pursued one another around Venice: one dressed as a plague doctor, the other in an elaborate headdress shaped like a Covid-19 virus.

Creepiest of all Manuela's masks was the *moretta*, also known as the *muta* (mute): a small black oval traditionally worn only by women, who held it in place by biting a button behind the mask's mouth. The fact that this rendered them unable to speak, and thus unrecognisable by their voice, only added to the appeal of the *moretta*, which was seen by Venetians in the Republic era as the height of eroticism and sensuality. Concealing the face and voice shifted the emphasis to the body, with costumes featuring plunging necklines and the wearers painting their nipples bright red, so they showed through the thin fabric of their clothes. 'The woman would lead the seduction game by choosing when to take their mask off,' Luisella said. 'If they took it off at all.'

Mask wearing in Republic-era Venice was by far at its most widespread during Carnival, but certain sectors of society – notably the aristocracy – wore masks at other times, too, enjoying the anonymity it afforded them while gambling, seducing, and otherwise enjoying themselves. Permitted periods varied, but in general mask wearing was allowed during the fifteen days of Ascension as well as several months from St. Stephen's Day (Boxing Day) until Shrove Tuesday. Predictably, the anonymity provided by masks created some problems. In 1268, men wearing masks were prohibited from playing the 'egg game', which involved throwing eggshells filled with rosewater in the vicinity of passing ladies and was apparently considered the height of flirting during the High Middle Ages. Not long afterwards, in 1339, a law was passed forbidding Venetians from visiting convents while masked, while laws also came into effect banning prostitutes and men who visited brothels from wearing masks.

The Republic fell in 1797, and the new Austrian rulers finally outlawed Carnival and the wearing of masks completely, disapproving of the debauchery and wary of the possibilities for anonymous crime. Carnival ceased to be a living animal and became dumbed down, never quite completely going away, but abiding quietly as a Halloween-like, rather cartoonish celebration aimed more at children than adults. The mask-makers largely disappeared, too, making Stefano's move to open his workshop, in 1977, an unusual one. 'When I went to the council to ask for a licence to make traditional masks, they were confused,' Stefano said. Perhaps he sparked an idea in the higher-ups, though, because just two years later, in 1979, Carnival officially returned, the authorities deciding it should be the centrepiece of Venice's modern tourism drive.

I asked Manuela how she felt about the tourist crowds which were once again descending on Venice, with pandemic restrictions having been lifted. 'When it was quieter, during the pandemic, the quality of our work was better,' she said. 'But we live for tourism now.' Resignation and regret jostled for supremacy in her voice. 'It's a complex relationship with tourism in Venice,' she added. 'But we need to keep creating high quality, to show tourists the real thing. It's offensive to show then something fake – they deserve to see the real Venice.' This is a sentiment I came across time and again: if Venetians were going to find their city sold completely to tourism, they were determined to at least control the narrative. 'We need to keep the quality high,' Luisella agreed. 'If not for high quality, Venice will be Disneyfied.'

Her words reminded me of those I had once heard from a local in another storied Italian city. Florentine psychotherapist Paolo Molino had said sadly to me of his hometown, 'Florence has become like Disneyland for art. I don't like that. I like lived places – I like to come and buy my sandwich from the *lampredotto* guy, to be able to walk without having to fight my way through crowds.'

Paolo's view was that Florence's artistic treasures – valued because of the ways they speak to us about the human condition – had actually reduced the city to the extent that it no longer counted as a 'lived place'. His comparison of Florence with Disneyland – of the Medici with Mickey Mouse, of *The Birth of Venus* with the Big Thunder Mountain Railroad – was similarly jarring, but it recalled to me the words of Jean Baudrillard:

'Disneyland is presented as imaginary in order to make us believe that the rest is real.' Baudrillard believed that the rest of America was not in fact real, but belonged to the postmodern order of the hyperreal – a world where information and media representations of things have replaced the experience of the things themselves; the signifiers have replaced the signified. Florence's artworks, commissioned by powerful families like the Medici in order to project power and promulgate mythology around themselves, were designed in their own time to create a kind of alternate reality. Centuries later, the world which they signified has been forgotten, known only by its signifiers in marble and oil, viewed on gallery walls, through glass screens, and remotely on postcards and photographs – a world of the hyperreal.

Modern Venice is an even more vivid example, particularly in the age of social media, the acme of hyperreality. 'When Carnival first came back, in the late seventies, early eighties, it was beautiful,' Manuela said. 'Young people wearing costumes of their own design, acrobats in the *campi* – it was a carnival of culture. Now people just come here to take pictures of people in costumes.'

The real Venice, a place for Venetians to live and work, is becoming separated from its signifier – the 'dream Venice' which tourists know and flock to, which finds its most potent realisation in the fantasy of Carnival. The Disneyfication of Venice is one of the prime concerns of Mattia Berto, an actor and theatre director striving to redress Venice's imbalanced relationship with tourism by recruiting locals to participate in performance art pieces in the city's streets and squares.

'I am a Venetian, but most of all, I am someone who is madly in love with Venice,' Mattia told me over the phone.

'Venice is the most beautiful city in the world, where you cannot find a berth and you cannot find a home. The relationship between Venice and tourism is a story of love and conflict. Venice cannot just be a touristic city; this is part of humankind's cultural heritage.'

It was Mattia's mentor, the director and playwright Maurizio Scaparro, who oversaw the public performances which characterised Carnival's riotous comeback. 'Venetians look with nostalgia at the way Carnival was in the 1980s, when Maurizio invited international artists – Marcel Marceau, the Floating Theatre by Aldo Rossi – to perform in Piazza San Marco and the city's other public spaces,' Mattia said. 'They were Carnivals of artistic geniuses, but also of the city and citizens, at a time when Venetians still loved to dress up and disguise themselves. Today, it's different – Venetians tend to flee from Carnival or complain about it.' In a further piece of sad symbolism, Maurizio Scaparro died on 17 February 2023, just as the modern Carnival was gearing up for its climactic weekend.

Mattia marked Carnival the same year with a giant, symbolic tug-of-war in Campo Santi Giovanni e Paolo, with 50 local residents involved to represent the 50,000 threshold below which Venice's population had recently dipped. 'The rope we are pulling between the real Venice and touristic Venice is almost broken,' he told me. 'I strongly believe Carnival has to get back to the street and to the urban spaces. I'd love a Carnival of citizens, something you build the whole year from shopkeepers to gondoliers, from schools to hotels; I'd love to see everyone expressing their own talent in this play of magic and disguise. Carnival is an incredible, cathartic, liberating time – let's try to make the city the protagonist, for the ones living here as well as for those visiting for a short time.'

All the Venetians I spoke to agreed that curbing visitor numbers is essential to the city's long-term survival. 'I've worked as a guide here for 23 years, and my parents and grandparents are both from Venice,' Luisella said, as we browsed the masks in Manuela's shop. 'But Venice is not just for Venetians – it's always been an international city. It's just when there are too many people that it becomes a problem.' A long-mooted €5 daily tourist tax was finally introduced in 2024, but locals are sceptical. 'It would be better just to limit numbers,' Manuela said. 'If you charge people to enter the city, they may think they have paid for the right to misbehave.'

Manuela passed me a chalk-white half-moon of a mask, which I tied behind my head before turning to look in the mirror. 'Bello!' said Stefano, looking at me hopefully. 'Very elegant. Like *Phantom of the Opera*!' I wasn't so sure. Yesterday's Campari, rather than being metabolised, seemed to have pooled directly in my eyes, which stared back redly at me like a Basset hound's; my hair stood up madly above the white face of the mask like wild grass on a neglected cliff of Dover. A rough few years on the absinthe for Michael Crawford. Still, at least it covered the bags under my eyes.

I paid for the mask and rushed back hotelwards to get changed before that evening's event. It was a soirée fit for Carnival's elegant heyday: a dance performance by the Isadora Duncan International Institute in the grand surrounds of the Palazzo Contarini Polignac. The show combined the naturalistic sweep of Duncan's dance style with the variegated costumery of Carnival – Roman tunics, Renaissance gowns and petticoats, and, of course, some magnificent masks, with the story of the Minotaur told through twisting bodies and a golden bull headpiece.

After the show, I spoke with the director, Jeanne Bresciani, a learned, elegant woman in late middle-age, who had once been the protégée of Maria Theresa Duncan, Isadora's adopted daughter. I sensed – in her, myself, and everyone else – the emboldening quality conferred by the wearing of a mask. I began, surprising myself as the words tumbled from my mouth, to tell lies: I gave a considered analysis of the gentrification which was occurring in my area of south London (I hadn't lived in London for five years) and told, in carefully moderated tones of false modesty, of my upcoming and entirely fictional feature on Japanese mail order priests for *Time* magazine. I suppose I didn't quite feel myself – but I didn't mind it. I felt a similar evaporation of inhibition in Jeanne. 'Journalists now are more handsome than in my day,' she twinkled at me from beneath her sequinned *colombina* eye-mask – a rather odd compliment, I thought, considering my face too was covered by a mask and I was as rough as a badger's arse. Still, I wasn't about to complain.

One thing that was not in question was the magnificence of our surroundings. Built on the Grand Canal in the fifteenth century, the Palazzo Contarini Polignac is a Renaissance-Byzantine pile once home to sewing-machine heiress Winnaretta Singer, whose family's legacy could be seen in the fabulous costumes which surrounded us: richly embroidered masks, fezzes and robes; dresses studded with crystals and adorned with feathers. No one makes them better than Marina Lazzaro, atelier at Scatola Magica, whom I was introduced to in the palazzo's portico. Marina started her costume-making workshop with her mother and two sisters more than four decades ago. For its entire history, their business has operated from an elegantly fading palazzo overlooking the Rio de Santa Caterina canal in the Cannaregio district. This was to be their last year there, she told me sadly – they were being evicted, the palazzo having been sold to become yet another luxury hotel.

Not that business shows any sign of abating. Marina's customers, of whom barely any are Venetian, are tireless in their commitment to the perfect Carnival costume. 'When you wear a costume, you become someone else – the person you want to be,' she said. 'Some of my clients are very old, in their seventies and eighties. But the costumes are never too heavy, and they never feel the cold. They just say, "I'll drink some more Prosecco and that will keep me warm!"'

Having taken that sentiment a little too much to heart, I slunk out the next morning in search of a hangover cure at the famous Caffè Florian. This splendid Baroque coffee house is where Marina's clients, festooned and gold-hatted, gather to compare their gladrags and show them off to the gathered crowds. Through vast floor-to-ceiling windows, passing Venetians peer in with a kind of tired amusement at these strangely dressed visitors, cosplaying as figures from centuries past. The tourists, meanwhile, gaze out at Venice – Queen of the Adriatic, La Dominante, La Serenissima – the beloved city that their footsteps abrade, their money restores, and their imaginations freeze in the past. Although magnified during Carnival, it's the same dance that plays out year-round: heavily outnumbered by tourists, Venetians have become spectators in their own city. 'It's a double theatre – the people inside watch those outside, and the people outside watch those inside,' Luisella had told me. 'The question is, which is the stage? And who is watching who?'

Byron's poetic channelling of Venice Carnival did not end with *'So, we'll go no more a roving'*. He slipped a more insightful line into another poem, 'The Carnival', explicitly about the festivities in Venice and found as part of the longer epic poem *Beppo: A Venetian Story*.

> *They've pretty faces yet, those same Venetians,*
>   *Black eyes, arched brows, and sweet expressions still;*
> *Such as of old were copied from the Grecians,*
>   *In ancient arts by moderns mimicked ill*

Byron may have seen the Carnival of his time as a modern 'ill mimicry' of the ancient theatrical arts; and Carnival today may be seen as a pale imitation of what it was in the days of the Venetian Republic. For those in attendance, though, it was and remains a wellspring of liminality: a chance to cast off the shackles of day-to-day life and become somebody else. That's partly afforded by mask-wearing, today as it always was; it's partly created by the simple but powerful sense of being at a special event, marked aside in the calendar as a time of difference and celebration.

For Venice, though, the mask is a particularly potent metaphor, in a city where, to use Baudrillard's lexicon, the signifiers have obliterated the signified. John Updike said that celebrity is a mask that eats into the face. The mask that Venice has made for itself – no longer plain white but ornamented with feathers and bedazzled with jewels – seems stuck fast, such that if you removed it, if such a thing were even possible, what lies beneath would be mangled and raw, so disfigured as to be, perhaps, unsalvageable.

So, the mask stays on. But a very pretty mask it is, and no mistake.

3

JESUS RAVES
Pilgrims, Passage, and
Threshold People

Andalucía, SPAIN

Ba-dum. Ba-dum. Ba-dum. The rhythm of a single drum echoed through the plaza like a heartbeat. Cows with scimitar horns, tied by ropes to the trunks of orange trees, swatted flies away with their tails. It was that time of early morning in Seville when things briefly are clear and cool, when the mind can work keenly before the fudge and haze of the hot day descends, like honey you have to swim through – but already the temperature was rising. A crowd was beginning to spill outside the doorway of the Church of El Salvador, most of them resplendent in Andalusian costume: the women in polka-dot, frilly Sevillian dresses, and the men in Cordovan hats and white button-down shirts with many pockets. The ladies appeared quintessentially Spanish, like flamenco *bailaoras*, but the men looked very English to me – somehow Wodehousian, as if dressed for punting on the Cherwell. One thing about their attire, though, was unmistakeably Andalusian. Around their necks, on green-and-white threads, hung silver pendants depicting the Virgin of El Rocío, the object of their devotion and of the five-day pilgrimage on which they were about to embark.

The Romería de El Rocío is one of Spain's largest and most elaborate fiestas, drawing – it is claimed – as many as one million people to the Andalusian countryside each May on a Pentecost pilgrimage to the Huelva town of El Rocío. Pilgrims embark on a walk – or, at least, a stretch of it – to the Hermitage of El Rocío, through the pine forests and wetlands of Doñana National Park, fuelled in equal part by religious fervour and cheap *fino*: a pilgrimage holier and more debauched than any other.

Some participants just tag along for one day; others walk the whole thing; still others hover around the event, dipping in and out of it, as I would be doing. Anybody can join the cavalcade, but the main protagonists are the members of the so-called Brotherhoods, of which there are more than one hundred across Spain, each one associated with a different church. The Brothers (both men and women) travel all the way to El Rocío from their respective churches, on foot and horseback, or in carts drawn by horse, tractor, or Land Rover. Depending on where they start, the journey takes between one and nine days. They travel by day in a giant convoy of horses, cows, dust, and electrified booze wagons, and set up each night in raucous campsites, drinking agricultural-grade alcohol from battered jerrycans and sleeping in tents or *carriolas* – flamboyant caravans adorned with flowers, pulled by stoic brown-and-white oxen, and fitted with bunk beds (and, in the fancier models, kitchens).

When they arrive in El Rocío, hungover but unbowed, the pilgrims spend several more days in worship and revelry before the final mass, which culminates in a remarkable ritual of violence inside the town church. A crowd rushes the altar in a moment of collective ritualised rage, climbing over a tall fence and seizing the Virgin of El Rocío, which they then lead on a procession through the town for the next eight or nine hours.

This a pilgrimage, but it's also a knees-up on a monumental scale, building up to a startling and transgressive act of ritual violence. As famous for dissolution as for divine grace, the Romería de El Rocío is a glorious collision of the sacred and the profane.

This may only be Spain's second most famous pilgrimage – it loses out on that front to the Camino de Santiago – but it must surely be Spain's greatest party. And the Spanish, perhaps more than any other people in the world, were *born* to party. Their programme of afterlife festivals alone – the skeleton-costumed flash mob which dances through the streets of Verges each Maundy Thursday, or Galicia's Festival of Near Death Experiences, in which fortunate survivors leap out of a parade of open coffins – brings to mind the comments of Federico García Lorca, the doomed poet laureate of Granada: 'In Spain, the dead are more alive than the dead of any other country in the world.' Having landed in Seville from Terminal 3 of Manchester Airport, I felt qualified to go one further: in Spain, the dead are more alive than the living in many corners of the world.

I would be walking with the pilgrims for two days before spending the weekend in El Rocío, seeing the remaining devotees arrive and joining them in their final, ecstatic descent on the Hermitage and its statue of the Virgin. I would need a translator and guide, however, and I had been making enquiries for months with a view to finding someone willing to accompany me on the Romería for a couple of days. Curiously, nobody seemed very keen, and I received several polite rejections on the grounds of health, safety, and the preservation of sanity. One email response, typical of the genre, read as follows:

> Just so you know, it can be very crowded and even dangerous. They drink a lot and use drugs, and I have seen people being beaten up inside of the chapel. Are you absolutely sure you want to do this?

I appreciated the sentiment of concern, although the message had the opposite effect to what had been intended. One thing was now abundantly clear: this was a pilgrimage I had to see with my own eyes.

Eventually, I found a company with shallow enough pockets and loose enough morals to send me a guide, whom I arranged to meet in the plaza outside the church. His name was Ruben, and he was a young graduate of the University of Seville's tourism programme. He looked boy scoutish – clutching a satchel, his collar fastened with an Andalusian green-and-white neckerchief, and his nose bridged with spectacles as thick and round as bottle glass. We'd barely exchanged pleasantries when he let slip that, in fact, he didn't much care for the Romería de El Rocío. 'I'm a conservative Catholic,' he said, with lemon-sucking prudishness. 'I don't think you should mix religion and partying.' Christ, I thought. They've sold me a dud.

We entered the church, which by now was heaving with devotees. The drawling mass began to crackle through the loudspeaker, and Ruben translated for me. At one point the priest embarked on a cautionary sermon about the opportunities for sin which would present themselves to tempt the pilgrims during this *fiesta inmensa*, as he referred to it. 'I know you will drink, I know you will lose yourselves,' he said. 'But always remember God.'

The mass finished, and a festival band, waiting in the choir, launched into song. The Romería has spawned a musical genre all of its own, of rousing singalongs with lyrics describing the glory of the Virgin of El Rocío:

> *Dios te salve, Maria, un rosal de hermosura.*
> *Eres Tu Madre mia, de pureza vrginal.*
> *Hail Mary, a rosebush of beauty.*
> *You are my Mother, of virginal purity.*

The crowd began to file out of the church, only making it a few metres into the plaza before turning back towards the door to watch the unveiling of the *simpecado* – a large, solid-silver palanquin, garlanded with paradise flowers and carrying a hallowed image of the Virgin of El Rocío, carried by each Brotherhood as the focal point of their procession from their church to El Rocío. The simpecado was manoeuvred to the centre of the plaza, and already a number of people were beside themselves, wiping tears from their faces as it passed them by. 'This is what propels the Romería – this love and devotion,' said an elderly man called Fernando who was standing next to me in the crowd. 'Look at all the old ladies – you'll see them reaching for the simpecado all the way.' And he was right – already there was a little gaggle of blue rinses and clattering earrings, grasping at the thing derangedly as if at a passing Popemobile.

A motto was emblazoned on the front of the simpecado: *Sine Labe Concepta* (Without Sin Conceived). There is nothing particularly special about the Virgin of El Rocío; she has not terrorised shepherds, demanded the initiation of grand housebuilding projects, or even so much as shed a single tear, unlike other celebrated Marian statues and apparitions. The Romería simply reflects the same virginal fixation which is universal in Roman Catholicism, and is particularly strongly felt in Spain. It is, nevertheless, an ironic preoccupation for a festival like this – unless, of course, you count it as a coincidence that there is without fail an Andalusian baby boom nine months after Pentecost each year.

As I pondered this, I felt something warm splashing on my leg and looked down to see that one of the two large bulls tied to the front of the simpecado was answering nature's call on the cobbled floor, not a yard from my foot. I forgave him; he had a long walk ahead.

Fireworks popped like gunfire, invisible against the bright morning sky, and the procession began its march, beneath the Moorish crenelations of the Alcázar, across the Guadalquivir to the potteries of Triana, and out for five miles or so towards the suburbs of Seville. It was slow going, with the simpecado stopping at various points for blessings. Beneath the red tower of a parish church, a sombre priest uttered an incantation before the silver litter; at a provincial police station, burly *guardia civil* made offerings of flowers, holding their hats with damp eyes. I sensed a disconnect between these pious officials and the religiosity of the crowd, which seemed folksier but no less keenly felt; it was still early in the morning, but bottles of beer and plastic cups of fino were already being knocked back with gusto. When they were in the proximity of the simpecado or belting out a song, the crowd seemed seized by a religious zeal – many were crying already – but during the blessings, people remained mostly quiet but seemed restless, whispering to each other and chewing on the rims of their cups, as if they regarded these solemn interludes as pieces of tiresome bureaucracy.

The procession got moving again, but suddenly panic descended and the whole thing ground to a halt once more after a woman, overcome by it all, collapsed in a cloud of sky-blue skirts. I used the break in proceedings to take stock of the logistics. Most people were on foot, but many others were on horseback – including some members of the Brotherhood we were walking with, holding walkie-talkies and operating in a semi-official herding capacity. Oxen pulled the carriolas, which were empty for the moment but would provide the pilgrims' accommodation each night. Many others travelled in classical style, on horse-drawn carts – some were pulled by elegant chestnut Andalusian horses, but a significant proportion were being dragged along gamely by mules, who cast their eyes to the floor and shuffled past their more glamorous cousins, looking embarrassed. 'Mules are cheaper to hire,' Ruben explained. 'This is the most expensive fiesta in Spain.'

In every hand was a bottle of beer or a glass of wine in outsized measures – pints of sherry in plastic cups were *de rigueur*. It is the alcoholic imperative, as much as the devotional one, which influences the way things are done on the Romería. Beside the carriolas, the other characteristic vehicle is the *carro*, a type of open-sided moveable bar, dragged by Land Rover, on which many pilgrims choose to spend the whole journey. At this point, Ruben came good – he recognised some of his friends from college, all dressed to the nines in traditional garb, who had clubbed together to rent a carro for the week, along with various of their family members and friends.

They invited us to hop on, and stuffed beers into our hands. The carro was a trailer, big enough to seat eighteen people on long benches arranged around a central bar, which had cup holders lined up along the top and refrigeration space in the bottom, full of beers, cured meats and cheese. Sometimes in life, you just have to throw your hands up and say: *that is a tremendous vehicle.* It was also the most Spanish thing I had seen in my life – people in Cordovan hats passing around boards of prosciutto and manchego, pouring sherry from steel teapots into plastic cups, and singing impassioned songs about the Virgin to the strumming of a nylon-stringed guitar.

I stayed on the carro getting happily drunk and having half-understood conservations with my new friends for the next few hours. The suburbs of Seville gave way to a network of highways, closed off to non-pilgrimage traffic, and then to a series of small towns, where we would disembark at little bars to use the bathroom and drink *tinto de verano*. We stopped in a shaded grove for a long lunch – jamón and goat's cheese, crusty bread and gallons of sherry – and a rest beneath an olive tree, before getting back on the wagon and rumbling on to the night's campground, as the sun slumped heavily over the Doñana to the west.

We were far from the first to arrive, and the campsite was already an ocean of activity. Each Brotherhood had set up their own area in a similar style. Carriolas had been arranged in circles like the spokes of a wheel, with groups of revellers perching on the back of them and drinking, much like an American tailgate party. Close by, wagons were lined up, resplendent in their garlands of vivid flowers which shivered in the warm breeze. Taking pride of place in the centre of each camp was the Brotherhood's simpecado, coruscating shards of silver in the evening sunlight.

Ruben had wandered off, so I chatted to his friend from university, José Luis, who was one of the only other English speakers in the group. 'I've been doing the Romería – walking the whole thing – since I was a kid,' he said. 'All of life is in the Romería – religion, partying, and healing, too.' He motioned to an older man, who was sucking on a cigarette. 'This is my father's first year. He's not much of a believer, but it was very important for him to come on the pilgrimage this year. He is very sick.' Before moving to Seville, José Luis had grown up in the town of Pilas, around halfway between Seville and El Rocío. 'In the villages around the Doñana, no one goes to school or work during the Romería,' he said. 'This is more important.' This atmosphere of defiance against the authorities is a central pillar of popular religiosity in Spain. I had sensed it that morning during the procession, with the crowd's lack of interest whenever a priest or a policeman appeared to bless the simpecado, and José's comments hinted at the same feeling. This is the people's pilgrimage, and the people make themselves pilgrims not because they are told to by a priest, but in spite of that fact – in devotion to their Virgin, as a personal prayer during a time of crisis, or to lose themselves and their worries in one of the world's greatest parties.

And so, the sun came down, and the night came on; the sparkling of the simpecados was extinguished by darkness, and the crackling of log fires mingled with throaty singalongs, the whinnying of horses and the clinking of cups. Dark-haired lovers embraced in dark corners, and, neglecting the cautionary words of the padre, the romeríos forgot to remember God.

Things stirred early the next morning – no matter that, for some of the pilgrims, the night had never got round to ending. Dawn broke somewhere back towards Seville, wanly at first, and then flooding the campground with golden syrup, illuminating plumes of dust and whirls of coffee steam, and warming the shivering flanks of the horses as the whole circus packed up and lit out again as quickly as it had assembled itself the evening before.

The whole Romería feels wrapped up in its own universe, never more so than when it suddenly becomes subsumed, as it did for us that bright morning, by the surreal landscapes of Doñana National Park. While the pilgrimage was leaving Seville, normal life was suspended to make way for it – people hung out of balconies and stood outside offices to watch it pass, and the route proceeded the wrong way along highways usually busy with motor traffic – conferring the feeling that this was a thing which ran along different tracks from everyday life. That feeling was compounded now as we reached the Doñana, not least because we were once again transgressing traffic norms – the national park is usually closed off to foot travellers, accessible to the public only on guided 4x4 tours, better to preserve its fragile ecosystems.

More than anything else, though, it's the landscape which marks the Doñana as a place apart. The dry scrub which we had been travelling through the day before had given way to a land of reed beds and glimmering ponds, where sand dunes the colour of baked pastry seemed to shift, like things with agency, while my back was turned. It's a place you could walk through alone and feel like you were being watched, but not in a threatening way; it just knows you're there. This feeling followed me through the morning and into the afternoon; when we stopped to eat a late lunch of cheese and ham *bocadillos*, I fought the urge to look over my shoulder, unable to shake the feeling that someone was staring at me from between the scrubby grass which tufted the dunes. The surreal atmosphere was enhanced by the fact that the convoy was perpetually enveloped in a cloud of orange dust and sand, kicked up by a million feet, tyres and hooves, giving the whole thing the veiled feeling of a dream.

I was stirred from my reverie by a death shriek – the searing caterwaul of Babi Ngepet, the demon pig, rising on a huge pillar of dust from a stand of eucalyptus trees. It was so loud and unholy a noise that it cut through the rumbling, the clopping of hooves, clattering of ice and the strumming of guitar strings, and made everyone stop and stare, and then wander over to the side of the road for a closer look. A pilgrim – a twenty-something man with his hat skew-whiff and ham in his beard – had come across a young wild boar, cornered it, and was now wrassling it like some low-rent rodeo bulldogger, kicking up a vortex of golden dust while his friends stood doubled over in laughter, swigging *rebujito* from plastic bottles and flicking cigarettes into the trees.

This kind of behaviour is, sadly, nothing new on the Romería. In 2019, four men were jailed for the abuse of rented mules on the pilgrimage, leaving the animals with harness wounds from which they were still recovering three years later.[11] In 2018, *El País* reported that 141 horses and mules had died on the Romería over the

---

11. El Refugio del Burrito

preceding decade, usually from colic or heart attacks stemming from extreme physical effort and lack of rest.[12]

Animal abuse is only the half of it. With little to no sanitation facilities provided, the pristine national parkland of the Doñana becomes a vast open-air public toilet for hundreds of thousands of pilgrims during the Romería, while many of them treat it as a dustbin, too, scattering cups and food wrappers on the path as they walk. As I have at festivals across the world, I heard several people lament that the Romería was not what it used to be, that it had lost its authenticity and slipped into decadence – but this sentiment is nothing new. As long ago as 2004, a journalist from *El Mundo* was complaining that the Romería was 'now, more than anything else, an outdoors orgy of limitless drinking, partying and, even, sex'.[13] Despite the cries of disapproval, though, there seems to be little appetite to stifle proceedings at the Romería. On the contrary, the only official pronouncement on the pilgrimage in recent years was a 2023 declaration from the Andalusian government that the Romería would be officially protected as an Asset of Cultural Interest.

The hubbub subsided, the convoy started up again, and my footsteps settled into a mantra-like rhythm as I fell into a passage of walking alone. To either side of the path were stands of pine, which fragmented the late afternoon sun into low, flat beams; seed heads and particles of dust seemed to hang in the light, almost still, as if pickled in a jar.

12. *El País*, 'El Rocío pilgrimage claims lives of more than 140 horses in last decade' by Javier Martín-Arroyo.
13. Cited in the *Guardian*, '"Pilgrims" turn wilderness trek into week of debauchery' by Giles Tremlett.

These moments of quiet were always there on the Romería and were surprisingly easy to find, despite the madness and the debauchery which were constantly in full swing all around me. Things did not seem to follow the usual, chronological order of things – quiet, late-rising mornings followed by slowly increasing levels of intoxication and madness, rising to a crescendo in the small hours of the night. Rather, at any given time the full spectrum of dissipation was visible, from sobriety to catatonia and everything in between. When I had woken up that morning, it was to the hiss of beer bottles being popped open; plenty of people clearly hadn't been to bed at all, and all through the morning and the afternoon I had seen many people sitting upright on the bench seat of their carro, snoozing like babies as full voices and aggressively strummed guitars filled the air around them. Now, I looked up and could see that there were other lonely walkers in the crowd, who, like me, were enjoying their own private moments in this cavalcade of chaos. As for Ruben, he seemed to have forgotten himself and his haughty, self-professed disapproval of the Romería, and had morphed into some kind of louche lounge lizard, slouched in the back of the carro with a sherry in his hand, a cigarette in his mouth, and a young woman on his knee. Maybe he wasn't such a fuddy-duddy after all. I felt strangely proud, but most of all grateful for him, and for his friends, who after all had spent the preceding two days keeping me in food and beer and talking to me, a stranger who didn't speak their language, for no reason other than that I had decided to turn up and tag along. 'You'll notice the people are very kind,' Ruben had said to me as we left the church, and he was right. 'Rich or poor, it doesn't matter on the Romería. We all have the same motivation:

to celebrate life and to see the Virgin. So, we help each other. We are all the same.'

Festivals and pilgrimages are both vehicles for the liminal state, in which hierarchy and division are dissolved. Pilgrimage is also the ultimate rite of passage – a spiritual journey carried on the legs of a physical one, from which the pilgrim emerges forever changed. Many rites of passage are private or semi-private events: bar mitzvahs, birthdays, graduation ceremonies, and so on. Others, though, assume festival form; they are regularly occurring, communal events, at which people gather together to undergo their personal journeys *en masse*. The ultimate example of the genre is the pilgrimage-festival – not those pilgrimages undertaken at any time of the year, in pious solitude, but those, like the Romería, which are tied to the calendar; events where you can reliably turn up and find yourself among a party of pilgrims.

Take the world's most famous pilgrimage-festival, the Hajj, which is explicitly inscribed as one of the Five Pillars of Islam – something which every Muslim who can is required to undertake at least once in their lifetime. During the Hajj, the white clothes worn by every pilgrim put everybody on a level playing field, regardless of their wealth or status in the world outside. On re-emerging into the world having completed Hajj, one assumes a new status, becoming a *haji*, a position afforded great respect. They are transformed. This is a power that festivals and rites of passage generally hold – they can change us, within ourselves and within society.

As a non-Muslim, I'm not allowed to join the Hajj – but pilgrimage is universal. It has, in fact, been growing in popularity in recent times, even though we tell ourselves we are living in an increasingly secular world.

The transformative effect of going on a pilgrimage appears to transcend religious belief. A 2022 study[14] found that 75% of pilgrims on the Camino de Santiago, many of whom do not profess to be walking the route for religious reasons, nevertheless experienced significant changes in their lives as a result of their walk.

While we are on a pilgrimage, we are in a transitionary phase, during which we travel outside of society's usual categories. This is when things get interesting, when the magic happens, when we slip into the twilight of the festival world. How shall we describe ourselves in this mode? 'Inbetweeners' is taken. Victor Turner's word, 'liminars', is too donnish for my liking. I prefer Arnold van Gennep's term: 'threshold people'. Anyone who has allowed themselves an immersive experience at a festival knows what it means to be a threshold person. Although our removal from society is only temporary, we often feel that this is a state in which we can truly be ourselves; and even if our experiences are not always happy or comfortable, they are often at least profound. The threshold people are the ones who are really living, although we are hidden out of sight; we are the dancers in the dark roots.

El Rocío has been described as Spain's strangest town. Its name means 'morning dew', but, while those beads of the dawn may glitter on the grasslands of the Doñana, the same cannot be said of the town itself,

---

14. 'Walking for well-being. Exploring the phenomenology of modern pilgrimage' by Anna Sørensen and Henrik Høgh-Olesen.

which is a kingdom of dust, kicked up by the horses and carts which remain the transportation of choice for the majority of the 1,500 permanent residents year-round – for there are no paved roads here. The town is a grid of dirt tracks and sandy paths, which bisect squat terraces of whitewashed, lemon-bordered houses, with wooden railings running alongside them for the tying up of horses. It is often compared, for good reason, to a Wild West film set, and the frontier-town feeling is never more pronounced than during the Romería, when the streets stream night and day with an endless procession of wagon wheels and riders on horseback. It has the desperate feeling of a gold rush descending on this dusty town, but the bounty does not lie in seams and veins in the belly of the earth; it's a feeling, sought at the bottom of the bottle, upheld on a high altar, and cradled in the crevasses of the human heart.

The smell of horse shit filled the air. The sides of the road were covered in fallen jacaranda flowers, so vivid as to look synthetic, like someone had peppered the pavement with lilac paintballs. Tented bars were blaring out Romería songs at ear-splitting volume, while makeshift stalls had been set up selling the predictable – hats, walking sticks and traditional dresses – alongside the less expected; I had to do a double take at a display of baby monkey dolls, dressed in nappies with dummies in their mouths. It all added up to the impression that a surreal circus had rolled into town.

I walked to the lakefront promenade which marks the southern boundary of El Rocío, and across the water of the Charco de la Boca I could see the wild horses of the Doñana, their eyes fixed bemusedly towards the town now filling up with their domesticated cousins. I walked into the church beside the lake: the Hermitage of El Rocío, the focal point of the pilgrimage. There was no mass taking place, but it was packed anyway, with red-eyed devotees staring in silence towards a huge, gilded altar centred around a statue of the Virgin Mary holding the infant Jesus. She looked ridiculous – a tiny wooden face staring out from a Baroque nightmare of crowns, golden halos, and brocaded skirts, the whole thing amalgamated into something not-quite-human: half worm, half golden god, like something from the mind of Frank Herbert.

Pig-wrassling, drunkenness, and public defecation may all be de rigueur at the Romería, but it was only here, gazing up at this strange effigy, that I had my first and only experience of pilgrimage law enforcement, when a security guard rushed over to admonish me for neglecting to remove my hat on entering the church. Shamed, I slunk into the gift shop, where the pious were queuing by the dozen to buy all manner of gilded tat: plates, amulets, and mantelpiece ornaments, all bearing the blank-eyed image of the Virgin of El Rocío.

It was Saturday, the penultimate day of the Romería. This is when the partying is ratcheted up to eleven – Sunday, by comparison, is a pious day, although it culminates in one of Europe's most potent outbursts of religious madness. The Brotherhoods were still arriving; the streets remained an infinite swarm of horses and carts, and of foot processions carrying their respective simpecados. There was something very Indian-looking about these parades, with their solid silver litters running on huge dharmic wheels, festooned with bright orange flowers, and pulled along by cows with great curving horns. Peering inside the palanquins, I half expected to see Ganesha, not Mother Mary, gazing back at me. They rattled as they passed, like washing machines spinning a thousand loose coins.

Although more than one hundred Brotherhoods now make the yearly pilgrimage to El Rocío, it all started with just one: the Hermandad Matriz of Almonte, a town nine miles to the north. I had made contact prior to the pilgrimage with Eddy Plasquy, a Belgian anthropologist who had originally been drawn by professional interest to the Romería and had studied the Almontese Brotherhood extensively. After almost 25 years, he had come to be considered almost an honorary member. I met him at the Brotherhood's *casa*, a traditional El Rocío house with a narrow doorway opening into something deceptively large, all wide, airy courtyards, tiled floors, and pictures on the walls which testified to this family's prominence: one photograph showed the smiling patriarch shaking hands with Sofía, Queen of Spain. It is the Almontese Brotherhood who still take centre stage at the Romería, when, in the early hours of Pentecost Monday, they engage in the event's climactic act of ritual violence, rushing the altar and fighting each other off to climb its high fence before seizing the statue of the Virgin and parading it around the town for the next eight hours in a heightened, furious trance.

'They call the storming of the altar *El Salto* – The Jump,' Eddy said as he poured me a Cruzcampo from the house's own beer tap. 'It's a kind of invented tradition. They didn't start doing it until the 1970s. It can't be a coincidence that it began with the downfall of the fascist regime; it was a wild expression of anger, of freedom.' Originally, the procession was held in daylight hours, on the morning of Pentecost Monday. But the ritual of El Salto was so transgressive – hordes of young Almontese men forming a hostile human ladder to climb over the gate which surrounds the altar, sending priests and curates scattering in their wake – that it began to be pushed further back into the night, so that it didn't interfere with hallowed rites such as the rosary. Nowadays, it takes place at around 3am, although the exact timing varies according to the whims of the Almontese Brotherhood, who are very clear that they will do it when, and only when, they are ready.

This tension between the Brotherhood and the Church may seem surprising in the context of such a religious event. But it speaks to the nature of Spanish popular religiosity, which is often marked by the same three pillars which uphold the Romería: a burning, almost mystical, devotion to the Virgin; ambivalence towards religious authorities; and a proclivity to partying. 'There's no contradiction for them between the drinking and partying and the religiosity. Many of the most fervent pilgrims don't even go to church,' Eddy said. 'The main thing is the Virgin, who they see as the mother of their mother. The Church has nothing to do with that for them. It's a distraction. But the priests are respected at the Romería – as long as they don't interfere.'

There is another knot of tension at the heart of this event, between the Almontese Brotherhood and the world at large. Word of the passionate pilgrimage to El Rocío was originally spread far and wide by holidaying Sevillians, who would escape the heat of the city for the comparatively cooler Doñana in the summer months. Further reports were disseminated by seafarers making sail from the port town of Sanlúcar de Barrameda, just south of the Doñana. Since the development of El Salto in the 1970s, interest in the pilgrimage has surged, and it is now a major tourist curiosity, although almost exclusively for Spanish visitors. It's not hard to see what attracts them to the event. 'It's theatre – people can come here and be somebody else,' said Eddy. 'The way the town looks, and the chance it gives people to dress up in costumes – it's like Walt Disney. But then the Almontese say, wait a minute – this is our pilgrimage, our Virgin, and it's serious.'

Therein lies the rub. The Almontese Brotherhood do not take too kindly to the Disneyfication of their beloved Romería, but, deep down, it seems they rather enjoy the attention, and the special atmosphere it bestows on the event. 'When people try to take pictures of the Almontese, they act as if they don't want it – but in fact they do,' said Eddy. I had noticed this myself as I walked around town with my camera, being admonished when I tried to take pictures of people, only to be beckoned back once I had lowered my lens and turned away. 'And on years where fewer people come, you hear them commenting on it,' Eddy said. 'Worrying about the local economy, and so on.'

Still, while the Almontese Brotherhood may be conflicted about the presence of outsiders – or 'foreigners', as they refer to anyone not from their small town – their own devotion to the Romería is unquestionable. 'Sometimes it's a little frightening, the extent to which the Romería dominates their thinking,' said Eddy. 'I have to take a step back. The whole year, almost, revolves around this.' As part of his research, Eddy carried out a study of given names, and found that since the 1970s, local people have even started naming their children 'Rocío', or variations on it. 'That never used to happen,' he said. 'It's abnormal.'

Even so, Eddy was keen to dispel certain myths about the Romería, beginning with the claim that it attracts as many as one million pilgrims and observers. 'Ridiculous. Impossible,' he said, and although there were huge numbers of people here, I was inclined to agree with him. Eddy also wanted to address rumours about the nature of the debauchery which fuels the Romería's climactic crescendo. 'Saturday's the festive day, but Sunday tends to be quieter – most of the people who take it really seriously stop drinking in the afternoon on Sunday and sleep. They'll be up all night, after all,' he said. 'There's this misunderstanding that they're all drugged up and drunk, but it's not true. If the occasional person does a big line of coke to get themselves geared up for it, they will be told to calm down before they go in. And if you were drunk, you wouldn't be able to stand upright in the crowd. Your head has to be clear.'

Eddy struck me as a very kindly and gentle man, but he said that even he, once he had gained the trust of the Almontese Brotherhood sufficiently to be allowed to join in with El Salto in years past, had felt a transformative rage welling up inside him. 'The anger you feel is real,' he said. 'Sometimes I feel it's like being in the trenches. You have to feel like you're in a war, or it doesn't work. You really have to cross a line; to transform yourself.'

This transformation often manifests itself in violence, particularly towards outsiders who dare to get too close to the Virgin. 'You could be two metres tall and weigh 150 kilograms; it doesn't matter. You could be Mike Tyson, and you're not getting in there,' said Eddy. 'Something changes in these guys when they enter the ritual. They're not completely out of control, but they're not fully in control, either. It's theatrical, but they're not acting. It's real.'

This performative conflict with the outside world which surrounds the Almontese Brotherhood's role in the

Romería is geared towards strengthening their own sense of identity. 'I can't think of another event where locality, and this feeling of being against the wider world, is so visible,' Eddy said. But there is another, different kind of community engendered by the Romería: the shapeless society of the pilgrims, a kind of home defined by the fact that it is not a place at all, but a journey between two points in space. 'It's about feeling a part of something, but it's an in-between community; a no-place community, where you meet others who also want to be in a no-place,' said Eddy.

The no-place is the essence of liminality; the state of being in between, and the special status it confers. The no-place is a motif that crops up repeatedly in world literature, such that it presents itself as a separate room in the human imagination – one that is usually locked, but to which we hold the key. The sound of the pilgrims in the dust, singing songs about the Virgin amid the whinnying of horses and the creaking of wheels, was the sound of a million voices, crying out in the wilderness – and it brought to mind Isaiah:

The voice of one crying in the wilderness:
'Prepare the way of the Lord;
Make straight in the desert
A highway for our God.
Every valley shall be lifted up
And every mountain and hill brought low;
The crooked places shall be made straight
And the rough places smooth;
The glory of the Lord shall be revealed,
And all flesh shall see it together'.

– Isaiah 40:3-5

If that isn't a paean to liminality, I don't know what is. The high mountains are brought low, the valleys risen up; the crooked made straight, the rough smooth. On this level plain, everybody gathers together in experience of the divine – or of something, anyway.

The same things are on display at the Romería, with everybody in their matching costumes which disguise social rank and class. The setting itself, the Doñana, is a liminal place – not just a scene of wetlands and moving dunes where the land meets the sea, but somewhere to which access on foot is actually prohibited at all times except during the Romería, visitors restricted to running on limited tracks, admiring the scenery through car windows.

The most famous piece of literature concerned with the no-place of the pilgrimage is, of course, *The Canterbury Tales*, written some 600 years before my adventures on the Romería, but a reassuring document of proof that pilgrimage has always served up the same heady brew of the sacral and the profane. Some passages could have been written right here, on the road to El Rocío:

'The Miller was coming up behind, half on and half off his horse. He was so drunk that he could scarcely keep his saddle ...'[15]

Chaucer's stories paint pilgrimage as a metaphor for life, such as in 'The Knight's Tale':

This world nys but a thurghfare ful of wo,
And we been pilgrymes, passynge to and fro.
This world is nothing but a thoroughfare full of woe, ·
And we are pilgrims, passing to and fro.[16]

---

15. Peter Aykroyd, *The Canterbury Tales: a retelling*
16. Geoffrey Chaucer, 'The Knight's Tale'.

Chaucer's pilgrims set out from London, making for Canterbury. As we follow them, and listen to their stories, they are in between, in transit between two poles – walking and riding through a no-place. The pilgrimage is a metaphor for the journey between birth and death, but also functions, as many festivals do, as a memento mori – a reminder that we must die, and in that light, to remember to live as fully as possible. When I took part in the Romería it had not long returned after being cancelled for several years due to the Covid-19 pandemic, and like many of the festivals I attended during this time, the whole event felt imbued with a kind of raving madness, tinged with indignation – the imperative to make up for lost time. The same thing was happening on a personal level; probably tens of thousands of the people there, as at any large gathering, were riding the wave of some kind of crisis, like José Luis's father, for whom the inward journey and outward effervescence of a pilgrimage-festival had attained fresh urgency and vitality in the light of his terminal illness.

For Chaucer's pilgrims, the looming spectre was the Black Death, which reached England when Chaucer was five, midway through its continental death march which killed one third of the European population. The young Chaucer would have seen many of his contemporaries die – the plague primarily affected children – before growing up as part of a survivor generation which still had the stench of death in their nostrils and were haunted by the plague for the rest of their lives in other forms, too: post-traumatic stress, a population crisis, a decimated economy.

These people would have carried with them the same instinct: that life, always mysterious and short, can be snatched away at any moment, and so it is vital to fill it while we can with meaning, joy, and defiance against the end – to rage against the dying of the light.

By early on Sunday evening, El Rocío was a ghost town; everybody was resting before the night's climactic ceremony. I joined them, retiring to my hotel for a few hours' kip before following Eddy's advice and arriving at the church at around midnight. The storming of the altar does not usually happen until around 3am, but it varies each year according to the whims of the Almontese Brotherhood, and even now, three hours before kick-off, the place was heaving. I'd resigned myself to a night of craning my neck towards the altar from a spot just outside the door, when a hand grabbed me by the wrist and pulled me into the warm glow of the church. It was José Luis, there with his father, Antonio, and a backpack full of warm beers. Over the next couple of hours, the church grew stuffier, and we grew drunker. Antonio repeatedly impressed upon me the singular power of the Romería – 'A holy party … is very beautiful' – and I could see that he was moved, although he did not speak of his illness.

As time drew on, the altar drew the congregation to it like iron filings to a magnet, squeezing the crowd even tighter. Apprehension was rising steadily; there were nervous glances towards the altar, and a couple of fruitless chants of '¡Salto de la reja!' – '*Jump over the fence!*' – until finally, at four minutes to three, a ruckus broke out near the front of the church. A small human pyramid had formed below the statue of the Virgin, and the bodies of young men could be seen writhing and kicking as they attempted to force themselves by any means necessary over the two-metre metal railing which cordoned off the altar. There were flying fists, gnashing teeth, and a howl that can only have signalled testicles being impaled on a finial, before in no time at all the Virgin, housed in a silver litter, was being carried down from the altar and being crowdsurfed on top of the scrum like an upright marionette. The statue, carried by its savage escort of barbarous pallbearers, proceeded quickly through the church; most people, myself included, took a few steps backwards out of harm's way, but more than a few fervid worshippers rushed forwards, forgetting or ignoring the received wisdom about outsiders getting too close to the statue. They were pushed back, often forcefully, for their troubles, but that didn't stop several mothers, perhaps imbued with hysterical strength, from braving the mob to hold their babies up to the statue head-first, presumably in hopes of some kind of godliness rubbing off on their soft young foreheads.

One man, having been pushed away from the mob by an elder, had ripped his shirt open at the chest and was standing alone, his neck bent backwards at an unholy angle, veins popping and spittle flying, screaming at the roof of the church. I seemed to be the only one paying him any attention; there were probably dozens of others like him, in a frenzy, out of control, ignored and lonely in the crowd. One of the many boons believed to be bestowed by the statue to the faithful is the curing of mental disorders. Judging by the scene unfolding before me, I wondered if this year's attendees, having shelled out untold thousands on carriolas, costumes, and Cruzcampo, should ask for their money back. But this was what they wanted, this madness – and I was loving it, too. Bakhtin's words were ringing in my ears:

'Carnival brings together, unifies, weds, and combines the sacred with the profane, the lofty with the low, the great with the insignificant, the wise with the stupid.' But which was which, and who was who?

I woke up in mid-morning to find my guesthouse deserted. The Virgin, five hours after having been removed from her altar, was barely halfway through her procession, and most of the town were still out watching it. I could hear it – a vaguely ominous babble down on the waterfront – but I had seen enough. In search of coffee, and perhaps a souvenir, I headed towards the market, but save for a few prowling cats, the tents were deserted, their canvas flapping in the breeze and their wares left out to glitter in the morning sun. My eye was drawn to a display of silver pendants, bearing the image of the Virgin – the same ones I'd seen hung around the necks of so many of the pilgrims. In one of the pendants, which was laid upside down, with its smooth back facing towards me, I caught my reflection. I looked vaguely demonic – burnt and bloodshot-eyed, sweat and grime on my brow and a dark, half-dry trickle running towards my upper lip. The dust had given me a nosebleed.

Just as a pilgrimage is not about the destination, but about the journey, religious festivals – indeed, religious practices in general – are not really about the object of their devotion. People engage in them because they present an opportunity to swim in the ocean of liminality, to travel, temporarily, along different tracks – and by doing so, to discover or alter something about themselves. When pilgrims make the climb up to Kyoto's Fushimi Inari,

Japan's most famous Shinto shrine – through galleries of vermillion *torii* gates which cascade up a mountainside, thousands strong, like fallen decks of cards – they lift their gaze towards the altar of the main hall and are greeted not by a trickster-fox, serene Buddha or smiling bodhisattva, but by a circular mirror: their own reflection staring back at them. We are all of us pilgrims, and this is why we travel far – in pursuit of ourselves.

4

HUNGRY GHOSTS
Food, Festivals, and Meaning

Phuket Old Town, THAILAND

'The whole island should be on fire, really,' said Phuket tour guide Jo Lecourt as a small boy discharged a flare gun at electrical lines a few feet above our heads. 'But we don't get many accidents, believe it or not. The gods must be looking out for us.' They have their work cut out during the Phuket Vegetarian Festival, a mind-frazzling extravaganza of roaring fireworks, technicolour palanquins, and gruesome ritualised mortification which erupts on Thailand's largest island in the lunar month of Jiuyue, which falls between late September and late October. Food is one of the most potent forms of expression in the festival world, and at this time in the calendar – for nine days only – the Taoists of Phuket celebrate the restorative properties of a wholesome vegetarian diet by cutting themselves to ribbons, spearing their cheeks with scissors and knives, and letting blood from sword-slashed tongues spill scarlet onto temple floors. Beyond the eating of meat, an information leaflet from the Phuket Museum informed me, certain other things injurious to the mind and spirit must be avoided during this time. Alcohol. Quarrelling. Tobacco. Sex. And all kinds of garlic and onion.

The origin myth of the Phuket Vegetarian Festival – also known as the Nine Emperor Gods Festival – is reasonably well established and goes something like this. In the 1820s, an opera company from the south of China were on tour and got stuck on Phuket during an epidemic of an unknown disease (variously given as cholera or malaria). The opera performers were Taoists, and in a bid to appeal to their deities for protection, they moved to purify themselves and make merit through various means: by abstaining from meat and sex, and by engaging in mutilation rituals such as spearing their cheeks with skewers. It worked, or so it seemed: the plague lifted, and the opera company returned home, but their legacy was imprinted on the island forever. Every year since, it has been the setting for one of the world's most bizarre festivals, a macabre theatre-play where no quarter is given to the weak, the haemophobic, or the faint of heart.

Apart from everything else, this event is a pyromaniac's dream. The acrid smell of gunpowder hung in the air, so strongly metallic that it seemed to emit an almost audible ring. It was comforting to me, transporting me back to the cap guns, French bangers, and victimless arson of a gloriously misspent youth. All around us, on every street corner, children were hurling firecrackers, cackling with joy at each crackle and spark. It was my first night in Thailand, and Jo was leading me through Phuket Old Town to see a firewalking ceremony, one of the several methods of self-mortification for the spirit mediums who are the festival's main protagonists.

We reached a piece of parkland, nothing more than a square patch of scrubby earth, and joined the crowd sitting around its perimeter. A constant drumbeat, tonal like an Indian tabla, settled into my brain like a mantra, sharpening and deadening my senses at the same time. A myna bird, rattling in a cage, squawked spikily in time to the rhythm.

In the centre of the arena sat a flaming mound of coals, being raked by a long chain held at each end by assistants dressed head-to-toe in white. All the devotees of the Phuket Vegetarian Festival dress in white because, apparently, it's important to look virginal when you're skewering someone's face with a sword. As observers, Jo and I were wearing white, too. Scattered about, though, were people dressed differently, in vibrant sleeveless tunics brocaded with golden thread and woven with symbols: yin and yang, dragons, tigers, and flowers. Each of them was surrounded by white-clad attendants and appeared to be in a trance: they were shaking like they'd just put down a pneumatic drill, their heads thrust to the moon, a glazed look in their eyes.

These people, Jo explained, were the festival's spirit mediums. They are known as *masong*, literally 'entranced horse', in reference to the hypnotic reverie in which they undertake their mutilation rituals and their perceived status as steeds for the gods. Masong generally start to feel their calling in adolescence, Jo said – they suffer unexplained illnesses and have seemingly paranormal experiences, seeing terrifying visions or speaking in languages they don't usually understand. Eventually the identity of the god who has chosen them – which could be one of many hundreds of Taoist deities – will be revealed during one of the masong's trances, after which follows a period of training with an older masong, in which the younger initiate will learn how to better control and deal with their periods of possession.

One by one, the masong were guided over to a corner of the ring and presented to the crowd like prize fighters, their shaking arms lifted skyward to applause from their adoring fans. One of the masong had escaped the watchful eye of his handlers and was wandering around unsupervised, shaking and jabbering wildly and holding a long wooden staff, which he began to swipe violently at a group of watching children who had encroached too far for his liking into the arena. An attendant noticed what was going on and ushered him away, an embarrassed look on her face.

The coals were ready. The masong were lined up and took turns crossing the bed of fire in bare feet, each one walking with a different gait representing the various gods they were channelling. One hopped across bow-legged, his arms loose and his swaying knuckles almost brushing the glowing coals. 'Monkey god,' explained Jo. Another man skipped across the coals like a child, with his long hair tied in pink-bowed pigtails. 'His god must be a little girl,' Jo said, her eyes narrowing uncertainly. 'I think.'

I had been told repeatedly that their trance state meant that the masong did not feel any pain during this or any of the mutilation rituals to which they subject themselves during the festival. We sat and watched at least fifty firewalkers, and around half of them, sure enough, were slow and stoic, deep in their trance, apparently unfazed by the searing temperatures being borne witness to by the soles of their feet. As for the other half, though – well, the best way to describe it would be that they hotfooted it. They couldn't *wait* to get it over with. Their lower halves spun in a blur like a *Looney Tunes* wheel-o'-feet, and on reaching the cool earth they hopped about like pogoing punks until they could unburden their body weight from their burning soles onto the shoulders of onrushing attendants.

I wasn't sure what to think. Some kind of divine intervention seemed to be at play, but with a roughly 50 per cent hit rate. Jo sensed my scepticism. 'This is nothing,' she said, with a wave of her hand. 'Just wait until tomorrow.'

I slid out of bed at 4.30am, half-man half-jet lag, my soul still in a plane seat somewhere above the Caspian Sea – an appropriately otherworldly frame of mind, it turned out, for the madness into which I was about to descend. It was still dark when we arrived at Jui Tui Shrine, but the black night was beginning to blush into a blue-mottled morning. The shrine was already packed with people. Clustered around the entrance were stalls selling vegetarian street food – deep-fried *popia* (spring rolls), deep-fried *jee jo* (sweet sesame balls), steamed sweet buns filled with bright green pandan custard. 'It might be vegetarian,' Jo warned with a wag of the finger as I hungrily grabbed a few items for breakfast, 'but that doesn't make it healthy.'

We ascended the steps into the shrine. Beneath crimson pavilions, inlaid with jade and embossed with gold, cosmopolitan committees were carved in teak and stone: representatives from the pantheons of Taoism, Buddhism and Hinduism. Figures from Chinese folk religion were there, too: Sun Wukong, the Monkey King born from a stone egg in Wu Cheng'en's sixteenth-century novel *Journey to the West*; and rows of heads on sticks, representing the imaginatively grisly torture scenes from the folk tale Fengshen Yanyi (*Investiture of the Gods*).

Masong, like those from last night's firewalking ceremony, stood bug-eyed and quivering, resplendent in ornate tunics of gold and cardinal red. Some carried wavy-bladed spears. One older man, clearly a veteran masong of some years, wobbled past me, coming close enough that I could see clearly how much skin he had in the game – his cheeks were so riddled with dark, coin-shaped scars that they looked like slices of lotus root.

Attendants bustled past, carrying statues of fearsome-looking gods and quivers full of burning incense which choked us with the scent of sandalwood. A more potent physical threat came in the form of pierced masong, who were beginning to file past us out of the temple with sharp objects sticking out of their faces at all angles. Some were only small skewers, thoughtfully bookended with pieces of plastic, oranges, or limes. Many others, however, were far more baroque and less health-and-safety considerate, their sharp edges glinting beneath the temple lanternlight. One girl shuffled past looking like she'd had a run-in with some pigeon spikes, which were wedged awkwardly through her bottom lip; a man followed her, I kid you not, with a table lamp fixed through his face.

Jo led me past them in the direction they had come from, up some steps into one of the auxiliary shrines where they were carrying out the piercings. Masong sat in plastic chairs as medical attendants wearing surgical gloves pierced their cheeks with various sharp artefacts. A queue of masong stood waiting their turn, surrounded by their teams of helpers. Jo approached one of them, a middle-aged woman in a cerulean-blue ceremonial dress.

She was a friend of Jo's named Kaewalee, whom we would be following through the day's procession. We were briefly introduced. She seemed completely relaxed, as if the situation unfolding around us was the most natural thing in the world. We stepped back to observe again from the corner, leaving her to her preparations. After a couple of minutes, Kaewalee suddenly folded over and began making violent retching noises. 'The spirit is coming,' said Jo. 'She's entering the trance.' Kaewalee stood up again, and suddenly the woman I had just met was gone, her eyes distant and dilated, her whole body trembling in time with the hundreds of other masong crammed into the shrine.

Kaewalee's turn came and she was helped into a plastic seat. As pink shards of cloud-light heralded the sunrise in the sky above, the first skewer pierced Kaewalee's cheek and was drawn through the other side by a medical attendant. Another followed from the opposite cheek, so that they crossed inside her mouth at a diagonal. She sat through the proceedings, trembling softly but serene and seemingly unbothered. Kaewalee's piercings, though, were relatively subtle. Over her shoulder I caught sight of something far more extreme: a young man being impaled from cheek to cheek with two full-size swords. I locked eyes on him just as the second sword ruptured his cheek. My stomach turned. Just as bizarre as the procedure itself was his lack of reaction. I was more upset by it than he was. He just sat there unmoved, blank eyes gazing towards the bruised sky.

Things like this, to varying degrees of extremity, were going on all around me. It was medieval in its goriness, but, given its ceremonial nature and the complete lack of reaction from the masong, strangely unviolent. After the initial shock I did not find myself repulsed by it, but fascinated, and mostly just baffled. Jo assured me that no anaesthetic was involved, and I believed her – I certainly didn't see any being administered – and, even more curiously, I saw barely any blood issuing from even the sword-sized piercings. I wondered aloud why anybody would choose to put themselves through this year after year. 'Being a masong isn't something you choose,' said Jo. 'The gods choose it for you.'

Kaewalee was ushered out of her chair to join the procession filing out of the shrine, and we followed, joining the throng while keeping her in sight. There is a procession on each of the Vegetarian Festival's nine days, each one departing from a different shrine and centring on that shrine's own masong. Jui Tui is the most famous shrine in Phuket Town, and today's procession was the biggest of the lot – there were 1,900 masong taking part in this parade around the streets of the Old Town, each one with a team of three or four attendants, and thousands more observers watching either from the sidelines, where I silently wished I was, or in the thick of it, where in fact I found myself to be.

A table lamp, as it turned out, was only the half of it. I spent much of the day in a state of slack-jawed awe, fluctuating between terror, shock, and morbid curiosity as I whispered my newfound mantra – '*What the fuck*' – under my breath a thousand times. There were plant pots, model galleons, G-clamps, and garden shears, none of them where you would normally hope to find them – i.e. independent of the human body – but, rather, transfixed to people's heads.

I saw a man with several metal measuring rulers stuck through his face, one with two full-size parasols piercing his cheeks, and – this hurts even to write – a group of three young men walking side by side, slashing their own tongues with daggers as casually as if they were filing their nails with an emery board. That would normally be the most memorable thing I'd see all year, let alone in a single day. But then the man walked past with the BMX frame through his face.

It was a scene that would make Hieronymus Bosch wince, and, to make matters worse, I was experiencing it all in a state of heightened anxiety, constantly looking over my shoulder for the unshielded ends of skewers and swords, which were sticking out from cheeks as their wearers pressed on unaware of their surroundings, wobbling like jelly, black-eyed and vacant. (I'm a sniff over 6 feet tall, which puts a 12-inch skewer sticking out of the average Thai's face at a 45-degree angle just about at my pupil level.) The procession follows a one-way system – you don't have a very wide turning circle when you've got a spirit level sticking out of your face – and there were not many gaps in the crowd through which to escape.

Occasionally, we would spot a Westerner among the teams of assistants following each masong. 'That's getting more common,' said Jo. 'One day soon we'll have our first Caucasian masong.' She shot me a mock-threatening look. 'Maybe this year.'

It was an unrelaxing experience, but I can tell you this unequivocally: there is no better or more instant cure for fatigue than joining a procession at the Phuket Vegetarian Festival.

As luck would have it, I had an excuse to slip away from the madness the next time the opportunity presented itself. I had an appointment to meet Jack Chaopreecha, an anthropologist at Phuket's Prince of Songkla University, who had spent years studying the festival. We met at a house altar – a shrine inside a family home which faced onto the street and was open to the public on festival days. Walls were bedecked with hangings of scarlet and gold, while black lacquerware tables bore statues of gods and bodhisattvas, metal drums full of smoking incense, and plates loaded with fruit and bottles of soy milk. 'Offerings for the deities,' Jack said. He explained what each of them meant. Dragonfruit represents abundance; pomegranates promise family harmony; green-skinned oranges deliver wealth and prosperity; pineapples bestow good luck for the coming year; and so on.

I remembered a sign I had seen the day before, affixed to a wall in the Phuket Museum: 'Foods are messages sent to the death world.'

Food offerings are a feature of religious practice worldwide, from the bread and wine of the Eucharist to the rum and black coffee poured out for Baron Samedi, Haitian Vodou's elegant Lord of the Underworld. In his authoritative tome on Mexico's Día de los Muertos, *Skulls for the Living, Bread for the Dead,* anthropologist Stanley H. Brandes writes of how everyday food items become holy artefacts according to their context: 'An orange resting on the kitchen table is placed there to be peeled and eaten. Put the same orange on a home altar, or leave it nestled among other fruit in a covered ceramic bowl on top of a relative's grave, and it becomes a sacred object.'[17]

For the most part, food offerings are understood to be symbolic, although the Catholic Church has been tying itself in knots over this issue for millennia. The concept

---

17. Stanley H Brandes, *Skulls for the Living, Bread for the Dead*

of transubstantiation states that the eucharistic bread and wine *literally* change into the body and blood of Christ during communion, while *outwardly* remaining as bread and wine. According to the Vatican's official *Catechism of the Catholic Church*, this occurs 'in a way surpassing understanding', in case you were thinking of asking any more awkward questions.

In 1995, the eyes of the world turned to a temple in New Delhi when it appeared that a statue of Ganesha was drinking its votive offering of milk. The phenomenon quickly began being spotted at temples across India, and by lunch, Hindu temples as far away as Canada reported ecstatically that it was working for them, too. Come teatime, the wonder had transcended the Hindu pantheon and was being observed at statues of the Virgin Mary. There is a lot of footage of this online, and it does indeed appear to show milk disappearing from spoons when held up to the mouths of statues.

Such was the mass hysteria, with milk supplies exhausted and temples nationwide overrun with queues of devotees, that the Indian government got involved, sending a team of experts from the Ministry of Science and Technology to investigate. The scientists put it down to a phenomenon called capillary action, whereby the surface tension of the liquid milk caused it to rise up out of the spoon when placed near the statue, either being absorbed into the stone or imperceptibly spilling down the front of it. They proved their theory by mixing the milk with food colouring; as the liquid disappeared, the statues changed colour.

Not everyone is willing to believe that a statue can drink milk, but many people still can't resist imbuing their festivals with a supernatural flavour, so they meet cold hard reality halfway. Brandes writes that although the Mexicans he studied did not literally believe that the dead consumed the food offerings laid out for them, they did believe 'that the spirits derive some nourishment and contentment from the smell of the food displayed in their honor'.[18] He quotes a man from the Puebla town of Huaquechula as saying:

> '[There] are those who say the dead do not return, but I know they do. I feel sure of this, because when we offer food to the deceased it loses its aroma and taste.'[19]

The sending of messages to the death world is a cross-cultural phenomenon, but who exactly is receiving them varies from place to place. In the case of the Phuket Vegetarian Festival, as I'd seen at the shrine yesterday, it's a broad church. There's the Nine Emperor Gods, the Taoist deities to whom the festival is officially dedicated – lords of the stars who control the fate of the planets from their celestial seat in the constellation of Ursa Major. Everywhere, too, are statues of the Buddha and his many associated bodhisattvas, while Hindu gods also play a prominent role in the festival, themselves having been introduced to Thailand through their longstanding intermingling with Buddhism. I'd seen statues of Ganesha and Hanuman among the procession, while proceedings on the first day are kicked off by the raising of a 30-foot pole, down which Shiva is believed to descend to bless the festival.

---

18. Stanley H Brandes, *Skulls for the Living, Bread for the Dead*
19. Ibid.

'Although it's often called a Taoist festival, it's not really appropriate to call the people who celebrate it now Taoists – that's not how they'd think of themselves,' said Jack. 'It's Phuketian folk religion – a mixture of Taoism, Buddhism, and animism.'

What isn't in doubt is that elements of the festival have changed over the last 200 years. There is no record of any of the original practitioners processing through the Old Town with bicycles through their faces, for example. Several local people had said to me that the festival was getting more extreme year on year; that it seems more 'fake' and engineered towards the ever-growing audience rather than genuine religious ritual. Jack even expressed some doubt about the spirit mediums' trance states. 'Sometimes they are not really in a full trance,' he said, 'so they have to pretend.' I wasn't completely convinced by this. It seems like a difficult thing to phone in, shoving swords through your face. There's being tourism-savvy, and then there's this.

'And another thing,' Jack said, as we compared pictures of the strangest sights we'd seen at the festival so far, many of them featuring masong gurning gamely into the camera to show off their new facial adornments. 'How do the gods know to stop and pose for photos?' This I couldn't argue with.

Jack and I sat on the red carpet in front of the main altar, looking out to the street, and ate deep-fried festival doughnut balls and longkong fruit. He pointed out that not only was everyone wearing simple white outfits, but that they had taken their jewellery off, too; this is yet another festival at which rich and poor are made equal, meeting on a level plane. Other people started to arrive – tourists snapping photos, and friends of the family whom this house belonged to. A small group of admirers had gathered around a masong, who had been in a procession the day before and now wore the all-white outfit of the regular devotees, his cheeks padded awkwardly with thick bandages. We were introduced. He'd been doing this for 32 years, he told me. 'Except during Covid,' he hastened to add, wincing as he tugged at a leaking dressing on his mangled cheek. 'I'm not stupid.'

Food seems to bring out the very strangest denizens of the festival world, and you don't need to take a long-haul flight to meet them. One of the first events I attended in preparation for this book was the Cooper's Hill Cheese Rolling in Gloucestershire, in which participants hurl themselves down a steep hill in pursuit of a huge round of Double Gloucester. What better way to get the ball rolling, I had reasoned, than with a nine-pound wheel of cheese? For the participants themselves, though, this is a vain pursuit. The laws of fluid dynamics mean that a cheese this heavy can never be caught once it gets up to speed. The cheese, in the race as in life, always wins – but the first person to cross the finish line behind it gets to take it home, along with the glory of being a champion.

Amazingly, no one has yet died in the pursuit – the cheese gods must be smiling on proceedings – but limbs have regularly been re-arranged extravagantly, with the event's history a litany of fractures, sprains, strains and stretchers. The 2023 event alone saw broken legs and ankles, concussions and seizures, while the winner of the women's race – Canadian Delaney Irving – smacked her head on the way down and crossed the finish line unconscious, only discovering her victory after she woke up seeing stars and clutching a prize cheese in the medical tent.

Back in 1982, eight runners – four adults and four children – suffered some extreme bad luck when they were struck by lightning during the race. Ten years later, one of the children, perhaps imbued for life with a performance-enhancing electrical spark, went on to win the race. He also snapped his thigh bone in half. Even onlookers are not safe; in 1990, an elderly woman was knocked unconscious on the sidelines by a runaway wheel of bouncing cheese.

A rearguard of ambulances waits at the bottom of the hill, as does a beefy human shield made up of Brockworth Rugby Club players and Young Farmers, whose job – which they take quite seriously – is to tackle to the ground any runners who reach the bottom at speed and are in danger of crashing into the metal fence.

What does this say about the contestants, tumbling in a vain tangle of arms and legs en route to twisted joints and snapped bones? The 2023 men's winner Ryoya Minami, who travelled from Japan to take part, probably spoke for all the participants when he was asked why he had entered: 'Because I love cheese.'[20]

What, perhaps more pertinently, does it say about the likes of me, the spectators who travel across the country – even across the ocean – to witness horror shows like these?

---

20. The *Guardian*, 'Woman wins UK cheese rolling race despite being knocked unconscious' by Nadeem Badshah.

It was the day after the procession, and I was gawping in unison with a thousand other spectators, craning our necks skyward to watch a man climb up a ladder of knives. It must have been 30 metres high, and each of its rungs was inlaid with a curving, cutlass-like blade. The masong ascending the ladder – likely one of the same ones from yesterday's procession, Jo said – didn't show any discomfort as he pressed his feet down on the blades, although he was biting down hard on a bundle of joss paper, which he threw to the waiting crowd once he reached the top of the ladder. There would be no respite yet, though – having reached the top, he then repeated the process in reverse, climbing back down the ladder to the ground. What's more, he carried out the climb in a kind of backwards crab position, facing away from the ladder and towards the crowd, held on only by his arms, which were bent uncomfortably backwards in a way which seemed to add an extra layer of difficulty to an already perilous task.

'This used to be more common, but most of the shrines don't do it anymore,' said Jo.

'Why not?' I said.

Jo lowered her voice to a whisper. 'A few people slipped and *died*,' she said, emphasising the last word by whipping her finger across her throat and clenching her teeth in the universal gesture for 'Whoopsie!' The crab-like stance of the masong made more sense now. You don't want to be slipping onto those steps throat-first.

We stood and watched dozens more masong climb up and down the ladder of knives. Strange as it may sound, the spectacle started to become a little boring. Once you've seen one person walking up a ladder of knives, you've seen them all. Besides, we had a special appointment to get to – we were meeting Kaewalee, the masong we'd been following in the procession yesterday, at a restaurant in town.

Kaewalee was sitting outside waiting for us when we arrived – a woman in her forties, her face bare of the make-up she'd been wearing yesterday, and her sumptuous tunic replaced by the standard all-white garb of the normal devotees. We had followed her for about an hour during yesterday's procession, and I had been struck by how serene she had seemed through the chaos, in stark contrast to my state of high-wired anxiety. Though she had exhibited the same glazed eyes and body shakes as the other masong, she had radiated a certain calmness, walking slowly and pausing often to offer blessings to groups of small children and hand them gifts – bracelets, amulets, and sweets like boiled gemstones. 'Her god is a grandma,' Jo had explained.

Although no less pleasant, the woman before us today was like a different person, laughing and making jokes, fun and boisterous despite the exertions of the day before. 'I was walking around for six hours yesterday,' Kaewalee said. 'I could never normally do that. I have asthma! But I don't remember any of it. I was in a trance.' There was surprisingly little evidence of the two large skewers which had transfixed her face the day before – just two tiny freckle-like spots, one on each cheek.

I asked how she had felt before the ceremony yesterday. 'Scared and excited,' she said – but she had no memory of the skewering itself. 'Only after my spirit has gone do I look in the mirror and see where the piercing has been.'

The splendid festival outfit she had been wearing yesterday had been specifically requested by her deity, she said – although, thankfully, she didn't have to pay for it. In the event, Kaewalee's company, for whom she works as a tour guide leading boat trips around the Andaman Coast, stumped up the money for her outfit. They even gave her several days off work to accommodate the festival. Companies like hers are happy for their employees to be involved, because it is deemed to bring good karma to the company and to wider society. This is the whole point of the self-mutilation practices, Kaewalee explained – the masong suffer for the rest of our sins, taking on the bad karma of the community.

Kaewalee has been a masong for 26 years, taking part in the festival processions ever since she was a newly graduated 23-year-old. Her spirit has been with her much longer, though – since she was 13, she told me. A series of accidents, illnesses and mishaps as a child prompted Kaewalee to visit a fortune teller. 'She told me I was going to die young.' But then Kaewalee's god found her. 'My health improved overnight,' she said. 'It saved my life.'

'When a god chooses you, you have the choice to accept or deny them,' she said. 'I think I would have died if I had denied mine, like the fortune teller told me I would.'

Being a masong, it turns out, runs in the family. 'My auntie was a medium, too,' Kaewalee said, 'so she knew what to do when my spirit found me. I had to eat a vegetarian diet for a year, and chant for 30 minutes each evening.'

Kaewalee's gift has now been passed on to the next generation, too. 'My son is fifteen, and he's been found by his god recently – but it's too early to tell which god it is,' she said. 'One day the spirit will enter him, and he'll write down its name in the Hokkien language. Then we'll take it to the shrine, and they'll translate for us.' Jo had told me that the youngest masong she'd ever seen was ten years old – a very young age to be either blessed from on high or initiated into a self-mutilation cult, depending on your perspective. Although being a masong runs in her family, Kaewalee's account did not imply that there was any pressure on her to go down that path, and although her position confers her with honour and prestige, it does not appear to bring monetary or professional advantages.

Kaewalee's spirit looks after children, she told me – that's why she was stopping to bless the groups of kids yesterday. 'In some ways me and my god are the same; in some ways we're different,' said Kaewalee. 'We both love children. But I love to smile; sometimes her, not so much! Sometimes she is calm like a princess, other times she's ready for war. She's often frowning.' Nor can she resist having a dig, apparently. 'When my god first found me, I was very skinny. Now, with every passing year she looks at my body and says to me, "What's happened here, then?"'

The spirit came to her suddenly and without warning, Kaewalee said. She was sitting at home one day, recovering from one of her many bouts of illness, when she was suddenly seized by the same trance state I had seen her in yesterday. On coming to, she had clenched in her hand a piece of paper bearing a word in Hokkien Chinese, apparently written in her own handwriting. Hokkien is a language of Fujian province in southern China and was spoken by the Taoists who originated the Vegetarian Festival back in the 1820s – it was not spoken, Kaewalee said, by her or her family. Kaewalee's parents took the paper to Jui Tui, their local shrine, and on translation it was revealed to be the name of a Taoist goddess. Ever since, Kaewalee has spoken Hokkien whenever she channels her spirit, despite, she claims, not usually being able to speak or understand it.

The phenomenon of people being able to speak a previously unknown language through apparently mysterious means is known as xenoglossy. It's distinct from the religious practice of talking in tongues, also known by the rather delicious word 'glossolalia', whereby worshippers unleash a barrage of random syllables unintelligible to either themselves or anyone else – gibberish, but gibberish projected so confidently that it could offer the illusion of language or meaning. Cases of xenoglossy, by contrast, are alleged to speak real languages, which they did not consciously have any prior knowledge of.

The Spiritualists of the nineteenth and early twentieth centuries went mad for xenoglossy, claiming that mediums could speak fluently in the ancient tongues of whichever Egyptian mummy, Zoroastrian priest or Sumerian warrior they happened to be channelling. The Welsh writer and Egyptologist J. Gwyn Griffiths, examining some of these claims in 1986, recounted the story of Ivy Carter Beaumont (known as Rosemary), a woman in 1930s Blackpool who claimed to speak a dialect of ancient Egyptian while channelling the spirit of a Babylonian princess. Griffiths' analysis of recordings made of Rosemary's speech revealed many linguistic inconsistencies, leading him to the conclusion that the recordings were a hoax and the passages of ancient language the work of an amateur Egyptologist making creative use of E.A. Budge's *An Egyptian Hieroglyphic Dictionary*.[21]

---

21. J.G. Griffiths, 'Some Claims of Xenoglossy in the Ancient Languages'.

Other cases cannot so easily be dismissed as hoaxes but rather suggest cryptomnesia – the bubbling to the surface of buried memories, in this case scraps of language either read or heard. Griffiths relates the example of a young woman who apparently exhibited xenoglossy in Latin, Hebrew, and Greek, before it was revealed that her scholarly foster father had read passages to her in those languages when she was a child.[22] Another revolved around a man as surprised as everyone else to find he had an apparently innate ability to speak fluent Russian, despite never having deliberately learned it. It was eventually established that when he was a baby his family had lived next door to a Russian teacher, whose lessons were audible through the walls and had implanted themselves in his infant brain.[23] A similarly prosaic explanation can be given for the feats of Therese Neumann, a German mystic of the twentieth century who related the events of the Passion in ancient Aramaic. The Aramaic phrases she used were later found in books which she was known to have access to, from where they could have wriggled into her subconsciousness.[24]

The most famous modern-day example of xenoglossy came in 2015, when the Australian media whipped themselves into a frenzy over the case of Ben McMahon, a young man who experienced a car accident and awoke from the subsequent week-long coma speaking fluent Mandarin. The words came out so naturally, McMahon later told, Vice's *Extremes* podcast, that he didn't even

---

22. Ibid.
23. The Center for Inquiry, Xenoglossy and Glossolalia.
24. Ibid.

realise he was speaking a language other than English until it became clear that the only person who could understand him was his Chinese nurse. Here's the thing, though: Ben spoke Mandarin before. He had studied it at high school and had achieved enough proficiency to have basic conversations. The Mandarin he was suddenly speaking after his coma was much more fluent, but it seems that the blow to his brain unlocked information that was already in there, that had been absorbed into his subconscious mind from language tapes and textbooks and had previously lain dormant. It's fascinating for what it implies about the untapped potential of the human brain. But it's not paranormal.

In Kaewalee's case, even though her family did not speak Hokkien at home, it's easy to imagine she could have picked some up at the shrine or during previous festivals, particularly the name of her god and phrases relevant to religious practice which she then repeated while she was under her trance. The apparently superhuman stamina and resistance to pain exhibited by the masong is easy enough to explain, too. Trance states are so effective in reducing or eliminating pain that there has recently been a revival of interest in hypnosurgery, which entails the use of hypnosis as an alternative to anaesthetic for certain medical procedures.

I had doubts about the exact nature of the masong's spirit mediumship, but the effect it had on their minds and bodies seemed unquestionable, despite Jack's reservations. Jo and I said goodbye to Kaewalee and headed back out into the Old Town, where we found ourselves on the periphery of another procession. This was like the one we had attended yesterday, with dozens of pierced, trembling masong, but featured a new element: the procession of palanquins, wooden sedan chairs housing statues of fearsome-looking warrior gods, hewn from black stone, being carried by teams of young men. Everyone standing around us on the sidelines held belts of bright-red firecracker strips, which they lit with glowing sticks of incense and threw into the air to herald the passing of each palanquin with a shower of sparks. The statues processed this way around town for miles, each one shrouded by a constant, deafening cloud of firecrackers. Every so often, the sedan chairs carried not a sculpture, but a human masong, each one showered with just as many pyrotechnics as the statues. The young assistants who carried them defended themselves from the firestorm with white towels wrapped around their heads like shrouds, secured by sunglasses to cover their eyes. The masong afforded themselves no such protection, standing tall, firecrackers bouncing off their tattooed torsos like bullets off an armoured car, trance-trembling like Carthaginian warriors charging into war on elephants' backs.

As the afternoon turned into evening, the procession didn't stop but rather expanded until it was filling the whole of the Old Town, the air thick with firecracker smoke and a constant barrage of pops, crackles and bangs. The whole festival lasts for nine days, during which time masong processions engulf Phuket Old Town once or twice a day; the one I had attended yesterday was the biggest, with around 1,900 masong, but every procession includes several hundred of them. For the first eight days, businesses stay open, and life mostly proceeds as normal in the Old Town, but today was the last day, when the whole place is consumed by the farewell ritual which sees the festival off on its final evening, with the chorus of firecrackers believed to send the gods back to heaven. It looked and sounded to me more like a warzone, a vision of hell.

People dressed all in white were gathered on every piece of ground where there was space for them, including on all the Old Town's roundabouts, which were doubling as launchpads for amateur fireworks displays. The firecracker-hurling, which earlier in the day had been largely confined to the processions and the palanquins, had now become completely indiscriminate, and little explosions were bouncing off everything, even the surface of the road, as motorbikes swerved to avoid them.

At one point, debris from a firecracker hit me in the chin, which I took as a cue to don eye protection in the form of my sunglasses. 'One of them *hit* me!' I said to Jo.

'Ah, come on,' she said, waving her hand dismissively. 'Is only small.' Jo told me that when she first attended the festival thirteen years ago, shortly after she moved to Phuket from Bangkok, she hated it. 'I got hit by firecrackers; I couldn't breathe through the smoke,' she said. 'I told myself, never again!'

She has been every year since. Partly, no doubt, this is because of her job as a tour guide, but it was clear that over the years her interest had come to transcend the purely professional. There had been incidents which made her question whether there was some kind of divine protective blanket covering the event. 'When I first came, people told me it never rains during the rituals,' she said. 'I didn't believe them, of course – but thirteen years later, I've never seen it rain during a ceremony, even when it's forecast. And then, when the festival ends, the heavens open.' Jo had also avoided personal injury during her visits to the festival – she told me about incidents where lit firecrackers had landed on her skin without leaving a mark.

Speaking from experience, it does indeed feel miraculous to emerge from the Phuket Vegetarian Festival unscathed, although judging by the number of ambulances streaming north towards Vichara Hospital, their flashing lights barely visible through the ocean of smoke, avoiding injury is by no means guaranteed.

Even so, I had felt myself getting swept along again, drawn into the festival world, over the course of my time in Phuket. I had been gratefully receiving blessings at the shrines and from passing masong, and had even been abstaining from meat and alcohol – just in case.

My involvement was nothing compared to Jo's, though. As I lingered on the sidelines, content to watch the farewell procession from a distance, she was itching to get stuck into the mayhem. I bought some noodles from a food stall, and when I turned around again Jo had assumed the uniform of some unhinged *Mad Max* acolyte, her face wrapped in a towel held in place by ski goggles. She stood in a wide stance, hands in the air, each one clutching a belt of firecrackers; she asked someone nearby to light them, then bounded off into the smoke, sparks flying off her like Blackbeard. I never saw her again.

I was lulled to sleep that night by a pyrotechnic orchestra and woke up late the next morning, stumbling out of my hotel bleary-eyed into the streets of the Old Town. Workers in wide-brimmed hats were sweeping up the millions of red firecracker papers which covered every road and pavement, like the aftermath of some strange wedding march. A few bloody tissues were strewn about, too – the only evidence of the grisly slaughterhouse scene which had descended on these streets for the past nine days. Despite the warning of storms throughout the festival, the weather had held out. Black clouds had rolled in that morning, though, and now they burst, sending great cascades falling from the sky, frothing in torrents in the gutters, firecracker strips and joss paper rushing down storm drains – the blessings and the filth carried off by the gods for one more year.

5

EGO ALTARS
Ritual Madness, Ecstasy,
and Altered States

KONYA, Turkey

The provincial tourism director unwrapped another Turkish delight, lit his eighth cigarette of our half-hour meeting, and looked me dead in the eye. 'We humans – all of us – only face one obstacle,' he told me confidently. 'Ego.' Above his head was a huge oil painting of Kemal Atatürk, the founder of modern Turkey, whose image adorns restaurants, offices, and private homes nationwide. Atatürk's sweeping, secularising reforms had made many religious groups illegal in Turkey in 1925, among them the Sufi mystical orders, led by influential sheikhs who Atatürk sensed were a threat to his authority over the nascent nation.

A little over a century later, Sufism is still technically illegal in Turkey. Yet here I was, in the Turkish city of Konya, along with hundreds of thousands of others – some tourists, but mostly devotees – to experience the biggest event of the Sufi calendar: the festival of Şeb-i Arûs. Konya has long had a reputation as one of Turkey's most fervently religious cities, thanks largely to its history as the home of the thirteenth-century Sufi mystic and poet Jalal al-din Rumi (also known as Mevlana) and the religious order which he founded, the Mevlevis. They are better known to the Western world as the whirling dervishes, named for their devotional practice of twirling themselves into a state of religious ecstasy in remembrance of God – an act designed to obliterate the ego, that universal obstacle which, in Sufi thought, stands between the human and the divine.

Mevlevi whirling is the most famous practice in all of Sufism, the mystical branch of Islam – a joyous and life-affirming tradition, rich in music, poetry, and dance, all geared towards helping the practitioner achieve union with the divine. Tradition has it that Rumi was walking through Konya's bazaar one day when he passed an area of goldsmiths' workshops. Between the rhythmic tapping of their hammers against the metal sheets, he began to hear the names of God, lifted his arms to the heavens, and started whirling around in ecstasy.

Rumi was born in either Balkh, modern Afghanistan, or Wakhsh, in what is now Tajikistan, in 1207. His family left Central Asia early in his life, fleeing the Mongol hordes of Genghis Khan, and settled in Konya, where a meeting with a mysterious wandering dervish named Shams-i Tabrīzī changed the course of his life. The word 'dervish' derives from the Persian *darvīš*, meaning 'poor' (equivalent in meaning to the Arabic *fakir*), and long before Rumi's followers begin whirling themselves into states of religious ecstasy, dervishes were wandering mendicants who gave glory to God through other artistic means: in the case of Shams, through religious poetry.

The meeting with Shams inspired Rumi to begin composing ecstatic religious verse of his own. Rumi's writing bears little resemblance to the austere vision of Islam which preoccupies the Western imagination today. His verse is sensuous, awash with wine and song, describing God as his 'lover' and likening the intoxicating experience of the divine to drunkenness by wine. His death on 17 December is the focal point of Şeb-i Arûs; in keeping with his wishes, it is not a solemn occasion, but a joyful one. Şeb-i Arûs translates as 'Wedding Night' – Rumi, like other Sufi mystics, did not lament the end of his time on earth, but celebrated it as the moment his life had been leading up to: his long-awaited 'wedding', or union, with the divine.

Rumi has long been among the most highly revered and widely read poets in the East, and now his work – or something resembling it – is gaining a reputation to match in the West. Earlier that morning, in my hotel lobby, I had picked up a copy of the English-language *Konya News* and opened it at a full-page spread entitled 'Hollywood's Love for Rumi'. The disembodied heads of assorted celebrities grinned emptily up at me from the page, while the accompanying text gushed proudly of their love for the 800-year-old Persian theologian and poet. Brad Pitt, the article said, has a Rumi quote tattooed under his arm. Pink captioned an Instagram photo of her children with one of his verses. Leonardo DiCaprio is poised to play him in a biopic, and Beyoncé and Jay-Z even named one of their twins Rumi in his honour.

These are not people renowned for their expertise in the field of Islamic mysticism. Nevertheless, thanks in no small part to their endorsement, Rumi has been described in recent times as the bestselling poet in the United States.

You may have gathered by now that there is a catch. These Hollywood saps who believe they love the poetry of Rumi are in fact enamoured with the dubious publications of American 'interpreters' who neither speak nor read the Persian in which Rumi's poems were written. These collections bastardise Rumi's poetry into social media-friendly fluff, gutted of all poetic subtlety and spiritual meaning. Particular care has been taken to excise anything remotely Islamic. It is this vapid dross which Hollywood's galaxy of stars have fallen for so ardently.

I turned the page of the *Konya News*. Amid the usual bumf about the local government breaking its own investment records, unprecedented levels of agricultural production, and an article beaming with pride about the performance of the Karatay trampoline gymnastics team, was a passage of unexpectedly poetic self-awareness. A piece profiling the city ahead of Şeb-i Arûs read, 'Konya is a sooty but bright light leaking from the back rooms of history.'

And so it is. Konya is a slow, smoky city. On my first trips to the Middle East, I had been delighted by road signs warning drivers to look out for camels crossing the road, a red triangle framing a humped dromedary silhouette in place of the more familiar outlines (to me) of a hedgehog, deer, or cow. This time, through the window of my taxi into Konya from the airport, I saw similar signs, on main roads no less, exhorting drivers to give way to crossing tortoises. It conjured a funny image – a city of 2.2 million people brought to a rush-hour gridlock by a maddeningly slow procession of little shelled reptiles. But the longer I spent in Konya, the less far-fetched it seemed. Konya looks like a modern city, all urban flyovers and high-rises, but it doesn't feel like one.

It's quiet both day and night, there are few bars and fewer drunks, crime seems unimaginable, and you'd be more likely to be propositioned on the backstreets of Riyadh. It doesn't exactly feel poor, but there is an atmosphere of neglect about the crumbling houses and scrubby yards which come to predominate as soon as you step off the main drags. Even its poshest buildings, the gleaming, sky-scraping office blocks and hotels, are artless; Konya saves its beauty for its exquisite Islamic buildings. In all, it is the kind of place which would gladly pause its day to allow a family of tortoises to cross a busy highway, with uncommon grace, courtesy, and a certain bow-headed humility.

The focus of devotion to Rumi today, not just during Şeb-i Arûs but at any time of year, is his mausoleum, housed within the Sufi lodge which he established here in the 1200s. Rumi had explicitly directed that a grand monument should not be built over his tomb – 'What better dome could there be than the sky?' – but his followers ignored this directive and built one anyway. I joined the throngs of devotees approaching the shrine, accompanied by a tour guide, Giray Özcas, a cheerful man in his early forties. Since I had arrived in Turkey, Giray and I had spent much time discussing the fiercely misplaced passion of Turkish football – on the day I arrived, the president of Süper Lig club Ankaragücü had run onto the pitch mid-game to punch a referee in the face for not giving his team a penalty – and Turkey's present problems with feral dogs, packs of which were rampaging across cities and attacking children on their way to school. ('He survived,' Giray reported grimly of a young boy attacked in this manner the day before, 'but they ate him down to his lungs.') Most of all, though, Giray had been educating me on the subject of Islam, in which he had found personal comfort in recent years after the death of his father. Earlier that day he had even taken me to Friday prayers at Konya's Selim II Mosque, despite my awkwardness about attending as an outsider.

'Come, whoever you are,' Giray had said, repeating the first line of a poem often attributed to Rumi. 'That is Mevlana's message.'

The verse he was referring to is one of Rumi's most famous, often rendered into English as follows:

> *Come, come, whoever you are,*
> *Wanderer, worshipper, lover of leaving, it doesn't matter.*
> *Ours is not a caravan of despair.*
> *Come, come, even if you have broken your vow a thousand*
>   *times,*
> *Come – come yet again, come!*[25]

This verse is widely known and quoted in the Muslim world as Rumi's, including by Mevlevis, but this is a misattribution. It does not appear in the earliest version of Rumi's manuscripts and is in fact thought to pre-date him. So, to be fair, the misrepresentation of Rumi is not the sole preserve of gormless Western celebrities. Still, the verse radiates with the outlook often associated with Rumi's poetry and with Sufism in general: a welcoming tolerance which transcends the boundaries of religion.

We entered the lodge complex, ducking to pass beneath a chain which hung at head level across the gate – a

---

25. *The Last Barrier* by Reshad Feild, 1976, epigraph; cited at
   https://www.dar-al-masnavi.org/three.fake.rumi.verses.pdf

feature designed to ensure that everyone enters the lodge in an appropriate stance of bowed respect. The lodge was arranged in a square, with the outer buildings housing the former dervish cells. At the centre of it all, beneath a conical roof tiled in the most brilliant turquoise, was the shrine built around Rumi's tomb, known in Persian as the *dargâh* – the portal, or threshold.

Above the door into the tomb was a sign in Persian reading, 'Those who have missing parts will find them here.' We entered – having taken a Turkish delight from a box offered by a smiling attendant – and passed through a veil of green velvet into a room of exquisite beauty. Ceilings were tendrilled with swirling arabesques, painted in vivid blues, reds and greens; Persian and Arabic calligraphy danced across the walls in flashes of black and gold. In the middle of the room was a glass case containing a small box inlaid with mother-of-pearl; an information sign indicated that it contained strands of the Prophet's beard. A couple of people stood close to the case, staring at it. Most of the attention, though, was directed to the side of the room, where an alcove contained Rumi's tomb itself, draped with thick dark green velvet woven with golden brocade. A crowd was arrayed in front of the tomb, several of them rocking quietly, muttering verses, their faces tracked with silent tears. 'They are lovers,' Giray said. People had travelled here from all over the Sufi world, and Giray identified them in turn based on their style of dress. There were Dagestanis in furry papakha hats, young men from Iran in white tunics and sand-coloured waistcoats, and an old man in a knit cap whose potent facial hair – long moustache forking down to intersect with a V-shaped beard like a square and compass –

identified him as being from the Sufi city of Erzurum, in the east of Anatolia.

There was one man whose aspect suggested less about where he came from, and more about his way of life. His black hair was short but unkempt, as if he cut it himself; his beard was as dense as sheep's wool; he wore the loose rags of a fakir, wrapped in a thick, camel-coloured shawl. I watched him for a while and realised he was not only rocking gently and mouthing words to himself, as many of the gathered crowd were, but was also subtly, slowly turning in circles – whirling, for no one other than himself.

Sufis have suffered persecution since long before Atatürk came on the scene, often from within Islam itself. Although Sufis are staunch monotheists, elements of their practice – the whirling, the ecstasy, the intoxicating musicality – do seem, whisper it, a touch paganistic. To me, that sounds like a good thing. There are elements in the Islamic world, though, which deem Sufism to be a heretical deviation from the Quran and from the *sunnah* – the practices for living set out by the Prophet Muhammad. This comes down to a difference in perspective which is paradigmatic, perhaps irreconcilable. Those of a more traditionalist bent consider the Sufi emphasis on personal experience of God, achieved through dancing, music, chanting and the like, to be a distinctly earthbound pursuit. Sufis, meanwhile, believe themselves to be engaged in the really important work of experiencing the divine, while traditionalist scholars are preoccupied with mundane legalistic arguments. The fifteenth-century Egyptian historian Al-Maqrīzī spoke to the reputation of Sufis during his time through a humorous verse: 'From Sufis in this age and day a mere six vows are due:

'To swank and sing, to dance and booze, to eat hash-cakes, and screw.'[26]

Salafi Muslims – those of the fundamentalist branch which emerged in the nineteenth century as a reaction to Western colonialism and has since gone on to spawn organisations including ISIS and Al-Qaeda – use the slur *innovator* to describe Sufis, possibly the only milieu in which this would be deemed an insult rather than a compliment. They also describe them as *quburiyyun* – grave worshippers – for their habit of venerating the shrines of Sufi saints. While I'm not sure this should be a pejorative term either, I couldn't argue with its veracity as I stood in front of Rumi's tomb, surrounded by people wiping tears from their faces and whirling in silent prayer.

Like many things life-affirming, Sufism has something of a preoccupation with death. Whirling is not quite art – rather than self-expression, *sema* (whirling) is referred to as self*less* expression. It is not simply that it diverts the whirler's mind from themselves towards God; it is believed to actually obliterate the self, a process known as *fanaa* (self-annihilation). The ego is known as the *nafs*, and sema is believed to destroy it. The ultimate, egoless state achieved through sema and dissolution of the nafs is called *khamra* – spiritual drunkenness.

'Many monks traditionally followed the discipline "eat less, speak less, sleep less",' said Giray. 'The Mevlevis go further. Their discipline is to kill themselves – to forget who they are.'

---

26. Cited in *Travels with a Tangerine* by Tim Mackintosh-Smith

I had been pestering Giray all week to introduce me to a Mevlevi, and he'd been making enquiries on my behalf. While we were inside the tomb he made a breakthrough, so we climbed inside a taxi to İrfan Medeniyeti, a cultural centre dedicated to the preservation of Turkish cultural traditions, to meet Mithat Özçakıl, a third-generation whirler.

A slender man in his early thirties, Mithat already seemed sage-like – white hairs were beginning to sprout amid his thick, ink-black beard, and crow's feet wrinkled the corners of his eyes when he smiled, which was often. I asked him to tell me his story.

'I was born in Konya, and I was born in the Mevlevi tradition,' Mithat said. 'Every December, my younger brother and I would come to watch our father whirling here at the ceremony. Generally, a young boy wants to imitate his father, and so it was with me; he started to teach me, and I performed my first sema when I was fourteen. That's nearly twenty years ago now – but I'm still a beginner.'

Mithat told me that modern-day Mevlevis are no longer subjected to the strict ascetic practices once required of new initiates to the order – kneeling in the same position on an animal-skin rug for three days and nights, for instance – but that there is still some physical hardship involved. To attain the delicate, toe-leaning balance required during the sema, students practise by whirling with an upright nail underneath one foot.

'At first, you cannot focus on your spiritual side during the sema because you're trying to be well balanced, trying to keep up your physical appearance,' Mithat said. 'But with time, you stop focusing on that and start focusing on the Creator. With every turn, we repeat the name of

God – *Allah, Allah, Allah* – but silently, with the heart, not the tongue. If you say it thousands of times, God sends his mercy. He turns his face upon us.'

Şeb-i Arûs is the holiest time of year for Mithat, as a devout Sufi and Mevlevi. And yet, it only exists in its modern form under the auspices of the Turkish Ministry of Tourism and Culture. Mithat and his fellow performers in the public Şeb-i Arûs rituals are far from mendicant dervishes, but rather government employees, who earn their bread filing paperwork when they're not whirling. Sufism is technically still illegal in Turkey under Atatürk's law, but after the government realised there was cultural prestige to be generated and money to be made – supposedly after the wife of an American diplomat lamented in the 1940s that she couldn't see the famous whirling dervishes of Konya – they brought back Şeb-i Arûs, turning what was traditionally a private ritual into a public performance.

The modern festival is a major tourist attraction, with 2.4 million tourists in 2024 – most of them international, and nearly all from across the Muslim world – flocking to sema performances throughout the week here at İrfan Medeniyeti and at other venues across the city. The climactic sema ceremony, on 17 December, is held in a huge purpose-built venue, is filmed for national television, and is opened with speeches by prominent politicians – including, on several past occasions, Turkish president Recep Tayyip Erdoğan.

For all the media spotlight and PR politicking, though, the modern Şeb-i Arûs is far from a zombified resurrection of a once-pure religious ceremony. On the contrary, for practitioners like Mithat, it has lost none of its transformative spiritual power. 'Sema is everything to me – it's my whole lifestyle,' he said. 'This order, this tradition, it shapes you – actually, it's better to say that it *reshapes* you.'

'Muhammad, peace be upon him, says, "Die before you die." All the clothes we wear during the sema refer to this. Our long white dress is like a shroud. Our tall cap is the tombstone of the ego. Our black belt divides our bodies into two – the animal half below, and the upper side, where the soul, mind and spirit reside. During the sema, our bad behaviour, our animal side, turns to our good side. Our ego and our lust turn to mercy.'

The idea of transformation through ego death is by no means confined to the realm of Sufism. The French, being as they are, understand this phenomenon in sexual terms – *la petite mort* (the little death) referring to the state of post-orgasmic loss of self. Psychedelic guru Timothy Leary, being who he was, spoke of ego death being primarily engendered by the consumption of large enough quantities of LSD – although as David Lenson wrote in his classic *On Drugs*, Leary's life and writing do not exactly point towards a loss of ego. This 'Hugh Hefner of the drug culture,' Lenson wrote, was 'an exemplary ego, not a dissolved one'.[27]

The festival world is a graveyard for the self, littered with altars on which the ego is lain. Its landscapes are riddled with deep wells and dark caves, reservoirs of ritual madness, ecstasy and altered states, of which its residents drink deeply in order that they might forget who they are. The Dionysian Mysteries of ancient Greece, like the sema of the modern Şeb-i Arûs, saw

---

27. David Lenson, *On Drugs*.

participants using music and dance to whip themselves into states of religious ecstasy. And like sema, the central imagery of the Dionysian rites was one of death and rebirth – this time that of the harvest and the changing seasons. Dionysus is of special interest to this book. Alongside being the deity of fertility, wine, ritual madness and religious ecstasy, he is the god of festivity itself – nothing less than our guardian angel. Rather pleasingly, one of Dionysus' associated qualities was *enthusiasmos* – root of the English word 'enthusiasm' – literally meaning 'infused with a god's essence' and thought by the Greeks to be delivered through wine. To this day, the Thessaly town of Tyrnavos celebrates the Dionysian festival of Bourani, during which townsfolk get good and hooned on tsipouro and chase one another around with giant wooden fertility-enhancing phalluses.

Alcohol is by no means the only mind-altering instrument in the festive arsenal. The Eleusinian Mysteries of ancient Greece – a series of yearly initiation rites into the cult of Demeter and Persephone – made use of an entheogenic drink known as *kykeon*, the ingestion of which seems to have engendered states of ritual ecstasy and revelation. Those who drank kykeon and experienced such visions (thought to have included Plato and Aristotle) were known as *epoptai* – beholders. The exact makeup of kykeon remains a mystery, but it's been theorised that it either contained ergot, the hallucinogenic grain fungus from which LSD is derived, or some kind of hallucinogenic mushroom.[28]

---

28. F.J. Carod-Artal, 'Psychoactive plants in Ancient Greece'.

Mesoamerican cultures made particularly extensive use of the rich bounty of natural hallucinogens available to them. The Olmecs licked the bufo toad, the Maya ate peyote, and the Zapotec – well, all of them, really – gobbled down psilocybin mushrooms with great gusto, seemingly for ritual purposes.[29] The earliest Western accounts of this behaviour came from horrified Spanish missionaries, who wrote wide-eyed accounts of events like Emperor Montezuma II's coronation, where the watching crowd dipped magic mushrooms in honey and ate them, slowly going insane while sacrificial prisoners had their hearts cut out on the pyramid steps above.

In the magnificent National Museum of Anthropology in Mexico City there lives a sixteenth-century statue of the Aztec god Xōchipilli, sitting on a plinth carved with various hallucinogenic plants. His mouth is open, and his jaw is gurning; his eyes look heavenward, great black bowls suggesting dilated pupils. His legs are crossed, and his raised hands are half-clenched, as if grasping at some unseen wonder.

The existence of artefacts like this – known as 'mushroom stones' – led the ethnomycologist Robert Gordon Wasson to Mexico, where he confirmed his long-held theory regarding the existence of a magic mushroom cult. Wasson and his wife were granted the rare privilege of taking part in a mushroom ceremony with an (unnamed in his account) indigenous group in Mexico in 1955, apparently the first foreigners allowed to do so. The terms in which Wasson describes his adventure ring with the same qualities of ego death as the Sufi sema.

29. F.J. Carod-Artal, 'Hallucinogenic drugs in pre-Columbian Mesoamerican cultures'.

Above left: *The galley burns at Up Helly Aa in Lerwick, Shetland.*

Above right: *The torchlit procession at Up Helly Aa.*

Right: *A Mari Lwyd in Chepstow, Wales.*

Above left: *The author at Venice Carnival.*

Above right: *Carnival masks at Papier-Mâché workshop, Venice.*

Left: *Pilgrims at the campsite on the Romería de El Rocío.*

Above left: *Pilgrims on the road to El Rocío.*

Above right: *A pilgrim pulls a* simpecado *in El Rocío.*

Right: *A spirit medium with swords through his face at the Phuket Vegetarian Festival.*

Left: *Jui Tui Shrine, Phuket Vegetarian Festival.*

Below left: *More ritual mortification at the Phuket Vegetarian Festival.*

Below right: *Whirling dervishes at Şeb-i Arûs, Konya, Turkey.*

Right: *Rumi's tomb in Konya.*

Below: *Decorations at the Rabat festa, Malta.*

Left: *Sunrise at the spring equinox at Mnajdra temple, Malta.*

Below: *Ashbourne, Derbyshire, dressed up for Shrovetide football.*

A musician plays a makeshift instrument at the Pèlerinage Gitan (Gypsy Pilgrimage), Saintes-Maries-de-la-Mer, France.

The Mass at the Pèlerinage Gitan.

Pigs wait to be sacrificed at a Torajan funeral, Sulawesi, Indonesia.

A Torajan burial ground.

'It was,' he writes, 'a soul-shattering experience.'[30] The 'bemushroomed person,' he says, 'is poised in space, a disembodied eye' – and this flight of the soul from the body is the literal meaning of the Greek *ekstasis*, from where we get 'ecstasy'.[31]

Wasson also gives us a clue as to the power and purpose of ego-dissolving practices in a communal, festival setting. '[You] feel that an indissoluble bond unites you with the others who have shared with you in the sacred agape,' he writes. Shattering the soul as private practice is one thing – to do it *en masse* is quite another, strengthening the bonds of the community as does every meeting on the level playing field that is the limbo of the carnivalesque.

The Australian anthropologist Marie Reay wrote of her experiences in the 1950s observing a mushroom festival among the Kuma people of Papua New Guinea. Once a year, the entire community would eat a locally blooming psychedelic mushroom, as a result of which around 10% of the population would enter a state which Reay describes as 'shivering madness'. Under this spell, women would simply gather in groups and start dancing, but the men would run amok, aggressively chasing and attacking members of neighbouring villages and their own. Those unaffected by the madness would remain hidden from the marauding men, but nonetheless seemed to encourage their behaviour from a safe distance. This 'mushroom madness' was also documented by other anthropologists and mycologists, and occurred not just among the

---

30. *The Road to Eleusis: Unveiling the Secrets of the Mysteries*, R. Gordon Wasson, Albert Hofmann, Carl A. P. Ruck
31. Ibid.

Kuma people but across the Waghi Valley in Papua New Guinea's Western Highlands. However, the phenomenon seems to have vanished from the valley sometime in the 1980s, despite the fact that the locals still gather and consume the same types of mushrooms to this day. When villagers were asked to explain the fading power of the mushrooms in the early 2000s, they 'expressed the belief that the associated spirits [believed to have cause the mushroom madness] have lost their power, since the people no longer believe in them'.[32] This seems to line up with one of the theories as to why only 10% of the population were ever affected by the mushrooms: namely, that the whole thing had little to do with psychedelic chemicals and was in fact a 'theatre-play' – a kind of collective hysteria.[33]

As a general rule, it is unwise to assume a placebo effect when offered a psychedelic mushroom. That could end up landing you in very strange waters indeed. But often, of course, that is entirely the point – the pursuit of altered states is a primary aim of many festivals across the world. 'Transformational festivals' is the name given to a wave of contemporary events geared in large part towards transformation of the self, often achieved through an obliteration of the ego via psychedelic drugs, deep meditation, yoga, and various other practices thought to expand or sharpen the mind.

The city of Ann Arbor, Michigan – where psychedelic plants and fungi were effectively decriminalised in 2020 – holds the yearly Entheofest, where seekers gather to eat

---

32. Roland Treu and Win Adamson, 'Ethnomycological Notes from Papua, New Guinea'.
33. Reay 1977, cited in Treu and Adamson.

peyote, attend workshops on how to grow psilocybin mushrooms at home, and listen to talks from speakers as diverse as Unitarian Universalist Reverend Mariela Simons-Perez, visual artist Barking Dog Darryl Brown, and Michigan Member of the US House of Representatives, Debbie Dingell – evidence, perhaps, that turning on and tuning in is going mainstream.

At Costa Rica's Envision Festival, meanwhile, unwashed trust-fund kids with tattoos in bad Sanskrit take to the rainforest for a week of music, chemicals, and workshops on yoga, mindful movement, and herbal medicine. Particularly common at festivals like this are lectures invoking the name of Terence McKenna, high priest of modern psychedelia, and a keen proponent of ego death:

> If the ego is not regularly and repeatedly dissolved in the unbounded hyperspace of the Transcendent Other, there will always be slow drift away from the sense of self as part of nature's larger whole. The ultimate consequence of this drift is the fatal ennui that now permeates Western civilization.[34]

The atmosphere of psycho-spiritual adventurism which was carried on the breeze in 1960s and '70s California directed many, like Terence McKenna, towards drugs. It also found different outlets; one was the study of world religions, particularly those of the East, and while the mania for Hinduism and Buddhism at this time is well-documented, a smaller number of young Californian

---

34. Terence McKenna, *Food of the Gods: The Search for the Original Tree of Knowledge: a Radical History of Plants, Drugs and Human Evolution*

seekers became drawn instead to Sufism, with its message of tolerance and possibilities of transcendence.

One of those was a young man called William Gamard – now Ibrahim Gamard – whom I had the privilege of meeting in Konya. Ibrahim has been a whirling dervish since 1976, although Parkinson's disease has diminished his ability to take part in the sema and to play the *ney*, the reed flute which accompanies the ceremony. I met him in a café in the rose garden outside Rumi's tomb. A small, elderly man with a long white beard, he was frail, physically reduced by Parkinson's, but mentally sharp – and clearly well enough to make the long journey from California to Konya, as he does twice per year: once in September, and again in December for Şeb-i Arûs. He led me to the offices of the International Mevlana Foundation, the UNESCO-accredited organisation which manages Rumi's legacy, and we sat in an upstairs room overlooking the dergâh.

'I discovered Rumi in 1975,' Ibrahim said. 'I read all six books of the *Masnavi* [Rumi's masterwork], and thought it was the greatest work of religious mysticism I'd ever read. I was living in LA at the time with my wife; our teacher was an Englishman called Reshad Feild.' Feild had earlier been a musician, and a member of folk-pop trio The Springfields, along with future solo star Dusty Springfield.

'Reshad had taught us rudimentary whirling – we made our white costumes and tall hats ourselves out of cardboard, and whirled every Thursday night,' Ibrahim said. 'In 1976, Reshad invited a Mevlevi sheikh from Konya called Süleyman Dede. We performed a sema with him, and he ritually placed the Mevlevi hat on my head, and I was initiated as a whirler. I've been one ever since.'

Ibrahim is a scholar of Sufism, too – he has translated Rumi's quatrains from Persian into English, and his third book about Rumi and the Mevlevis was published in 2022. He is from the old school of Western Rumi enthusiasts, so enamoured of the words, the whirling, and the states of religious bliss they engender that he learned Persian and devoted his life to studying Rumi – a far cry from the sanitised Rumi 'interpretations' which have since become million-selling self-help manuals for Hollywood celebrities.

I asked Ibrahim about the annihilation of the ego through sema. Could he explain what such a thing feels like? Is it even possible to put into words? 'After my first sema was over, I stepped outside the auditorium and it felt like the whole sky had opened up inside me,' he said. 'That was my first experience of an ecstatic state from sema.'

Ibrahim is uniquely placed to analyse the effects of sema – not only has he experienced them himself, but he worked for decades as a clinical psychologist. I suggested that the mental state engendered by sema is a kind of trance. 'Trance is a word that's very misleading and complicated,' he said. 'It seems to explain everything, but really it explains nothing. It's a difficult thing to explain – the Sufis often liken it to taste. You can't describe the taste of cinnamon to someone who's never tried cinnamon. But once you taste it, you're in love with it.'

'The best term would be "peak experience". It's a very intensely concentrated state. You have to not only hold up your arms for a long time, but on each step you're praying silently – "*Allah, Allah, Allah*" – and you're supposed to be at a certain distance from the whirlers next to you. The skirts are not allowed to touch; you should be whirling at the same rate as the others. It involves tremendous concentration. From the spiritual side of that concentration sometimes come these peak experiences.'

I asked, rather tritely, if these peak experiences could be visions of the Face of God. Ibrahim smiled. 'That's too grandiose,' he said.

Nevertheless, under different guises, peak experiences of this kind are a feature – in some cases, an objective – of many different festivals. The concept of the peak experience originates with Abraham Maslow, the American psychologist most famous for his concept of the hierarchy of needs. Maslow conceived peak experiences as those transformative moments of high intensity, which engender an escape from the small self, connection to something bigger, and feelings of great happiness – the type experienced on mighty mountaintops, beneath glittering auroras, or in the depths of a mushroom binge. The annihilation of the ego is a key characteristic. 'The peak-experience itself can often meaningfully be called a "little death," and a rebirth in various senses,' Maslow wrote.[35]

Maslow listed several things common to peak experiences which are identifiable in the sema: first, that 'the whole universe is perceived as an integrated and unified whole' – as with the shedding of the ego and unity with the divine. Second, 'there is tremendous concentration of a kind which does not normally occur', just like Ibrahim had reported of whirling. Maslow also wrote that 'perception in the peak experiences can be relatively ego-transcending, self-forgetful, egoless, unselfish' – so that checks out, too. Ibrahim had told me of the new mode

---

35. Abraham Maslow, Religions, Values and Peak Experiences.

of perception which follows the ego death, in which the whirler experiences every aspect of reality as beautiful reflections of the attributes of his sheikh, or of God. This too is mirrored in another of Maslow's criteria: 'The world seen in the peak-experiences is seen only as beautiful, good, desirable, worthwhile.' Wasson described something similar in his account of his mushroom trip: 'All that you see ... has a pristine quality: the landscape, the edifices, the carvings, the animals – they look as though they had come straight from the Maker's workshop.'

Finally, Maslow wrote: 'People during and after peak-experiences characteristically feel lucky, fortunate, graced.' Ibrahim, while acknowledging some of the strangeness and contradictions of the modern, government-mandated Şeb-i Arûs festival, ended our conversation with a similar sentiment. 'Despite all the difficulties and imperfections, people are still affected,' he said. 'Their mood is affected through the music, the whirling, and the occasion. It exposes them to some kind of spiritual grace.'

Maslow was not entirely positive about the ritual role of peak experiences. He warned that mystics can be prone to chasing the dragon, seeking ever higher and wilder experiences to the abandonment of reason: 'If the sole good in life becomes the peak-experience, and if all means to this end become good, and if more peak-experiences are better than fewer, then one can force the issue, push actively, strive and hunt and fight for them. So, they have often moved over into magic, into the secret and esoteric, into the exotic, the occult, the dramatic and effortful, the dangerous, the cultish.'[36]

---

36. Ibid.

Perhaps one role that festivals play in society is as a time-limited stage for the peak experience. The masks of Venice Carnival would not hold half as much power if they were worn year-round. The explosion of ritual violence which marks the end of the Romería de El Rocío would likewise lose its potency if it happened more often, and the same can surely be said of the travails of Phuket's masong, who, if they attempted to live their festival lives in the everyday world, would certainly fit Maslow's cautionary criteria: dramatic and effortful, dangerous and cultish.

Maslow believed that peak experiences are biologically grounded rather than supernatural, and suggested that all religions are attempts to communicate the mystical peak experiences of their founding prophets – a problematic task, he said, given that a significant proportion of the human population are either unable or unwilling to have peak experiences themselves. The situation is further complicated by the fact that many of these 'non-peakers', being better suited than solitary, mystical types to system and hierarchy, often end up in positions of influence in society, including in major world religions: '[The] two religions of mankind tend to be the peakers and the non-peakers, that is to say, those who have private, personal, transcendent, core-religious experiences easily and often and who accept them and make use of them, and, on the other hand, those who have never had them or who repress or suppress them and who, therefore, cannot make use of them for their personal therapy, personal growth, or personal fulfilment.'[37]

---

37. Ibid.

It is easy to see how this conflict between mysticism and jurisprudence is played out in the attitudes towards Sufism held by some Muslims. It's also easy to identify the non-peakers of the world. They are those who are resentful of mysteries; who equate morality with law; who believe that science has made religion redundant; that the use of psychedelics or pursuit of altered states is never anything more than distasteful hedonism; that there is nothing in the nature of reality beyond human understanding; nothing to be learned from the ways of mystics and visionaries, nothing of value in festivals or rituals which appeal to something, imagined or otherwise, greater than our small selves. I would venture as far as to say that, generally speaking, if you enjoy festivals, you're probably a peaker; if you don't, you're probably not.

Before I left, there was somebody Ibrahim wanted me to meet. We walked downstairs and entered a wood-panelled office, where there sat behind a desk a grey-haired woman dressed in a black suit, her green eyes illuminated by jade bracelets and a bright emerald ring. Ibrahim introduced her as Esin Çelebi Bayru, the vice-president of the Mevlana Foundation, and Rumi's granddaughter 22 times over. She was busy – more so than at any other time of year – but I stole a brief conversation with her.

'Şeb-i Arûs is our biggest day; our happiest day,' she said with a smile. 'Mevlana's death was the day of his union with his greatest lover – Allah – so he wasn't sad about it. He wished joy and celebration, so that's what we do. With music, concerts, workshops, and the sema, we celebrate.' The sema is not limited to the public performances, she explained, but is practised privately in Mevlevi homes at this time of year, too. 'But sema is not just a Mevlevi tradition,' she said. 'It's a natural human behaviour. As soon as a child starts to walk, when they are happy, they spin around. Adults dance; musicians turn around the fire beneath a desert moon. Whirling is about enthusiasm and happiness – when you feel inspiration from your soul, you start turning and whirling.'

I said goodbye and stepped out from the Mevlana International Foundation into Konya's hazy winter air. The streets were quiet, but for a few prowling dogs and the muffled sound of music coming from a black tent which had been erected in the square outside the Selim II Mosque. I entered and stood at the back. It was packed, with everybody's attention given to the stage, where a six-piece band was playing. There was a guitar, a flute, a rebab, two drummers, and a woman strumming a *dutar*, a two-stringed Iranian lute. Three of them doubled as vocalists – two singers, and another man who gave long spoken sermons over the music in Persian and Arabic. Apart from the music itself and the notable absence of alcohol, the atmosphere was identical to the quieter corners of a Western music festival – the family tent, perhaps. Small children were hoisted on their fathers' shoulders, the crowd cheered as the band broke into numbers they recognised, and a group of young men standing in front of me sang along in full voice, their arms around each other's shoulders.

It was 17 December. That evening saw the headline event of Şeb-i Arûs: the final sema. Rumi's 'wedding night'. When the event was first resurrected in the mid-twentieth century, it was on a small scale – a handful of whirlers performing sema in the Konya Public Library. Over the years, as more people learned of the opportunity to see the forbidden dance of the dervishes, the event outgrew the venue, moving to a soulless sports stadium before the construction of a purpose-built sema hall in the east of the city, the Mevlana Cultural Centre. This was where Giray and I travelled to now. The atrium was lined with pop-up stalls, selling Rumi books, little statues of dervishes in mid-whirl, and neys, the reed flute played during the sema. There was an excitable babble in the air, and people of all kinds milling about. I saw the dervish who had been whirling at Rumi's tomb, chatting with another man similarly attired; next to him was a group of young men and women in suits, who kept pressing headsets to their ears and rushing off to attend to important-seeming tasks.

The time came to enter the auditorium, and we blagged our way into seats on the front row. Before the spiritual matters came an interminable slew of politicking guff, delivered in long speeches by an increasingly eminent roster of bigwigs culminating in the Minister for Culture and Tourism, Mehmet Ersoy. I listened to the speeches in translation on a headset. It was your usual self-congratulatory stuff about how the world looked up to Konya as the home of Mevlana, the universal poet. But they each finished their speech by saying, 'I salute you all with love.' Which was nice.

Ironically, given that Ataturk made Sufism illegal as part of his creation of the secular state of Turkey, the whirling dervishes have been co-opted by today's nationalist government as a symbol of the country's cultural heritage. They bring in tourist money throughout the year, particularly through tourist shows in Istanbul, but Şeb-i Arûs is by far the most lucrative single event in the calendar. Ibrahim had pointed out to me that tying the event to 17 December was an artificial move, designed with tourism in mind – the date of Rumi's death would traditionally have been marked on the Islamic lunar calendar and so would change every year, as do festivals like Mawlid, the anniversary of the Prophet Muhammad's death. There were even rumours, Ibrahim said, that the tourism ministry was planning on moving Şeb-i Arûs to spring or summer to attract more tourists.

Still, economic motives have likely always played a role in festivals of all kinds – as have questions of authenticity, as reflected in Byron's complaints that the Venice Carnival he experienced was a pale imitation of the event of the past. At least in modern Turkey the authorities recognise that cultural traditions can be an asset, rather than a threat, and are worth preserving.

Finally, the politicians cleared off, and the ceremony could begin. The lights were dimmed but for one, which shone on an orchestra of singers, drummers and woodwind players. A heavy silence hung like a velvet shroud over the huge auditorium. One of the vocalists began to sing, strong and clear, mellifluous and muezzin-like, undulating through a Quranic verse. Then began the drums, quietly at first, slowly swelling to a galloping, trance-like beat. The whirlers entered the arena in single file, twenty or more processing in a row of long black robes and tall, green, cylindrical hats – tombstones for the ego. They knelt in a row along the perimeter of the arena, as bouncing notes rose from the orchestra – a plucked rebab – alongside a chant-like humming from several singers. They gave way to the soft, earthy strains of the ney, the reed flute, which Rumi himself is said to have played, and which appears in the opening lines of his *Masnavi* as a metaphor for the spiritual journey of the Sufi. As the reed is cut from the reed bed, the human soul is torn from its union with God for a life on this earth. In its journey to the ceremony hall, the reed is taken from the river, left to dry in the sun, punctured with holes – and still, only rarely is it enough for it to play a beautiful tune, a song of lament for its separation from the divine. I thought of those Mevlevis in times past, turned away from the order for wincing or shifting their legs while kneeling for three days and nights on a sheepskin; I thought of Mithat, twirling his foot on an upright nail.

The ney solo reached its end. The Mevlevis, who had been kneeling still and silent throughout, suddenly sprang into life, raising their arms into the air and slapping the stage once in unison – an almighty sound, representing the blowing of the Horn of Jibreel and its announcement of the Day of Resurrection. One by one, they stood, spread out across the stage, and began to shuffle across it, a few steps at a time, their arms crossed beneath their black cloaks. In turn, they threw off this outer layer to reveal white tunics and skirts – their grave clothes – and began to whirl, as the sound of the drums and the voices swelled once again to a long, rousing plateau.

As the whirlers approached where I was sitting, close to the edge of the stage, my face was wafted by breezes from their spinning skirts; I smelt the frankincense they were perfumed with. They whirled anticlockwise. Ibrahim had told me that this has been misinterpreted by Westerners as representing the orbits of the solar system, but that it actually represents the anticlockwise circumambulation of the Kaaba undertaken by pilgrims to Mecca. 'Mystically, the whirler is whirling around the Kaaba of the heart,' he said. They were mesmerising to watch, gliding across the stage as they whirled, their left feet bearing all the weight, their right legs swinging constantly like weathervanes in a stiff breeze. They had their own little meteorological systems, their feet kicking up chalk from the arena floor and their skirts whipping it into dust devils. It seemed at once choreographed and free – they maintained a perfect, consistent distance from each other, and their skirts never touched, even though their eyes were closed; they seemed to be running on tracks and lost in a rapture at the same time.

All the whirlers were male; female Mevlevis do whirl privately, but do not perform publicly as part of the modern Şeb-i Arûs. They varied in age from about 12 to about 65, although most of them were adults. The younger ones seemed more bound to the occasion, with looks of concentration on their faces – I thought again of Mithat, starting out when he was 14, fretting about his technique. The older men, though, were deep in a reverie, overtaken by some kind of peak experience. They would throw their hands up in the air spontaneously, and as they passed me, I heard them letting out strange noises, little involuntary barks and moans. All the while, they whirled, whirled, whirled, their skirts spinning constantly and their heads still, leaning far to one side, glued to their shoulders.

Eventually, the music began to calm and then stopped altogether, like the settling of a storm. Most of the whirlers stopped, too, but some had carried on, lost in the dance, and had to be quietly brought back down to earth. They raised cupped hands in *du'ā'* – supplication – and wiped them over their faces. This is how Muslims end their prayers, but I saw from those standing closest to me that some of them were wiping away tears, too. Some people in the audience had stayed in their seats and were doing the same, clearly moved by what had been a profound experience. Others were filing out and chatting happily, like they'd just been to the cinema and had already forgotten which film they'd seen.

I joined the departing throngs and found Giray in the foyer. We compared notes on the ceremony, and I asked him why the whirlers bent their heads to one side. He wasn't sure, but he seemed happy I'd asked. 'I do this, too! My friend told me I seem like a Sufi, because I always lean my head to the left-hand side,' he said.

'Because you're a spiritual man?' I asked.

'No,' Giray said quietly, casting his eyes to the floor. 'I'm left-handed and I have a big head.'

Beware of false prophets.

6

THE GOLDEN THREADS
Festivals as Roadmaps of Religion

Rabat, MALTA

It was 19 March – the festa of San Ġużepp – and the streets of Rabat were dressed for the occasion. Pennants and streamers of red, white and gold hung between the balconies of the old town, while the pavements were lined with colourful plinths, seven feet high and topped with ornate floral sculptures and towering statues. There was King David plucking his harp; Archangel Gabriel thrusting a cruciform sceptre to the heavens; and Melita, personification of Malta, clutching a red-and-white national flag which flapped in the afternoon breeze. Everything had been given a fresh lick of paint, so that the statues looked like those of ancient Greece and Rome once would have done: alive and brightly clothed. I'd never seen a place so dressed up, festooned like a castle town on the wedding day of the princess; some of the streamers even met at giant cloth crowns suspended above the street, befitting a royal jamboree. On Juliet balconies, girls stood with their hands in hats, sprinkling those of us on the streets below with colourful confetti.

It was early afternoon, and the streets were a throng of people chatting and laughing, drinking Cisk, Malta's ubiquitous beer, out of plastic cups. The sweet, oily smell of sizzling dough rose from street stalls selling the festival speciality, *zeppoli* – balls of deep-fried choux pastry, filled with ricotta and slathered with honey. Children chased one another, chewing on blocks of nougat bigger than their heads. Monks in dark brown cassocks strafed along the pavements looking purposeful, while rotund nonnas cut straight through the crowd like bowling balls, swatting aside anyone standing in their way with a swing of a grocery bag, a tut, and a dark incantation.

At the heart of all this feverish activity was the L'Isle Adam Band Club, the headquarters of the local marching band, who would be making a procession through the town later that afternoon. Inside, it resembled a bar on race day, all summer suits and colourful dresses; at the back was a garden, with circles of drinkers standing at tall, round tables.

I sidled up to one of them and wriggled my way into a conversation with a group of friends, visiting for the festa from Valletta. The group's composition – broadly bohemian, with a wide age range and diverse accents – would ring a bell with anyone who has hung around in time-warped, ex-colonial places with large expat populations. There was a French Canadian named Grégoire who wore a spotted bandana knotted round his neck, had a notebook poking out of his breast pocket, and said he was a novelist; a Maltese poet called Adam in an army surplus shirt and dark sunglasses; and an attractive English couple, both artists, the man older than the woman and with an elegantly wasted air. They smoked cigarettes and drank beer and anisette. It felt like I was in Paris in the 1920s, hanging out with the Lost Generation.

'The festa is all very civilised at this stage,' Adam said. 'There's the marching band, and then later they make a procession with the statue of Saint Joseph through the town. It's very calm and traditional to begin with.'

'What happens after that?' I asked.

'Cocaine, mostly,' said Adam. 'Cocaine and Eurodisco.' I expressed surprise; Rabat didn't seem like that kind of place. 'Maltese love getting fucked up,' Adam said. 'We're the Brits of the Mediterranean.'

Malta's festi – the local celebrations of Catholic saints' days – are a highlight of the social and cultural calendar for the Maltese, and were inscribed on UNESCO's Intangible Cultural Heritage List in 2023. There are over one hundred of them each year across the islands of Malta and Gozo, most of them exhibiting the same rip-roaring melange of pyrotechnics, fresh paint, and sacral dissipation which was on display in Rabat that day. They are held throughout the year, although the vast majority happen in the summer, with dozens of festi taking place in each of July and August.

Word got around that something was about to happen, and the crowds inside the bars and cafés decanted themselves outside, swelling the streets even further. From around the corner came a muffled cacophony of woodwind, brass and drums, becoming clearer as it moved towards us down the street. This was the L'Isle Adam Band, and they were dozens strong: men and women, old and young alike, in dark suits and blue ties, their rosy-cheeked heads topped with sailors' hats.

The crowd cheered the band along, and waved balloons of blue, white, red and gold; occasionally one would be let go, and children would chase after it, stamping on it delightedly when it fell to the floor. Teenagers were play-fighting with silly string and confetti. Chants broke out which bore no relation to the jazzy strains of the marching band: first a blast of 'Seven Nation Army', then several throaty rounds of 'San Ġużepp! San Ġużepp! San Ġużepp!'

Even by Catholic standards, the Maltese venerate their saints deeply. Mary is deified to the same level as Jesus, Gozitans are Georgiani (followers of St. George) first and Christians second, and virtually every realm of life – agriculture, fertility, travelling, trade, family, leather tanning, martyrdom – is watched over by a smiling patron saint. Collectively, you might be tempted to say, they make up a pantheon comparable to polytheistic Pagan religions, although this suggestion would of course be shot down in flames by the Church. Malta is a religiously homogenous kind of place. Government statistics in 2023 revealed that 83% of the population identify as Roman Catholic, and the local variety is staunchly conservative: Malta was the last country in the EU to legalise divorce, finally taking that step in 2011, while abortion remains prohibited in virtually all its forms. 'Vilification of religion' itself was illegal until 2016, prior to which insulting or making fun of the Catholic faith carried a maximum sentence of six months' imprisonment. 'Lord forgive them,' Malta's archbishop Charles Scicluna wrote on Twitter when this archaic law was repealed; 'they do not know what they do.'

Even so, it is easily possible, if you know where to look, to detect echoes of the pre-Christian past. I wandered away from the festivities into Rabat's side streets and descended into St. Paul's Catacombs, a hypogeum originally built by the Phoenicians and Carthaginians in the first millennium BC, and in use for several centuries afterwards. At ground level, the site is a collection of little stone pavilions, sheltering steep staircases cut downwards into the rock floor. I descended them in turn, entering lamplit rock-cut caverns containing unusual features known as agape tables: flat, circular platforms carved out of the stone, at which early Christians, in a hangover of pagan practice, would gather for meals to commemorate the dead. Carvings of menorahs and crosses alongside older Roman and Phoenician artworks indicate that Christians and Jews were buried here, alongside the pagan burials, with no attempts to divide them – a legacy of a more religiously tolerant time.

Today, Maltese Pagans are stigmatised against – one local told me that she had heard priests devote sections of their sermons to preaching about the dangers of tarot cards, and a writer friend of mine, who grew up in Malta, put it bluntly: 'People are extremely Catholic and traditional for the most part. You don't want Doris next door knowing you worship the sun.' In short, Malta is the kind of place where, to the majority, 'Pagan' still implies 'barbarian'. Even so, a contemporary Pagan community exists quietly on Malta, and, as it happens, the day after the festa of San Ġużepp marks one of the most significant festivals in their calendar: the spring equinox. Malta is scattered with millennia-old megalithic temples which are some of the oldest and most atmospheric religious buildings on the planet, and collectively make up one of the world's most significant ancient spiritual landscapes. Very little is known about the culture or religion of the people who built them, but today, the temples have become sites of spiritual significance for modern Maltese Pagans. I would be joining them the next morning to mark the spring equinox at one of Malta's most famous megalithic temples, Mnajdra, where I hoped to learn more about how festivals can provide not just a grounding in the changing seasons, but a link to the past and a roadmap for how religious traditions evolve from and inform one another. The chance to experience the equinox with Maltese Pagans directly after taking in such a paragon of Maltese Catholic festivity as the Rabat festa was too intriguing to pass up. But first – with several hours still to run until the proceedings in Rabat really ramped up that afternoon – I had yet another festival to get to.

I squeezed into my tiny rented Fiat and rumbled off into the countryside to the north of Rabat. Malta is semi-arid and sees less rain with each passing year; in the summer months, the archipelago lies like a dead lizard, cracked and sizzling beneath the hot sun. In the spring, though, the islands erupt with life, a green blanket sprouting with wildflowers. Outside my window, amid fields of spiky agave and smooth pads of prickly pear, burst a riot of yellow: crown daisies, buttercups, and giant fennel, its inflorescences bobbing in the breeze like heads of hogweed dipped in gold.

I pulled up at Vincent's Eco Estate, an organic farm which on that St. Joseph's Day – a public holiday across Malta – was playing host to a secular, fête-like festival called the Green Family Fiesta. There were face-painting stalls, pony rides, and a bouncy castle, around which desperate-looking parents, wild-haired and baggy-eyed, were chasing after their crazed children. I made a beeline for the quieter area beyond this, an artisans' market, where childless couples strolled, bright-eyed and straight-backed, stopping to browse at wooden stalls selling organic soaps, spoons carved from plum wood, hand-painted ceramics, and the like. I had come here at the invitation of Rosalind Dougall, a Maltese Pagan who had offered to tell me more about Malta's mysterious megalithic temples. She was there overseeing a stall representing her boutique, Fata Morgana, a Pagan and fantasy shop which sells tarot cards, incense burners, ritual candles, and all manner of other witchy paraphernalia. A Pagan shop at a secular festival held on the holiday of a Catholic saint – is Malta more cosmopolitan than it appears, I wondered, or was this yet more evidence of the levelling, egalitarian power of festivals?

Rosalind greeted me warmly, a friendly woman with facial piercings, long dark hair and a black T-shirt covered by technicolour, mosaiced dungarees. Her stall exhibited the same contrast as her outfit: a black gazebo sheltering a vibrant array of tie-dyed throws, jazzy bath bombs, and planetoid charms cut from searing blue sodalite. It all looked awesome, I thought: a cosmic vignette, set in a black void against the blue sky and the bright green fields.

Rosalind explained that some Maltese Pagans have taken to gathering in the ruins of the megalithic temples for communal rituals and festivals. 'There are certain temples which allow Pagans to get married in them now,' she said. 'And others which people can use because there are no fences. Most people respect them, but some people don't – they leave crystals scattered there, candles burning down to the stone. It drives me crazy.'

Mnajdra, the temple I would be visiting the next morning, is of particular significance during the equinox because it seems to have been built as a calendar – at sunrise on the spring and autumn equinoxes, its inner chamber floods with light. A handful of surviving prehistoric buildings across the world exhibit similar features. Loughcrew, a passage tomb in County Meath in eastern Ireland, is bathed with light at sunrise on the equinoxes, just like Mnajdra. At the Karnak temples near Luxor in Egypt, a sanctuary to the sun god Amun fills with light at sunrise on the winter solstice, a time of religious significance for ancient Egyptians as a period of agricultural rebirth. Among the Inca ruins of Macchu Picchu there sits a calendar stone known as Intihuatana – 'the place the sun gets tied up' – which casts a shadow throughout the year except for two very specific times: midday on the spring and autumn equinoxes. A wealth of archaeological finds at Mnajdra and the other Maltese megalithic sites, particularly a huge number of figurines with exaggerated female body parts, have been taken as evidence that these were fertility temples, and it's tempting to imagine that the equinoxes, with their significance as turning points in the agricultural year, would have been occasions for religious festivals held at the temples. But Rosalind was keen to caution against drawing conclusions.

'We don't know what the ancient religious traditions were in Malta, even though we have a rich history – there are theories, but we just don't have enough information,' she said. 'So, most modern Pagans here use deities and pantheons from the Mediterranean region: Greco-Roman, or Egyptian. For me, it makes sense to use regional gods, or the gods of people who colonised Malta and brought their gods here – the British and the Celtic gods, for example.'

This is not unique to Malta. Pagan gatherings tend to be eclectic – it's common for one person to be invoking the Wiccan mother goddess while another prays to Freyr, while an evening's programme might include tarot readings, meditation, magic circles, and any number of other diverse practices. Syncretism has its limits, though, according to Rosalind. 'I can't imagine working with the Nordic gods,' she said. 'If they had to come to Malta, they'd get heatstroke.' Her sense of humour around the subject reflects the fact that, for most modern Pagans, there is no contradiction inherent in even the same person working with deities from different pantheons, because their practice is rooted in personal experience, not theological dogma. There's a sense that deities are seen for what they are: mythological figures created to help people tell fundamental stories, to root themselves in vivid experience of the universe, and to foster a connection between themselves and the natural world. The cardinal points of the year – the equinoxes and solstices – are particularly potent times in this regard, as I was to find out the following morning.

First, though, I had the end of the festivities in Rabat to return to. I said goodbye to Rosalind and trundled back to town, where I arrived just in time for the procession, joining a throng of spectators on San Pawl Street. The church was bedazzled, covered with large round light bulbs of the kind you'd normally find on a dressing room mirror. I craned my neck to see the statue of St. Joseph (San Ġużepp) emerge from the church door – I couldn't get closer than 50 yards – cloaked in gold and carrying the baby Jesus, both adorned with gilded halos. The party was paused for a moment, as a veneer of piety fell over the hushed crowd – big-bellied men rocked and burped quietly, clutching their cups of Cisk, while the more zealous spectators gazed intently at the statue as it moved through the crowd, hands pressed to their hearts, eyes damp with emotion.

As quickly as the procession had begun, it was over; the mask of religiosity was lifted, and the revellers got back to the serious business of getting biblically drunk. Workers were sweeping constantly to clear mountains of white paper confetti strips, which covered the floor like fallen snow. Kids had it stuck to their clothes and hair, and were bending down to scoop it up and throw it at each other in lieu of the snowball fight they will likely never have in Malta; snowfall has dusted the archipelago seven times since 1858.

The atmosphere in the L'Isle Adam Band Club had slackened considerably. In the garden, a man in a Cisk-branded straw hat had devised a game: he stood with a lit cigarette up each nostril, exhaling plumes through his mouth, while his friends approached him in turn holding balloons, which they popped against the smouldering cherries – the challenge being for him not to flinch and subsequently cause a cigarette to fall out of his nose. That was his game, and he was very good at it; each popped balloon elicited a roar of approval from his comrades, while he stood shaking and silently laughing, eyes closed and streaming tears, puffs of smoke emanating from his mouth like a choo-choo train.

I walked through the streets of the town. The festivities had spread from Rabat itself to the adjoining walled city of Mdina, Malta's ancient capital, which fell from prominence in 1530 and has been known ever since as the

Silent City – a nickname that was hard to reconcile on a night like tonight.

It felt like things were at a tipping point; it was nearly time for the cocaine and Eurodisco, as had been prophesied. I didn't much fancy that – it wasn't that kind of holiday – so I wandered out to the edge of town, to a viewpoint with a bench where I sat and took in the majesty of Rabat's imperious position, high on a hill. Beneath me, yellow flowers frothed in the green fields of the place they call Wied il-Buzbiez – the Valley of Fennel. Buttercups sprouted amid the tombstones in a graveyard down the hill, while behind me, the bells of the church tower chimed, mingling with the cries of children and the laughter of revellers. The smell of fennel sighed upwards from the valley, as fireworks tore holes in the sky above the Silent City.

I slipped out of my hotel at four o'clock the next morning and rumbled through the sleeping stone streets of Rabat and out, suddenly, into an empty countryside, nothing visible in the dark but rugged, sun-bleached limestone walls and dust rising from the rutted roads. A signpost signalled my arrival – Ħaġar Qim and Mnajdra Archaeological Park – and I climbed out of my car and into the chill of the morning.

Roosters crowed; dogs howled in sympathy. The corners of the sky began to glow pink in the first sign of the coming day – one of two each year (one in March and one in September) in which the sun passes over the equator, and day and night are more or less the same length across the whole planet. The significance of the equinoxes as turning points in the year has been recognised by societies probably since at least the dawn of agriculture, and as such these dates have been bestowed with spiritual significance by cultures across the ages.

Nowadays, Heritage Malta, the organisation tasked with caring for the country's historic monuments, opens Mnajdra early on the equinoxes, to allow people to experience the sunrise illuminating the temple just as people did here thousands of years ago. Of the dozen or so people gathered there, most were like me – camera-toting history nerds or amateur archaeologists. There were a couple of people in attendance, though – one man and one woman – who I sensed were there for more personal purposes. They had travelled alone, bedecked in bangles and boho clothing, the woman in a floaty dress and the man in patchwork harem pants. The rest of us passed the time by making small talk, but these two stood off in separate corners, keeping themselves to themselves; the woman sat perched on a step, her eyes closed as if in meditation.

A Heritage Malta tour guide arrived and led us to the temples. On the way, as we walked across scrubby fields which dropped down sharp cliffs into the Mediterranean Sea, we passed a small pop-up tent. It had been erected close to the cliff-edge, looking out to the ocean, right next to a sign that read 'No Camping!' The guide prodded the tent with a stick, and from its doorway emerged a ragged-looking man of the trustafarian type, wearing a Baja jacket, his white, bleary-eyed face framed with matted dreadlocks.

'Can't you see the sign?' the guide said. 'Camping's prohibited. This is a World Heritage Site.'

'I wasn't camping, man. I was only sleeping.'

'It damages the carob trees!' the guide hissed, followed by an admonishment in Maltese, before turning back to us, shaking his head and saying, 'Only in Malta' – that expression of self-effacing exceptionalism that you hear in every country in the world.

Soon we reached Mnajdra, a complex of buildings close to the cliffs – large limestone slabs stacked on top of each other in a prehistoric game of Tetris. Both Mnajdra and its neighbour, Ħaġar Qim, remain mightily impressive, built more than 5,000 years ago – before Stonehenge – and still standing tall. We walked beneath the lintel which crowned the doorway of the so-called Temple Calendar and assembled around the edge of a circular room to wait for the sunrise. 'Shhh,' our guide said. 'The birds are starting.'

The dawn chorus echoed beneath the tabernacle, and at 6.30 sharp, the rising sun appeared through the temple's open doorway, slanting a thick beam of light into the chamber, lengthening our shadows, and casting aglow an empty altar at the back of the room. I caught myself holding my breath, as if exhaling would knock this timeless cosmic dance off-kilter. But this was a robust phenomenon – it had been happening for 5,000 years, after all – and there was something energising and life-affirming in that fact alone. After a couple of minutes, the sun passed on, the chamber was cast back into shadow, and the group moved out of their private moments and back into a communal one, with eye contact, broad grins, and whispers of appreciation at what they'd just seen. 'You've just witnessed the workings of the oldest known calendar in human history,' said our guide, beaming with pride. 'Congratulations!'

We were a disparate group at Mnajdra that morning, and I suspect that most of the people there would, like me, not have described their reasons for being there in religious terms. But it was a festival, alright – we had gathered in a special place on a special day of the year in pursuit of a shared experience – and, in fact, it was the closest thing that I could recall to a festival experience that I could describe in personally spiritual terms. I felt more of a connection to the people around me there than I had at virtually any other festival, where I often felt, to a greater or lesser extent, like an observer. But this was just awe-inspiring – the moment when the blank altar was cast aglow by the just-risen sun was one of those moments that makes you proud to be human, amazed and even slightly unsettled that people living 5,000 years ago had the means, imagination and inclination to create buildings like this. The mystery surrounding the temple builders only added to this impression, because it forced me, in the absence of any other defining information, simply to think of them as fellow human beings, rather than a distinct cultural group to which I was an outsider. I understood fully, in that moment, why Malta's modern Pagans were taking to these ancient sites for their own communal rituals. I was also surprised by how rare and powerful it was, in the modern world, to actually notice this turning point in the year which ordinarily would pass me by completely – to actually *see* the equinox in the form of a fleeting beam of light against a temple wall. I realised, too, what people mean when they talk about being grounded in the earth – my shoes, for a moment, felt stuck fast to the stone beneath my feet.

The group started to drift out of the temple. The woman I had seen meditating by the stones earlier had taken a seat on a bench; I joined her. Her name was Maria, and she was, as I had correctly surmised, a Pagan. She comes to Mnajdra on this day every year, she said, to bask in the vernal sunrise, press her beating heart to the cool stones, and foster a connection to the Mother Goddess, for whom she is certain that these temples were built all those years ago.

'This temple is a calendar, and the builders believed that the womb was a calendar, too,' she said. 'The light enters through her legs and hits the altar – the brain – so the equinox is like an orgasm. The operation of the sun is to fertilise the earth. These people did not differentiate between the physical and the symbolic so much as we do now.'

Maria had come from her home on Gozo, the second-largest island in the Maltese archipelago, a 25-minute ferry ride north of the main island. Gozo is something of a hub for alternative types: a quiet, rural sort of place, which, although dotted with towns and villages which are even more traditional than those of the main island, also has plenty of quiet coves and rural settlements where hippies, seekers, and New Agers of all stripes feel free to practise their own ways of living, undisturbed. Gozo also has megalithic temples of its own – the mighty Ġgantija, which are the largest in Malta.

With the whole day still ahead of me, I decided to go there. I drove to Malta's northern shore and boarded one of the many daily ferries which ply the Gozo Channel. Gozo is described in the guidebooks as 'quiet' and 'sleepy', but Malta is a densely populated country, and popular with tourists, and on sunny days like this, Gozo's ferry port and major attractions are choked with day-trippers. I extricated myself from the mob and walked up a steep hill, inland from the harbour. In the village of Għajnsielem, in the shadow of a mightily impressive neo-Gothic church,

I came upon easily the strangest place I was to see during my time in Malta. A rickety wooden arch, hung with an antique lantern, framed a path in whose drying cement someone had used a finger to crudely inscribe the words, 'Welcome to Bethlehem Għajnsielem'. Square stone houses, fringed with threadbare palm-thatch awnings, were connected by dusty paths and footbridges lain with rotting planks; piled in a corner were decaying fishing boats which would never see the sea; and in a mock amphitheatre, Roman columns had collapsed against each other, supported against a backdrop of mouldy plywood. Bethlehem in Għajnsielem is a theatre set – or, officially, 'animated nativity village' – used by locals to stage their annual nativity play each year. The rest of the time it stands empty, slowly falling apart. The only souls I saw, although I suppose people must come to feed them, were some half-dead cats and caged birds: two once-mighty peacocks, and a turkey, which seemed like the cruellest Christmas joke.

It was one of the saddest and weirdest tourist 'attractions' I'd ever seen. Pagans on Malta are persecuted for minding their own business, and meanwhile, this is what the Christians are up to? Not for the first time on this trip, I got the impression that double standards were at play.

From Bethlehem I took an Uber to the temple of a giantess. That, at any rate, is how Gozitan folklore explains Ġgantija, a complex of megaliths said to have been created by a primordial giantess, swollen from a diet of honey and fava beans, who had an affair with a local man and built a temple to celebrate the birth of their resulting child. The giantess tale is seen locally for what it is – only a story – yet is deeply entrenched enough for it to have given the temple its very name: 'Ġgantija' derives from the Maltese word for 'giant'. While there is no evidence for any direct continuity between the religion of the temple-builders and the later giantess legend, Ġgantija still figures prominently in the itineraries of 'goddess tours', undertaken by organisations and private individuals seeking connection with a divine feminine energy perceived to radiate powerfully from the megalithic temples of Malta.

The theory that Malta's temple builders practised a goddess religion became absorbed into the feminist movement in the late twentieth century. 'The prevailing belief was always that there was a Maltese goddess,' said Anna, a Pagan who'd agreed to show me around Ġgantija. 'With the Neopagan movement and feminist movement in the 1970s there was a famous archaeologist called Marija Gimbutas, who put forward the idea that the Maltese statues were part of a palaeolithic goddess religion. She was more than an academic – she was a witchy leader, too. She came to Malta and was doing ceremonies in the Ħal Saflieni Hypogeum.'

The Maltese archaeological establishment, startled at this blurring of the lines between the scientific and the experiential, rejected Gimbutas, and today, Heritage Malta's official line plays down the goddess angle. Displays in Valletta's National Museum of Archaeology refer simply to 'figures of the corpulent type' without specifying gender – and, indeed, many of the figures are sexually ambiguous in appearance. 'I don't think there was just a goddess; I think there was a male deity as well,' Anna said. 'They found lots of phallic objects in the temples, too, for example. But that's not the only reason the establishment has moved away from the goddess theory. It's the Church; it's misogyny; it's anti-spirituality; it's all these things. Nowadays some people claim the figure represents a sumo wrestler. I mean, come on. It's crazy.'

My guide at Mnajdra had apologised for repeatedly tripping over his terminology – after a lifetime of calling the buildings 'temples', he had recently been instructed to start referring to them by the more general term 'megaliths'. 'Heritage Malta are trying to desanctify these buildings,' Anna said. All the ancient temples are spiritually charged places, she explained, but the more famous ones, like Ġgantija, Ħaġar Qim and Mnajdra, aren't so easy for Pagans to use as sacred spaces anymore, being busy with tourists and tightly managed by Heritage Malta. 'They let people use them for rituals, but you have to pay a lot of money, so when people do carry out ceremonies at the temples, they tend to choose the quieter ones – Xemxija outside St. Paul's Bay, or Tal-Qadi near Naxxar,' she said. Veronica Veen, a cultural anthropologist, has written of how women who wished to become pregnant would gather to circumambulate and sit upon the Stone of Qala, another megalith in Gozo.[38] Dawn Saliba, a Maltese-American writer and academic, has written of modern Maltese Pagans 'enter[ing] the ancient structures in an effort to experience transcendence' – gathering at the Qala Stone to leave an offering of fava beans to the Ġgantija goddess, or performing 'widdershins' (an anti-clockwise circumambulation) around a bonfire on the occasion of Samhain. She also quotes members of the Pagan community as calling for greater access to

---

38. Veronica Veen, *Goddess, Giantess, Farmeress: Female Images of Malta.*

Malta's megalithic temples for the purpose of religious ceremonies.[39]

None of the Pagans I spoke to in Malta were under any illusions that their religion bore any resemblance to that of the people who built the temples, and Anna corroborated what Rosalind had told me about the diversity of Maltese Pagan practice. In the context of a ceremony, she said, individuals will invoke their chosen gods, and their different beliefs are generally respected. 'Hades, Anubis – you hear all sorts,' she said. Amid these cosmopolitan assemblies, though, there tends to be one consistent presence. 'There's always a Sleeping Lady on the altar,' Anna said. 'The Goddess of Malta.'

The goddess tours which run to Malta pitch the megalithic temples as sacred sites, but just as pertinent as the locations they choose are the activities included on their itineraries. There tends to be an emphasis on art and creative expression – on drawing or writing while inspired by the spiritual atmosphere of the temples. The same impulse, it seems to me, is often channelled at festivals, particularly the likes of Glastonbury, where revellers can often be found practising self-expression – singing, dancing, craft workshops, and so on – while drawing on the special 'energy' of the physical place. 'Art has a role to play in opening people's minds to spirituality,' said Anna. 'Many people are willing to have these kinds of ecstatic experiences through theatre or music, but not through religion.'

I thought of my friends back home, mostly atheist and self-consciously secular; often, in fact, actively anti-

---

39. *Think Magazine*, 'Malta's Paganism: A Dance Between Archaeology and Anthropology' by Dawn Saliba.

religious. I knew that many of them would scoff at the idea of someone having a mystical experience at a communal ceremony inside an ancient temple, yet they would enthusiastically report having experiences of the exact same type themselves, engendered by live music or mind-altering drugs, their tabernacle a festival tent.

I got the ferry back to Malta and drove south as the sun began to set. Valletta looked pharaonic in the golden hour. The setting sun blazed the limestone a fierce gold, and waterfront residents pushed their Egyptian-blue window shutters ajar for a glimpse of it honeying the harbour as it sank beneath the Dingli Cliffs, over to the west where the island falls into the Mediterranean Sea.

There is something about Valletta on a golden evening which invites a sundowner, so I took a seat and ordered a Blue Label beer outside Caffe Cordina, an old Valletta institution where I'd arranged to meet Dr Huw Groucutt, an archaeologist. Huw arrived soon after: a warm Welshman brimming with passion for and knowledge of Malta's ancient past.

'It's complicated,' was Huw's answer when I asked him to clarify what we know, scientifically speaking, about Malta's temples and how they relate to the festival calendar. 'Things like the Mnajdra sunrise phenomenon can't be an accident, but you have to contextualise them in an agricultural society. Farming, festivals ... in the modern world we have this split between the ritual and the mundane. In the past, people probably didn't have that.'

I had been struck, even in the context of Malta's busy festive calendar, just how many festivals were going on at this time of year. There was the Rabat festa, the spring equinox, and the Green Family Fiesta, all within two days – and it was Easter the following week. I had wondered if the equinox, and its perennial significance to the agricultural year, could be something to do with this burst of festive activity – the autumn equinox mirrors this effect, being associated with a huge number of festivals, often harvest-related, across the world – both today and for the temple builders, 5,000 years ago.

'Some people have argued that what happened at the temples may have been quite similar to the modern festi,' agreed Huw. 'Take the Rabat festa – it's surely not a coincidence that it's at this time of the year. Some archaeologists have gone a bit far with the notion of continuity, but I think history does repeat itself in some ways.

'Certainly, these temples probably were places where there were communal gatherings, even though the format may have changed. The form that Christianity takes in Malta is very interesting – Mary is as important as God or Jesus; some people have even argued there's a continuity going back to the Mother Goddess, who later becomes absorbed into the Virgin Mary. I don't think that's really true, but I think it's perhaps tapping into an underlying logic.

'In Paganism often there are different deities for different parts of the landscape; Christians have different saints. Operatively, a lot is actually the same.'

There has been excited theorising among folklorists for centuries about the extent to which it is possible to draw an unbroken line of descent between modern festival traditions and ancient antecedents with which they appear to share certain characteristics. A theory first documented by the Venerable Bede in the eighth century claims that Easter grew out of an earlier festival based around the renewal of life heralded by the spring equinox, a fact signposted by the very word 'Easter', which supposedly derives from the name of the Germanic spring deity, Ēostre. James Frazer and Mikhail Bakhtin, meanwhile, both believed that the carnivalesque qualities of the Feast of Fools, whereby someone of low social class would oversee festivities in the guise of the Lord of Misrule, represented a direct continuation of the Saturnalia of ancient Rome, where masters would serve their servants at the banquet table.

Similar debates were had in the context of the witch trials of the fifteenth to eighteenth centuries, with observers tying themselves in knots over whether or not the people prosecuted were practitioners of a pre-Christian pagan religion which had continued to operate in the shadows throughout the Christianisation of Europe. The pro-continuity idea was most famously expressed in folklorist Margaret Murray's witch-cult hypothesis – which was later discredited, but not before proving hugely influential on the development of modern Paganism. Similarly, most scholars nowadays dismiss the idea of any direct continuity between the Saturnalia and the Feast of Fools, and others, such as the historian Ronald Hutton, have also cast doubt on the idea that Easter grew directly out of an existing pre-Christian tradition.

In any case, to grasp for tangible proof of continuities between religious traditions – unbroken chains of festival behaviour, ritual, or oral transmission, for example – is to miss the point. The real continuities are in the human heart and mind, within our biological, emotional, and spiritual hardware. The impulses which lead humans to create religions – the yearning for transcendence beyond our mortal bodies, the connection to each other and to the rest of the natural world, the desire to understand at least a little of the great mystery which underpins and infuses it all – these are the real golden threads, which run through the generations; threads which we cling onto for dear life, trailing behind us in the hope that, when the time comes, they will lead us out of the maze.

Huw was now echoing my own instincts – that the important continuities are not the ones we can trace above ground, intact links of ceremonial or festive practice stretching into the distant past. Rather, we should be examining the impulses that lie beneath, subcutaneous, out of sight, surging through our veins; forever dancing in the twilight world of the cellular and the subconscious.

'It's not about continuity; it's about recreation, convergence – the same things happening over and over,' he said. 'Each time it's a bit different, but the threads are very similar.'

For us earthbound mortals, there is no more graspable golden thread than the shifting of the seasons – the movements of the sun and stars in the sky, and the way they correspond to the nourishment of the earth. Whether you're a Maltese Pagan invoking the Mother Goddess, a farmer tilling his fields hopefully beneath a harvest moon, or a raver seeing in a secular solstice at Stonehenge, there is an undeniable energy about these times of year – times for rolling in the grass or summoning dust devils from the dry earth; times for howling at the moon.

7

US & THEM
Festivals and Tribalism

Derbyshire, ENGLAND

There was something uncanny that day about Ashbourne, an ordinarily mild-mannered market town in the Derbyshire Dales. The springtime sun lit the red-brick Victorian architecture in a handsome glow, while bunting and streamers swayed in the soft breeze, hanging from branches and eaves like the dressing for a village fête.

And yet, despite this genteel visage, the implication of violence hung over the town. All the shop windows were boarded up. Signs were stuck to lampposts warning visitors to '*Park here at your peril*'. Elderly couples peered past net curtains, looking out at a threatening world with concern etched on their faces.

On the street, though, things were different; those townsfolk brave enough to venture outside radiated a tangible air of excitement. They stood chattering animatedly on street corners, their faces plastered with arrows of warpaint, many of them wearing branded hoodies bearing the name 'Up'ard' or 'Down'ard' – a sign of their allegiance for the next two days, during which time an ancient, ultraviolent ball game would swallow their hometown.

That game is known as Shrovetide football, and it is not bound by many rules. Here are a few exceptions:

- The ball may not be carried in a motorised vehicle.
- Cemeteries and churchyards are strictly out of bounds.
- Murder and manslaughter are prohibited.

Everything else is pretty much permissible in this centuries-old tradition, one of the oldest and largest 'football' games in the world, considered the ancestor of football, rugby, and many other modern ball games. The precise genesis story of the Ashbourne version of the game has long since been lost, obscured by the passing of time and by a fire which ripped through the public records of the Royal Shrovetide Committee in the late nineteenth century. It is known to have been played for hundreds of years, however; there is an oblique reference to the game in a 1683 verse by Peak District poet (and cousin to the Baronet of Ashbourne) Charles Cotton, titled 'Burlesque; Upon the Great Frost':

Two towns, that long that war had waged,
Being at football now engaged
For honour, as both sides pretended,
Left the brave trial to be ended
Till the next thaw, for they were frozen
On either part at least a dozen;
With a good handsome space between 'em
Like Rollerich stones, if you've seen 'em,
And could no more run, kick, or trip ye
Than I can quaff off Aganippe;

Till ale, which crowns all such pretences,
Mull'd them again into their senses.

Games like this, known as medieval football, folk football or mob football, were once commonplace across England, with two large and amorphous teams wrestling for control of a blown-up pig's bladder, which they would attempt to manoeuvre to either end of the town. In most cases, the game was stamped out by the authorities during the nineteenth century, particularly after the Highway Act of 1835, which made it an offence 'to play at Football or any other Game on any Part of the said Highways'.

The city of Derby, ten miles southeast of Ashbourne, is known to have staged its own medieval football game until 1846. Its most celebrated player was a man with the mighty moniker Tunchy Shelton, a prize fighter of local repute described as a 'ranting, roaring, tearing, swearing, leathering swash of a Derby man'.[40] His special move was to use his thick skull like a battering ram, headbutting his way through the scrum with the ball in his hand.

The Derby game, like Ashbourne's, was played by two teams divided on geographical grounds, one from the north of Derby and one from the south. One theory even has it that this game was the origin of the term 'derby', used in a number of sports to describe a match between two teams from the same town.[41] In this case, it was

---

40. *Derbyshire Life*, 'Why Derby's Royal Shrovetide football became a thing of the past' by Ian Collis.
41. Others have suggested that the term originated not in the Derby area at all but on Merseyside, with face-offs in different sports, perhaps horse racing or rugby league, on the Knowsley Estate, seat of the Earls of Derby.

the parishes of two churches, All Saints' and St. Peter's, who faced off against each other. Tunchy Shelton was a St. Peter's man, and was known to have said he would have died for the cause – a sentiment apparently shared by many of his teammates, and probably by their opponents, too. The Derby game was eventually shut down by a special constabulary force, who needed assistance from the heavy cavalry of the Dragoon Guards, such was the scale of resistance put up by the people of Derby in the face of attempts to suppress their beloved game.

Most of the other versions of mob football ended up going the same way: squashed by the authorities. A few isolated incarnations of the game have survived into the present day, however. Versions are still played in the Northumberland town of Alnwick; in Atherstone, Warwickshire; and in Kirkwall in Orkney, alongside a few other places. Similar games can be found elsewhere in Europe, too: *choule*, a Normandy equivalent which has been revived as a regional tournament since 2011; and the *calcio storico fiorentino*, a Renaissance-era Florentine game which is still played as a tournament each June around the time of the festival of Saint John the Baptist, with the final held on his feast day, 24 June.

The Ashbourne game, which is by some distance the largest and best-known surviving example, plays out like this. Two teams are chosen based on the geographical threshold of Henmore Brook, which runs through the centre of Ashbourne. The Up'ards are those born north of the brook, and the Down'ards those born to the south. They form a scrum of people, hundreds strong, within which the two teams try to manoeuvre a ball – by any means imaginable – towards one of the two goals. The game lasts for up to eight hours on both Shrove Tuesday and Ash

Wednesday, starting at 2pm and ending at 10pm, unless a goal is scored after 6pm, in which case play ends for the day.

The goals stand three miles apart on the site of two former water mills, Clifton Mill and Sturston Mill; both have long since been demolished, and stone plinths, inset with millstones, now represent the focal point for the two teams, who score a goal – or 'goal a ball', as the local parlance has it – by knocking the ball against the relevant plinth three times.

There is no demarcated playing field. With the exception of the aforementioned cemeteries and churchyards, along with private gardens, nowhere is out of bounds, and the ball is carried through farmers' fields, town centre streets, and across Henmore Brook itself as the two teams attempt to will it towards one or other of the mills. Clifton Mill was the site, in the 1860s, of one of only two documented deaths directly associated with the game, when a young man fell inside a water reservoir and drowned. The other casualty happened much more recently, in 2007 – a 51-year-old man named David Johnson was found collapsed after the Tuesday's play, still wearing his rugby shirt, shin pads and boots.

More than just an expression of English eccentricity, Shrovetide football is an example of the power of festivals to stir up powerful feelings of tribalism, even on a temporary and contrived basis. 'On those two days, chaos reigns,' a local told me at the 2023 event. 'But go into [local pub] the Greenman afterwards, and it's like nothing had happened – it's a big love-in.' The heat of battle sees the mob football game create the same conditions as many other festivals: liminality is generated, inhibitions melt away, and the normal rules are turned upside down. Agreeable shopkeepers are turned to rabid beasts, students grab their teachers in headlocks, workers gouge their bosses' eyes.

In 2023, footage of the Atherstone ball game, showing a descent into a mass brawl, went viral on social media. A ragged-looking young man is shown climbing on a boarded-up William Hill betting shop, raining punches down on those beneath him as they literally tear the shirt from his back; a burly builder type rises to the top of the mob in a crowd surf, kicking his high-vis-trousered legs like pistons, his workers' boots smashing into any face stupid enough to get in the way.

Such scenes are not a regular occurrence at the Ashbourne game, which has assumed hallowed status among the local community. You get the impression from talking to locals that reversion to such base instincts would be considered highly unsavoury, although such outcomes are not exactly hard to imagine either, in a game where another of the oft-repeated rules states that unnecessary violence is, merely, 'frowned upon'. There are running jokes, delivered non-ironically, about the idiocy and even inbreeding which must characterise any of the other towns who dare to play games of their own resembling Shrovetide football. 'They say a few fingers were lost at the Atherstone game this year,' a man told me in Ashbourne's Greenman pub, the setting for pre- and post-game drinks and very much the spiritual heart of Shrovetide. 'But that's okay – they've got a few to spare over there.'

The thugs caught on camera defiling the Atherstone game in 2023 might have you believe that mob football is little more than an excuse for mindless, consequence-free violence. Ashbournians, however, would tell you that their game is about much more than that: a sacred local tradition, which might seem to tear the town in two, but actually results, counterintuitively, in a strengthened sense of community. Indeed, the only people for whom the two Ashbourne teams reserve more violence than each other is outsiders – and woe betide any non-Ashbournian who sets foot into 'the hug', as the Shrovetide scrum is known, and is caught doing it.

This kind of behaviour is central to the social identity theory of psychologists Henri Tajfel and John Turner, who wrote of how we think of the world in 'in-groups' and 'out-groups'. Watch the news for five minutes and it becomes painfully clear that it is inherent to the darker side of human nature to divide the world into categories of 'us' and 'them'. We all knew this already, but neurologists have now proved it, with research showing that, as we grow older, our brains become more responsive to faces we associate with in-groups as opposed to those we associate with out-groups.[42]

Festivals have a powerful role to play in this. According to academics Howard and Jane Giles: 'An important characteristic of the in-group dichotomy is that groups mark their identities communicatively by ... the festivals and pageants that highlight their unique traditions and rituals.'[43] Festivals are one of the methods that cultural groups use to communicate, to themselves and to the wider world, *This is who we are; this is what we do.* Other forms of cultural expression serve the same purpose – music, architecture, artistic styles, and so on. Exclusivity is inherent to the in-group/out-group mentality, because we define ourselves, for better or worse, in opposition

42. João F. Guassi Moreira, Jay J. Van Bavel, and Eva H. Telzer, 'The Neural Development of Us & Them'.
43. Howard Giles and Jane Giles, 'Ingroups and Outgroups'

to other people. This explains why people can be so protective about who gets to be a protagonist in their culture's festivals. The attitude of the Ashbournians during Shrovetide football is identical to that of the Almontese Brotherhood during the Romería de El Rocío – outsiders can watch, but they cannot be involved.

These constructed cultural identities tend to map onto the geographical world, giving meaning and justification to the brute physical facts which are usually the bottom line when it comes to group characterisation – we live here, they live there. In the words of Norwegian scholars Karl Jaeger and Reidar J. Mykletun, 'festivals can contribute to the development of identities through storytelling, explaining who we are ... Tales about a place may be used to mark out spatial boundaries and confirm that a defined piece of space actually means something, and delineate who belongs in that space and who does not.'[44]

Shrovetide football turns a couple of muddy riverbanks, once the site of industrial mills, into wellsprings of symbolic power – ostensibly playing a role in deciding who comes out on top between the Up'ards and the Down'ards, but actually bringing them together as one whole, affirming who is an Ashbournian and who is not.

The medieval football games which were once popular across England had analogues in other countries, too. The Ponte delle Tette, which we visited at Venice Carnival, is not the only Venetian bridge to bear an anatomical name; also notable is the Ponte dei Pugni – the Bridge of Fists.

---

44. Karl Jaeger and Reidar J. Mykletun, *Festivals, Identities, and Belonging*

In the seventeenth century, rival factions representing the different *sestiere* of Venice would meet on the bridge (as well as on several others across the city) to engage in a mass brawl, with each side aiming to push as many of the opposition into the canal as possible. (Nowadays, there are protective metal railings on each side, but there were no such concessions to health and safety in the 1600s.) The authorities frowned upon the practice, and eventually outlawed it in 1705 after a particularly enthusiastic edition devolved into serious violence, with knives and stones being wielded as weapons.

As the harvest moon rises over the Japanese island of Okinawa each October, the city of Naha plays host to a giant tug-of-war, lasting three days and comprising some 25,000 participants, who make up two teams representing the East and the West. The tradition dates back to the seventeenth century, a period of war between the Ryukyu Islands (of which Okinawa is a part) and Japan – but while ostensibly this represents a battle between two sides, Okinawans will tell you that the coming together for the event, the creation of the great rope from braided straw, the design of the traditional costumes, all have the effect of engendering *yuimaaru* – co-operation.

The Greek town of Vrontados, meanwhile, on the island of Chios, is set ablaze each Easter by the Rouketopolemos, a mock war between two rival churches. Members of each congregation fire rockets towards the opposing church, with the aim of hitting their bell tower. In the light of the following day, each tower is inspected for scorch marks, which are totted up to determine the winner. Invariably, both sides claim victory, with the only way to settle it being to do it all again the following year. Tradition has it that the event harks back to the end of the Ottoman occupation, a celebration of the islanders having their freedom and their munitions returned to them. Again, this mock battle is in fact a symbol not of division, but of togetherness. It's deemed an important one, too – people have died after being hit by stray rockets, and damaged property is par for the course, but occasional calls for the Rouketopolemos to be cancelled have been fiercely resisted.

These events differ in their manifestations, but all are vehicles for social identity. By playing or celebrating Shrovetide football, Ashbournians are saying, to themselves and the world, 'This is us; this is ours.' It is for this reason that, as I discovered, Ashbournians guard their game jealously. Like many festivals which draw a large crowd, Shrovetide is experiencing some problems with overtourism. Here, though, the people involved with the game are taking much more proactive steps than the money-hungry authorities in, say, Venice or Konya. They can't get rid of the crowd, exactly – the Ashbourne game *is* the crowd, and anyway, it's played in a town in the open air – but they are turning their back on the watching world, refusing to promote the game and certainly not making a habit of speaking about it to unscrupulous writers. Most of the people I spoke to, once it became clear my interest in the event was more than just sporting, only agreed to speak to me on condition of anonymity, lowering their voices to a whisper or dragging me into pubside ginnels, away from prying eyes and ears. The official Royal Shrovetide Players Committee rebuffed me: 'Over the last few years we have distanced ourselves from speaking to the media ... We play an ancient game that we want to protect. The popularity of the game is its biggest threat.'

One of those who did deign to speak to me in an official capacity was Tim Baker, a local historian who serves as the curator of Ashbourne's museum. A whole culture has grown up around the game over the centuries, with much folklore surrounding its origins. One story suggests the 'ball' was originally the decapitated head of an executed criminal, à la the infamous Mayan ballgame. This is unlikely in the case of the Ashbourne game, according to Tim, because there wasn't a castle here – but he had another theory. 'The pagans used to sacrifice a virgin, decapitate her, then play ball with her head,' he said. 'Wherever the head landed was deemed to have the blessing of her fertility. So that's a possibility.'

Beyond the origin myths, Shrovetide has developed its own vocabulary; as well as Up'ard, Down'ard, and 'goal the ball', there's the 'hug' (the scrum in which the ball is carried), and the 'turner-up', the person bestowed with the honour of kicking off proceedings on the Tuesday by launching the ball into the hug from a purpose-built plinth in a town centre car park. A touch of stardust is occasionally provided by the turner-up; celebrities afforded the honour include Brian Clough and then-Prince Charles, who opened the game in 2003, as a plaque on the side of the plinth proudly announces. The Ashbourne game is officially known as Royal Shrovetide Football, the only game of this kind to bear such a title. 'In 1922, Princess Mary was married at Westminster Abbey on Shrove Tuesday,' Tim explained. 'The people of Ashbourne sent her a Shrovetide ball in celebration, and she gave the game the royal title by way of thanks.'

Tim has had a personal connection to the game since birth. Shrovetide is in his blood – members of his family have been playing for more than 200 years, and his great, great, great uncle, Joseph Burton, goaled seven balls over his illustrious career, the most that anybody ever has. Tim is not a player of the game – 'It's men of a rare breed that play Shrovetide,' he told me – but it has nevertheless been a lifelong love affair for him. When he was a child, his family's milk was delivered by Philip Tomlinson, who was also a long-serving president of the Shrovetide Committee and is now spoken of in hushed tones as a legend of the game. Young Tim had been going to watch the game since he was three and quickly developed a passion for it. Tomlinson was aware of this, and when Tim was sixteen, he was given the task of painting the official Shrovetide ball, an honoured position which he has held ever since. He's unlikely to ever give it up – 'It's a position that's generally held for life,' he said.

The balls themselves are made locally, sewn from leather by a man named Terry Brown; their bodies are filled with cork, so that they float when they inevitably end up in the river. The design of the balls varies each year, but is sure to include royal insignia befitting of the Ashbourne game's title – the Union Jack, and the Tudor Crown. There are often nods to the home nations – the 2023 ball featured a huge Welsh dragon – or to local life, with the 2024 ball bearing the image of a tractor. If a ball is goaled, it becomes property of the goaler, but occasionally they make their way onto market, and they fetch a high price; in 2020, four balls sold for the princely sum of £12,500.

Tim has also channelled his fascination with the game into archiving it, assembling dozens of boxes' worth of press cuttings, artefacts, and official documentation.

There is a lot of material on Shrovetide football in the historical record, much of it relating to the many legal attempts which have been made to suppress it over the years. 'Most of the medieval football games across England were eventually stopped by the intervention of law, but our ancestors fought for their right to continue, holding events in town to raise the funds needed to go to court,' Tim said. In 1860, local police attempted to stop the game being played, but were foiled by local woman Elizabeth Woolley, who smuggled a ball inside her skirts and launched it into the waiting crowd from the upstairs window of a shop.

Much has changed since that time. The game has become a spectator sport, which, in its own modest way, attracts the glare of the international media spotlight and sees out-of-towners outnumber locals in the watching crowd – a worrying development, according to Tim. 'We've made Shrovetide famous, and a hell of a lot more people come to watch it now than 40 years ago, when I was watching it as a kid,' he said. 'It's a global phenomenon now, but that has a downside. Nowadays people come here for a piss-up and the chance for a brawl.'

Even team allegiance, once considered immutable and sacrosanct, has become muddied over the years. 'I'm afraid we've fallen foul of what I call the Manchester United syndrome,' said Tim. 'The game's been very Up'ard dominated over the last 30 years or so, and now we see a situation where people tend to pick the winning team to either play for or support, just because they win. That's worrying to me, as a historian and as an Ashbournian. The game does strengthen the town's identity – but at what cost?'

Tim went on to express a sentiment which I was to hear several times during my trip to Ashbourne: that the game had gone soft, compared to the old days, at least. He said that his grandfather would tell him of times in in the 1920s, '30s and '40s when men would turn up to the game still in their workwear, with vengeance or grudges on their minds. 'In those days,' he said, 'debates were settled with fists.'

Things are different now, but it still gets pretty tasty. Punching, kicking and biting are all de rigueur, and the directive about unnecessary violence being 'frowned upon' is little more than a sop to health and safety, delivered with a nudge and a knowing wink. Tim acknowledged that tempers are tested in the hug, and that violence even between close friends and family members is not uncommon. He insisted, though, that it was all played in a good spirit. 'It's friendly strife,' he said. 'People in the same family face off against each other for two days, and then they're fine again.'

The time for turning up was approaching. I wandered through the town centre, where the streets were full of an excited rabble all heading in one direction: towards the car park and the plinth, where the ball would be turned up by one John Tomlinson, a local farmer and son of local legend Philip Tomlinson. In those years when the event is not blessed with the presence of future kings or celebrity football managers – i.e. most years – it is local characters such as these who tend to be afforded the honour of turning up.

An elderly woman, being buffeted by the boisterous crowd, asked if she could hold onto my arm as she shuffled along. She gripped it like a vice, and it struck me that she would have been quite handy in the hug herself, had she come of age in a time when women were encouraged to take part. Her name was Peggy and she was an Up'ard, having been watching the game since long before Clifton and Sturston mills were knocked down, in 1967 and 1981, respectively. She had even brought her newborn son here when he was just two weeks old. 'We nearly got crushed! But he'll grow up tough,' she said of her boy, who presumably by now was pushing pensionable age himself.

Toughness was something of a fixation for Peggy, who, like Tim, yearned for the days when Shrovetide football was even more of an orgy of unalloyed violence than it is today. 'My father used to come straight from work at the quarry – he goaled two balls in the '40s,' she said. 'People used to get teeth knocked out by steel-toe boots, all sorts. Half the town couldn't walk for a week afterwards. Men were men back then – Shrovetide used to be about revenge.' She said this with the same misty-eyed longing which people of her generation usually reserve for remembrances of houses being blown to bits during Second World War air raids. It should be noted that women, although in far smaller numbers than men, have long taken part in the game, and have goaled balls on three occasions – Doris Mugglestone and Doris Sowter in 1943, and Nora Wibberley in 1957.

We reached the car park, and Peggy insisted I escort her to her usual spot, barely ten metres away from the plinth, right on the edge of what would become the hug – that much was evident from the outfits of those standing around us, rugby shorts and shin pads and boots caked with years of Shrovetide mud. 'Superstitious type, me,' said a man in ankle-high walking boots which looked like they'd been dredged up, attached to a bog body. 'I've been wearing these twenty years. They're never getting cleaned. They bring me good luck.'

'Never been injured, then?' I asked.

'Just some snapped ankle ligaments, a broken wrist and a few crushed ribs,' he said, proudly. 'And I saw a ball being goaled with my own eyes in 2008.' This is what, for most participants, passes for glory at Shrovetide football. It is a low-scoring game – most years end 1–0, with a 2–2 draw in 2011 being a veritable goal-fest by Shrovetide standards. The vast majority of participants never get close to the ball, and that includes the players who train the hardest: the 'runners', who remain vigilant on either edge of the hug, waiting on the off-chance that the ball falls to them and they get a few golden seconds of unimpeded running to make up a few yards towards their goal before getting subsumed once more by the hug. They prepare for this year-round, training like sprinters to maximise their acceleration and power. Most of them never touch the ball.

One young man, who told me his name was JP, was looking to the plinth with mad, staring eyes, his jaw milling a wad of chewing gum with industrial force. I'd seen that face enough times, in festival fields and darkened warehouses, to assume the man was all hepped up on goofballs. But no stimulants had been ingested, and not even so much as a drop of Castle Rock Harvest Pale had passed his lips in the Greenman that day, he told me. He was high on pure anticipation – a rocket-fuel fervour propelled by the prospect of unbridled partisan violence.

It was the time for turning up. From the plinth, Tomlinson led the gathered crowd in a throaty rendition of 'God Save the King,' and then chucked the ball, underarm and two-handed, with the awkwardness of a man who does not do a great deal of throwing giant cork balls into baying mobs. There was a collective intake of breath, followed by an airlock silence; where Peggy and I were standing, at some kind of frontier, half of us – the spectators – took an unconscious step backwards, and the other half, the players, motioned forwards to join the scrum. Time seemed to teeter on a cliff-edge; the sun beamed down on the hug, catching whirls of steam which rose from it like the breath of a great, sleeping beast – and then the thing awoke: the ball reached the mob, an army of hands grasped towards it, and one pair broke through, grabbed it, and sucked it back down into the underworld. The onset of violence was swift and extraordinary, like someone had flicked a switch – fists were windmilling and arms and legs sticking at unlikely angles out of a whirl of motion, like a dust-up in a cartoon. To my right, Peggy was looking on approvingly, nodding slowly – serene in aspect, yet with an unmistakeable flash of malice behind her horn-rimmed spectacles.

The hug started to move, an amorphous mass with a hive mind of its own, absorbing the occasional spectator at will. Along with contempt for the non-locals who attempt to get involved with the hug, the overriding attitude of Ashbournians towards innocent bystanders who get injured during the game tends not to be one of sympathy, but rather of eye-rolling disdain. Despite the significant personal risk which playing in Shrovetide entails, 'most of the injuries are to spectators who get too close to the hug – broken bones, cracked ribs,' Tim had told me. 'People get knocked over like skittles.' As for collateral damage, to houses, businesses, and cars, 'occasionally we have issues with broken windows. But it's down to people to get them boarded up, isn't it?' The game is not at fault. The game is sacrosanct; it is beyond reproach.

Over the course of the day, the hug shifted to and fro over town, flat, low, and sliding, like a puddle of liquid mercury, growing here and diminishing there as onlookers hurled themselves into the hug or limped out of it, retiring through injury. There were usually smiles on even their wincing faces, and the spirit throughout was consistent: one of cheerful violence, like the play-fighting which strengthens the bonds of brothers.

The hug spent hours tussling in the streets of the town, 'stifled by huge crowds of followers', as the *Derby Telegraph* would later lament in their coverage. I was among those crowds, keeping a safe-ish distance from the hug, and several times I was close to leaving after a long, dull period of nothingness – before a thrilling glimpse of the ball, and its accompanying flurry of kicks and fists, re-energised me and kept me watching. There were no balls goaled that day, which meant a full day's play until 10pm – so I did as the locals do, and broke up periods of standing and watching the game by going to the Greenman for a pint and, at dinnertime, heading to a local curry restaurant, where I was lucky to get a table; the waiter told me happily that this was their busiest night of the year.

I headed back out in the darkness towards the end of the day's play to catch up with the hug, which by this time had made it to the fields on the fringes of town and had shrunk noticeably. Things had slowed, after eight hours' play, to a crawl; the ball was visible more often, and its carriers were jogging with it rather than running full pelt. Where this morning the hug had emanated a static roar, it was now possible to hear individual cries of encouragement from players trying to motivate their teammates, and when the whistle blew at 10pm, it was with a sense of relief that the players began to trudge back through the darkness towards the Greenman, where Up'ards and Down'ards licked their wounds and showed off their battle scars, laughing off their individual bust-ups with hearty hugs and 'has-to-be-done' shrugs, their libations mulling them back to their senses – players, once more, on the same team.

8

NATION FÊTES
Festivals, Nation Building, and Ethnic Identity

SAINTES-MARIES-DE-LA-MER, France

Cries of '¡Ole!' rang out like a call to arms, punctuating scattergun phrases of flamenco guitar and plaintive songs of yearning and despair. The musicians were a group of middle-aged men – *gitanos* (Spanish gypsies) from Andalucía – arrayed around a table outside a bar in the Provençal seaside town of Saintes-Maries-de-la-Mer. Two or three were strumming acoustic guitars; another blew a clarinet. One old man seemed to be playing an instrument of his own creation: a tambourine folded back on itself and taped to a metal bar, which he tapped rhythmically with fingers clad in metal guitar slides – junkyard instrumentation of the kind you'd normally expect to hear on a middle-period Tom Waits album. All the while, above the music, they were singing, singing, singing, from the tips of their toes to the top of their lungs; singing like their lives depended on it. Their voices were clear as a bell and their playing metronome-tight, despite the table before them sagging with a complement of drinks which could have felled Alexander's army. A woman whirled in a flamenco dress, cinnabar-red, ruffled and spotted with black; her eyes half-closed, she moved to the raucous music in a quiet ecstasy.

I was attending a national celebration unlike any other: the Pèlerinage Gitan (Gypsy Pilgrimage), which sees Romani communities from across Europe converge on Saintes-Maries-de-la-Mer each May in a continent-wide caravan. The festival centres on a procession from the town church carrying a statue of Black Sara, the Romani patron saint, into the Mediterranean Sea in a remarkable parade of pilgrims, flanked by the snow-white horses for which this region of France, the Camargue, is famous.

The procession is just the ceremonial centrepiece, though, of a vibrant kermesse which overtakes this ancient seaside town for several weeks, with revellers camping in the streets, drinking plum brandy by the gallon, singing in full voice, and feasting on the foods traditional to their respective cultures. Many festivals exist to celebrate national or ethnic identity, but this one is particularly special: a boisterous gathering of disparate languages and cultures from across Europe and beyond, united by their nomadism and their fierce pride in their Romani cultural heritage.

'The pilgrimage is the most important international event of the gypsy people,' Yohan Salles, president of the Comité des Tsiganes (Gypsy Committee) for the Provence-Alpes-Côte d'Azur region, had told me via email over the run-up to the festival. 'It is the oldest, and it is the only one which brings all the ethnic groups of the gypsy people to a single place for a single goal: to find each other, to share and celebrate both Saint Sara and also our people, our culture and our future.'

I left the square with the flamenco singers behind and walked past a makeshift stall whose tabletop was assembled with tiny plastic cups filled with a straw-coloured, petrol-like liquid. 'Țuică', read a hand-drawn paper sign. '€1'. Romanian plum brandy. I took one at the vendor's urging and knocked it back with some difficulty – petrolly not just in appearance, it turned out. I squeezed through a crowded street into another square, this one also alive with music – but this time it was the clicking tongues and dancing mandolins of a Hungarian band, and the nimble accordion runs and guitar picking of gypsy jazz. The latter genre found its most famous expression through legendary guitarist Django Reinhardt, who was a familiar face here at the Pèlerinage throughout his short life; before he died in 1953 at the age of 43, he was working on the music for a Catholic organ mass, with the dream that it would be annually performed at the Pèlerinage. Other musical luminaries to be associated with the festival are crossover stars Gipsy Kings, who are said to have formed at the Pèlerinage in the 1970s and have since achieved worldwide success with their blend of pop, flamenco, and Catalan rumba.

It wasn't just the music bringing a cosmopolitan flavour to proceedings. The aromas of diaspora cuisine rose from bubbling cooking pots, mingling in the air in a glorious farrago: sweet, earthy beetroot borscht, the gamey smell of rabbit stew, and the sweetness of fried cornbread delighted my nostrils in turn, as people stood with paper plates and wooden forks tucking into apple pie, dumplings, and stuffed vine leaves. This was a communion of cultures, soundtracked by a polyglot orchestra – a babble of Hungarian, German, English, Portuguese, and everything else, united by the universal exclamation '¡Ole!' and its associated handclaps, which people seemed compelled to join in with, apparently unconsciously, even as they were mid-conversation, eating, or otherwise engaged.

And then came another battle cry. In a parking area beside the beach, a long-haired, bare-chested man stood on the steps of his wooden caravan on an upturned fruit crate, his matchstick legs clad in leather trousers, his sinewy forearm bearing a tattoo of a stick-man devil holding a pitchfork, its head crowned with an angelic halo. He looked brilliant, this merry prankster, a poster boy for a pirate nation – like a Romani Keith Richards. In his right hand he held a megaphone, which he raised to his mouth. 'Vives Saintes-Maries!' he bellowed, throwing his head back to reveal a mouthful of gold fillings. 'Vive Sainte Sara!' After each call, everyone in the vicinity roared back in kind. Without thinking, I found myself joining in, swept up in the rapture. This was to become a recurring theme of my time at the Pèlerinage, and something I had felt at festivals of different kinds the world over. Although this is a pilgrimage, it is a festival, too, infused with the qualities of the carnivalesque. And the carnivalesque is infectious – perhaps inherently so, thanks to its social levelling power, its matchmaking of mésalliances, its irresistible predilection for profanation. Animals get swept along by the carnivalesque, too – look out for it, the next time you're at a festival. Dogs chase their own tails, and each other; cats steal away from food stalls with fish in their mouths; parakeets dance around telephone wires. Like us, they are cutting loose, emboldened by an atmosphere designed to enable just that. They are having fun.

The day was falling away, the dipping sun honeying the white stone of the Church of Saintes-Maries. Flamenco was still ringing out in the church square, the bars and cafés warm with the atmosphere of revelry and the greetings of long-lost friends – sounds of home which are intelligible across any language barrier. Tomorrow, this would be the heart of everything, the setting for the occasion which the festivities had been leading up to: the Mass, followed by the procession of Saint Sara to the sea. That evening, I'd arranged a meeting with somebody at the centre of it all: Vincent Bedon, the head chaplain for all the Romani communities in France. I met him outside the church, a short, slight man in priestly vestments and rimless spectacles. He greeted me and led me into a vestry which was, if anything, even rowdier than the festivities outside – photocopiers clanked, phones rang incessantly, and black cassocks swished around every corner.

'It's a bit of a crazy time,' said Vincent, smiling wearily and rubbing his eyes. 'We have two national pilgrimages: Lourdes in August, and Saintes-Maries in May. Lourdes is a mild place and a mild pilgrimage. This one? Not so much.'

Vincent is no stranger to the hustle and bustle. 'Before I was a priest, I lived in London, where I was a trader in the City – Japanese securities,' he said. 'And then I made my best trade. And here I am.'

As he spoke, he lifted his sleeve, revealing another possible clue as to his erstwhile worldliness: a huge, pitch-black tattoo of a cross on his right forearm. He laughed as he saw my eyes widen. It was just a transfer, he explained, which he had got the previous day at the market here in Saintes-Maries. 'Only €8! Everyone thinks it's real,' he said. 'One guy told me having tattoos means you've been to jail,' he added, with a hint of pride.

The tattoo depicted a symbol of the region which I'd spotted adorning restaurants and trinket shops across town: the Camargue cross, which combines the shape of a crucifix and an anchor, overlaid with a heart symbol. The arms of the cross end in small serifs, which curve to three points in a representation of the tridents used by local cattle farmers. It's a striking symbol for a unique region, which is the perfect setting for such a singular event as the Pèlerinage. Like the nomadic Romani themselves, the Camargue has a shifting, in between quality – a tidal interzone between the Rhône River Delta and the Mediterranean Sea. Sandy beaches give way to muddy marshes, home to salt-encrusted succulent plants, half terrestrial and half marine; swaying tall grasses are the only feature of a pancake-flat landscape which seems to stretch infinitely like a salt pan, the horizon difficult to pick out, flickering through heat shimmers, sand bars, and clouds of mosquitoes.

For most of the year, however, the town of Saintes-Maries itself is an unassuming place. Reverting to its historic atmosphere as a somnolent fishing village during the winter months, it becomes a buzzy beach resort in the summer, popular with working-class French families – although its low-slung, light stone buildings, topped with terracotta tiles, better recall seaside resorts across the border in Spain. Why, I wondered, had the Romani chosen such a seemingly unremarkable place for their pilgrimage?

The answer, Vincent explained, begins with the three saints who gave the town of Saintes-Maries its name. 'The Gospel of John talks about Saint Marie Jacobe and Saint Marie Salome standing before the Cross,' he said. 'Later, they are said to have been with Mary Magdalene at the tomb when they discovered Jesus had risen.'

They were accompanied by their maid, Sara, a mysterious figure documented in the apocryphal gospels. 'Saint Sara is said in the Testament of Galilee – an apocryphal writing from the late first or early second century – to have been one of those to discover the empty grave, and to have run to tell the apostles the good news,' Vincent said.

The story goes that the Three Marys, along with Sara, set out onto the Mediterranean Sea on a sail-less boat with no oars. Divine grace carried them here to Saintes-Maries, on what was then the marshy southern coast of Gaul. Tradition has it that this spot was a pilgrimage site as early as the sixth century, though it seems more likely that the Marys became more closely associated with the region after the discovery of bones, held to be the relics of the saints, in 1448. Only in 1838 was the town itself formally renamed from Notre-Dame-de-la-Mer to Saintes-Maries-de-la-Mer.

Sara's mysterious origins and outsider status made her a natural fit for the wandering Romani, who had arrived in France in around 1418, not long before the relics were discovered at Saintes-Maries. Depictions of Saint Sara often show her with a dark complexion, and tradition commonly holds her to have been Egyptian. When the first Romani arrived in Europe from India, the Europeans mistakenly thought these dark-skinned newcomers had come from Egypt, too. This is the root of the word 'gypsy': a contraction of 'Egyptian'.

'When the gypsies arrived in Europe, nobody really knew who these people were,' Vincent said. 'To be satisfied, the locals had to give them a name, and they gave them many – *bohèmien, tsigan, kalderash, roms,* Egyptians. The names were varied, but they had a common meaning: these people are not from here.

'Sara is also depicted as being in a very humble condition, just like many of the early gypsies were. So, when the gypsies arrived in France in the fifteenth century, they took her for their patron saint.'

Sara's name in the Romani language – Sara e Kali – suggests another link with an ancient Indian past, sharing her name with the dark-skinned Hindu goddess Kali. The Romani Canadian scholar Ronald Lee has written that the ceremony surrounding the statue of Sara at the Pèlerinage – placing it on a platform covered in flowers, carrying it to a body of water (in this case the sea), and submerging it while the crowd throws flowers into the water – has strong parallels with the way that Kali and her twin goddess Durga are worshipped in India. 'In other words,' he wrote, 'the Roma who attend the pilgrimage to Les Saintes Maries in France and in other related ceremonies elsewhere honouring black female divinities, are in fact continuing to worship Kali/Durga/Sara, their original goddess in India.'[45]

Being misunderstood has always been a central pillar of the Romani experience, from the false assumption about their place of origin to the discrimination they face today virtually everywhere they go. Yohan had told me that his job as president of the regional Romani committee largely focuses around 'resolving all the problems that we [the Romani] encounter as a community – absenteeism,

---

45. Ronald Lee, 'The Romani Goddess Kali Sara'.

housing, resistance to our travelling way of life, discrimination'.

According to the Council of Europe, there are an estimated 400,000 Romani people in France, making up 0.21% of the population, although estimates vary widely, as they do for Romani communities in countries across the world – a result of their itinerant lifestyle and the fact that many individuals are not registered with local authorities. As is the case across Europe, they have faced discrimination since their arrival in France in the fifteenth century. In 1802, a concerted campaign was launched to clear Romani people from the French Basque Country, with a view to rounding them up and sending them to Louisiana – a plan which collapsed only when the colony was sold to the United States in the Louisiana Purchase of 1803.

Forced evictions of French Romani have continued into the modern age. In 2010, the French government drew international ire over their decision to deport tens of thousands of Romani to Bulgaria and Romania, while in 2016 the European Roma Rights Centre and the Ligue des droits de L'Homme (Human Rights League of France) claimed that 60% of Romani families in France had experienced eviction from their homes. As many as 17,000 of those that remained were living in makeshift camps, often without access to clean water or electricity.

Even here at their own event, the Pèlerinage, they face stigma and suspicion, which was barely concealed by many of the non-Romani locals I spoke to prior to the event. 'The gypsies are settling in little by little … their market starts today,' came a slightly nervous report from a contact at the tourist board, a few days before I arrived. 'But the village remains fairly calm. For the moment.'

I had received a less diplomatic account from a tour guide in Arles, Saintes-Maries' northern rival to the title 'capital of the Camargue'. 'Yesterday, the gypsies lit a fire in the football stadium. And another one on a roundabout,' he said. 'But on the day itself, you will be fine. They're not allowed to fight on the saint's day. So, it will be quite calm.'

I didn't personally witness any violence at the Pèlerinage, either on the saint's day itself or on the two days surrounding it, but tension between the Romani and the local authorities was simmering in the build-up to the event. I saw Yohan's name in several news reports in the days prior, in his role as the president of the Comité des Tsigane, defending the pilgrims' right to set up a market for the duration of the festival in the central Place des Gitans. This market had been held here every year since 2000, but this year the authorities had declined to grant the required licence. In protest at the restrictions, the Romani had used their caravans to blockade major access routes into town; the situation was eventually resolved and the licence granted on 16 May, barely a week before the main festival day.

The Romani even face continuing attempts by the local community to undermine their legitimacy as the originators of the Pèlerinage. 'The Camarguaise and the gypsies compete with each other,' Vincent had told me. 'Everyone wants to be the first to claim the procession, when we know perfectly well it was the gypsies who did it first. We have very early photos which show it was only the gypsies doing this. Why is this place famous? Thanks to the gypsies. And now they want to take it from them.'

The story of the Pèlerinage, however, is not as simple as that of a traditional Romani festival, sticking true to its ancient origins in the face of local resistance. The relationship between Romani culture, that of the wider Camargue region, and the modern Pèlerinage is a complex one, which sheds light on questions of tradition and authenticity in relation to even longstanding festivals.

The Pèlerinage is undoubtedly an ancient pilgrimage, with Romani faithful having travelled here to pay their respects ever since the relics of the saints were supposedly found beneath the church in the fifteenth century. Many of the outward aspects for which the pilgrimage is now famous, however – particularly the incorporation of the white Camargue horses and the traditional dress worn by their herders – were a more recent invention, the creation of an early twentieth century Provençal cattle farmer and writer called Folco de Baroncelli.

Keen to preserve the Camargue's rich and unique cultural traditions, which he feared were in danger of fading away, Baroncelli encouraged local farmers to maintain purebred lineages of the Camargue cattle, a primeval breed armed with huge, curving horns; short and stocky like the Camargue horses, but jet-black instead of white – their photographic negative. He also helped codify the rules of the *course camarguaise*, a local bloodless form of bullfighting which involves attempting to grab pieces of cloth wrapped around the bulls' horns, which (largely thanks to Baroncelli) remains very popular in the region to this day. Baroncelli helped the local cattle herders – known hereabouts as *gardians* – to form a self-identity akin to the North American cowboy or the South American gaucho, even influencing their style of dress, which still reflects his own penchant for brimmed hats, straight-leg trousers and floral shirts.

Perhaps more than anything else, Baroncelli had a keen eye for branding. The Camargue cross, which I had seen earlier plastered on Vincent's forearm, was created by local artist René Georges Hermann-Paul at the behest of Baroncelli, who desired a logo to represent his 'Camargue nation'.

Arguably, Baroncelli's greatest achievement was his role in legitimising the Pèlerinage in the eyes of the local authorities. An advocate for the Romani community, who had long had a presence in the Camargue and had been making their pilgrimage to Saintes-Maries since the fifteenth century, Baroncelli was instrumental in convincing the town council to tolerate their annual visit. In 1935, he convinced the church to allow the pilgrims access to the relics of the Marys and the statue of Saint Sara, and gathered a band of local gardians to help guide the procession from the church to the sea, effectively creating the ceremonial aspect of the Pèlerinage Gitan that survives to this day.

The fact that many characteristics of the modern pilgrimage are either revivifications or innovations on the part of Baroncelli does nothing to dampen his standing among the Romani, for whom he is an ally and a hero. Nor does it do anything to delegitimise the Pèlerinage; on the contrary, his efforts have made it more vital and true, perhaps the only place in the world where international Romani communities are allowed to legitimately gather and celebrate their identity. In culture, in any case, flux is the only constant. Those looking for pure, unchanging, monolithic representations of an ancient culture are wasting their time looking here, or at any festival, or anywhere.

Baroncelli understood that festivals are potent vehicles for the shaping of identity, whether that of a place or its people. This fact is well understood by governments the world over, nearly all of which encourage their citizens to celebrate and consolidate their collective identity on an annual national day. Every 15 August, the skies over India are darkened by a canopy of kites, flown in gardens, parks and streets as symbols of untethered freedom from British rule. On 16 September, Mexico's plazas become a riot of banda brass bands and street food vendors, serving traditional dishes in the red, white and green of the national flag – *chiles en nogada, bistec a la Méxicana*. In Oman, meanwhile, the pristine parkways of Muscat are lit up in the same tricolour of red, white and green to celebrate National Day each 18 November – giving the dissonant effect, to the European observer, of Christmas decorations glittering beneath the desert sun.

The power of festivals to unite people behind the cause of a nascent nation was not lost on the Founding Fathers of the United States, where independence from the British Empire has been celebrated each 4 July for nearly 250 years. Future president John Adams wrote in 1776, the year that the Declaration of Independence was signed, that Independence Day would be 'the most memorable Epocha, in the History of America. I am apt to believe that it will be celebrated, by succeeding Generations, as the great anniversary Festival. It ought to be commemorated, as the Day of Deliverance by Solemn Acts of Devotion to God Almighty. It ought to be Solemnized with Pomp and Parade with Shrews, Games, Sports, Guns, Bells, Bonfires and Illuminations from one End of this Continent to the other from this Time forward forever more.'

Adams seems to have been a little confused about exactly what kind of event he was advocating – guns, sports and bonfires are not the first 'solemn acts of devotion' which spring to mind, but then again this is America we're talking about. He was clear about one thing, though: a special day in a nation's history requires special commemoration. Observances today usually include fireworks; barbecues and picnics; hoisting of the American flag and other manifestations of the red, white and blue; and the nationwide consumption of non-casual quantities of light beer.

In places, however, the celebration of 4 July has been elevated to a uniquely American art form. The apogee of Fourth of Julyism is surely the Nathan's Famous International Hot Dog Eating Contest, a gala of gluttony which sees competitive eaters descend on a Coney Island restaurant each Independence Day. The competition's founding myth relates that, on 4 July 1916, four immigrants to Coney Island were engaged in an argument over who was the most patriotic American. They decided to settle it the same way any reasonable person would: by seeing who could eat the most hot dogs. In the years since, Nathan's has attracted the leading lights of competitive eating from around the world, from Takeru 'Tsunami' Kobayashi, a small Japanese man who once gave a Kodiak bear a run for its money in a televised eating contest, to Korean-born Sonya Thomas, known by the immortal sobriquets 'Leader of the Horsemen of the Oesophagus' and 'The Black Widow', the latter for her ability to regularly defeat men five times her size. The competition's dominant force is Joey 'Jaws' Chestnut, who set a new world record in 2021 by eating 76 hot dogs and buns in ten minutes. In days to come, when the mists of time have obscured the borderline between fact and folklore, Joey Chestnut's labours each 4 of July will be forever entwined with the founding values on which his country was built: life, liberty, and the pursuit of flatulence. He is a down-home hero; nothing less than America's Hercules.

The United Kingdom, incidentally, is one of only two countries, along with Denmark, which does not have an official national day. Britain's constituent nations have their own saints' days, but their celebration barely registers, with the exception of Scotland, where St. Andrew's Day is a bank holiday, unique among British national days. The Welsh St. David's Day does not get much attention once children get beyond school age – it's hard to get excited over daffodils and leeks, and I say that as a born Welshman – while the English celebration of St. George's Day is largely confined to flat-roofed pubs which sell Carling. The United Kingdom reflects this collective indifference by not having an officially designated national day, saintly or otherwise. The joke goes that the Brits don't need a national day, as they're responsible for so many other countries having their own independence days.

The British social psychologist Michael Billig called this kind of thing 'banal nationalism' – ordinary expressions of national identity that also include things like national sports teams, flags hung on embassy buildings, and the use of collective language like 'ours' and 'us' in the context of nationhood or ethnic identity. The celebration of national dishes – Hungarian goulash, Malaysian nasi lemak, Qatari machboos – is another form of banal nationalism, which is defined in opposition to more explicit forms of nationalism, like waging wars and drawing borders. The wording doesn't quite sit right with me, though. I can't be the only one who thinks that a steaming bowl of Vietnamese pho or Burmese mohinga, or a plateful of chicken satay from a Javanese street stall, is much *less* banal than the glum mechanics of geopolitics: grey men in grey suits starting wars by remote control in the tinned air of government offices. Politics is overrated. Culture, food, festivity: this is the stuff of life.

In Billig's analysis, although he doesn't express it in quite these terms, national days could be said to exhibit many of the properties of the carnivalesque – they are occasions when life is drawn out of its usual rut. 'Certainly, each nation has its national days, which disrupt the normal routines. There are independence day parades, thanksgiving days and coronations,' Billig writes. 'These are conventional carnivals of surplus emotion, for the participants expect to have special feelings, whether of joy, sorrow or inebriation. The day has been marked as a time when normal routines are put into abeyance, and when extra emotions should be enacted.'[46] For Billig, the very fact that these days are set aside as 'special' is enough to consolidate feelings of nationhood and shared identity throughout the year – even if the participants find themselves unsure of how they're supposed to be celebrating. Billig writes of a British survey, the Mass-Observation Project, which asked British citizens to report how they celebrated the coronation of King George VI in 1937. A woman, perhaps irreverently, wrote in her diary:

> Troubled by vague necessity for waking husband with suitable greeting. Sleepily wondered whether a 'God Save the King!' would be appropriate (husband likes Happy-New-Years and Many-Happy-Returns). Finally awoke enough to realize that a shaking was sufficient.

Billig writes that national days 'are patterned so that the national flag can be consciously waved both metaphorically and literally'. At the Pèlerinage Gitan, it is not the flags of nation states which are waved –

---

46. Michael Billig, *Banal Nationalism*.

nations and borders mean little, other than as symbols of oppression, to a people defined by their nomadism. Rather, it is the ethnic flag of the Romani people which can be seen everywhere, flying from caravans, tattooed on wrists, even decorating the corners of car and van numberplates in place of the European Union flag usually seen in this part of the world. The Romani flag is an attractive one: two horizontal stripes of light blue and green, representing the heavens and the earth, superimposed by a bright red *dharmachakra* – the dharma wheel common to Hindu, Buddhist and Jain symbolism, which is also found on the national flag of India. This is a relatively recent addition to the Romani flag, added at a meeting of the World Romani Congress in 1978 to reflect modern understandings of the Indian roots of the Romani people. Prior to this, there had been not one official Romani flag, but many different ones, which were unique to individual groups and often bore symbols evoking the Romanis' then-supposed descent from ancient Egyptians. When the 'gypsies' were misunderstood as having come from Egypt, this misinterpretation did not remain on the outside, but fed back into Romani culture itself, affecting Romani understandings of their own past.

This is an example of the phenomenon known as the pizza effect, whereby the (often mistaken) perceptions of outsiders go on to influence the perceived culture itself. The phenomenon gets its name from the anthropologist Agehananda Bharati, who in 1970 made the claim (which itself turned out to be based on a misunderstanding) that pizza as we know it was invented not in Italy, but in the USA by Italian Americans, who then exported it back to Italy in the twentieth century.

Other examples include the now-yearly Day of the Dead parade in Mexico City, which was only held for the first time after appearing in fictional form in the 2015 James Bond film *Spectre*; and the present-day popularity in India of postural yoga, which was invented in the Indian subcontinent but only became popular there after becoming a phenomenon in the West and then being re-exported to its original homeland.

Another of these feedback loops can be identified in early French perceptions of the Romani. During the twentieth century, Romani people living in France were known as *bohèmiens*, based on yet another false assumption about their origins – this time that they had arrived in France from the Central European kingdom of Bohemia (precursor to the modern Czech Republic). While the term originally had pejorative associations, it came to be adopted by young, anti-establishment Parisian intellectuals, who fancied themselves in tune with the nomadism, free-spiritedness and artistry which they had romanticised as characterising the 'gypsy soul'.

Typified by doomed poets like Arthur Rimbaud, the original Parisian bohemians eschewed the steady jobs, sensible marriages and fixed abodes aspired to by straight society, but it wasn't long before the movement forgot its commitment to poverty, the perceived glamour of the lifestyle having been seized upon by members of the bourgeoisie who exported it to Britain and America. By the turn of the twentieth century, the celebrated 'Queen of Bohemia' was not a starving Parisian poet, but New York socialite Aimée Crocker, who spent her vast inherited fortune on sumptuous pearls, Far Eastern artefacts, and the wildest parties west of West Egg.

The bohemian movement in turn has had an inestimable influence on modern, secular festivals. Glastonbury, for example, could be said to be the ultimate 'bohemian' gathering, in the modern sense of the word: a time for music and dancing, colourful clothes or none at all, voluntarily spartan living, and open drug use (light policing, in particular relaxation of drug laws, is probably the most obvious way in which modern music festivals like Glastonbury fit Bakhtin's criteria of the carnivalesque). How the original bohemians would have felt about Glastonbury, however – with its £12.50 cheese toastie vans parked beneath signs saying things like 'Eat the Rich!' – we can only speculate.

By the time I'd said goodbye to Vincent and stepped out of the vestry into the warm evening air, the town was a whisper; the musicians had disappeared from the squares and the bars had closed their doors, the carousing of the afternoon replaced by soft murmurs which snuggled against the warm yellow glow of the glass windows. There would be only muted festivities that night – a mark of respect for tomorrow's ceremony. I walked back to my hotel, as the stone houses became sparser, giving way to trembling grasslands, dotted occasionally with the thatched cottages of the gardians. It was still; almost threateningly so. The air felt charged, like a jumper rubbed against a balloon. Something was about to happen.

I woke up early the next morning and it was already hot as I sat drinking coffee in the little garden of my hotel. I looked out over the marshland which stretched backward some eighteen miles all the way to Arles, eerily flat and unpeopled by anything other than ghostly horses, Stygian bulls, and hot-pink flamingos. The wetlands shivered. In the caravan parks between me and the centre of town, life was beginning to stir; chihuahuas yapped and rattled their chains. I walked along the main road into town, past rows of open-doored riot vans, where bored-looking gendarmes lay across seats, playing on their phones.

I had a few hours to kill until the Mass, so I went to check out the market on the Place des Gitans which had caused so much controversy in the build-up to the festival. It was a mixed bag, to put it lightly, with mundane products peppered amid a cornucopia of contraband usually unseen this side of Khao San Road: knuckle dusters, butterfly knives, gas stoves, jump leads, laser pointers, drill bits, carpets, acoustic guitars, gypsy headbands, bars of soap. Groups of young men browsed through stalls laden with bling, nodding approvingly as they inspected golden rings inset with the logos of BMW, Mercedes, and assorted other German car manufacturers.

I made for the church, where, despite it being two hours before the Mass was due to begin, huge crowds had already gathered. I spotted Vincent from afar in a gaggle of priests, all resplendently attired in long white robes branded on the back with golden Camargue crosses. Old women were trying to hawk pin badges, many of which bore the same curious automobile logos as the rings I had seen at the market. Their sales tactics were aggressive, largely consisting of grabbing passers-by by the scruff of the neck and attempting to stick them with a badge, regardless of any expression of interest. This happened to me twice in quick succession before I managed to extricate myself from the pin-wielding crones and found my way to the church's side door, where I squeezed my way into a spot right beside the altar, amid the most pious devotees.

This ancient church was once a Mithraic temple, a heritage I could easily imagine as I admired its rear chamber, semi-circular and colonnaded, bare-walled and Pantheonic. These thick stone walls have withstood barrages from Vikings, Saracens, and French revolutionaries, but any hopes I had that they would provide a cooling effect were swiftly crumpled – it felt even hotter in here than it did outside. The essence of the swamp was among us. I looked out towards the huge main door, half open beyond a sea of devotees, letting in thick beams of white sunlight which illuminated whirls of steam rising from their heads.

It was evident, early on, that those gathered there were trying their best to maintain an atmosphere, on this holiest of days, of staid and sombre piety. But staid and sombre are not within the wheelhouse of the Pèlerinage Gitan. It soon became clear that this could not keep up the appearance of an ordinary Catholic mass for long. As the service unfolded, the veneer of soberness began to rattle like the lid of a pressure cooker, jets of steam escaping in the form of flamenco singing, cries of '¡Ole!' and frenetic handclaps, which occasionally escaped from the crowd seemingly involuntarily, peppering the liturgy like splashes of hot sauce on breakfast eggs. There was a sensuality about proceedings, which the priest encouraged the congregation to linger over, soak up and savour. 'Shhhh,' he exhorted time and again through his microphone when he sensed the atmosphere was getting a little too fervid. '*Écoutez.*' The simmering tension was almost audible, like the buzz of a fridge. Some people were already overcome; I could hear them sobbing quietly.

About half an hour into the service, I heard a scratching noise which seemed to be coming from the church roof, and I looked up to see movement in an alcove some twenty feet above my head, recessed into a stone wall. A large wooden chest, painted dark green and buttressed by iron brackets, was being manoeuvred into the alcove, while disembodied hands fastened it with ropes. This was the reliquary which Vincent had told me about, containing the mortal remains – so it was claimed – of saints Mary Salome and Mary Jacobe. The story goes that, in 1448, a hidden cave was discovered underneath the floor of the church, within which was found some broken pottery, an altar, and the remains of two bodies, which were apparently emanating a sweet odour. They were taken to be the remains of two of the Three Marys, and a pilgrimage was born – along with, in time, a new name for the town itself.

Over the course of the service, the reliquary was lowered towards the altar, not three feet away from where I was standing, inching closer as the sense of fervour rose inside the church. Once the chest was perhaps ten feet above our heads, those in the immediate vicinity began passing around long, thin, white votive candles, lighting them, and lifting them towards the descending reliquary. Their reaching towards it seemed at once desperate and involuntary, as if they were drawn to it like flowers bending towards the sun – they strained, grunted, leaned over one another, pushed themselves onto their tiptoes. All eyes were on the reliquary now. The voice of the priest was rising; every 30 seconds or so, he would lead rounds of 'Vives Saintes-Maries! Vive Sainte Sara!', chanted in unison by the gathered thousands, their eyes glazed, many of their faces tracked with tears which mingled with the sweat dripping from every brow. The smell of frankincense wafted from swinging thuribles, infused with a less welcome aroma – was that burnt hair? I looked to my side to see a votive candle, held vainly at arm's length by a woman desperate to reach the reliquary, singeing strands of a ponytail on the back of a girl's head. I adjusted the angle of the candle so it was out of harm's way. Neither the burner nor the burnt seemed to notice – their eyes were fixed on the prize.

The mercury rose further – the chanting, and the heat. A bead of sweat rolled down my cheek. I closed my eyes. There were no drummers in the church, but I swore in that moment I could hear them, striking a march from far away in the ocean, coming closer, closer still – and syncopating the rhythm was the pounding swell of Camargue hooves, riding in from the spray, mingling with the voices and the smoke.

The reliquary finally approached the altar, meeting the mass of votive candles which extinguished their flames against its painted underbelly. Hands grasped to help the box onto the stone altar; many people were crying, shaking, and muttering prayers as they rocked back and forth. The moment the reliquary landed on the altar, a similarly excited hubbub began to break out down the steps from where I was standing, in the middle of the congregation. This was Saint Sara being released from her crypt: a statue maybe three feet tall but shrouded in layer upon layer of white silk robes, sequinned and brocaded with floral motifs. Her head was circled by a halo of flowers, from the middle of which peered out a face, ebony in complexion and topped with a jewel-encrusted crown. As the gate to Sara's crypt swung open, so too did the huge church doors; the tension had resolved into a rapture; steam seemed to rush out of the church as if sucked into the afternoon air by a vacuum cleaner. The procession to the sea is a march for release, for Sara from her crypt, and for the faithful from the oppression – of the heat, of the gendarmes, of the strictures the Romani face everywhere they go.

Sara was jostled forward through the crowd, led by a train of priests in their white robes, Vincent at the front. The statue was carried on a wooden palanquin by pallbearers; those closest in the crowd stretched their arms out of their sockets for a brush of their hand against Sara's robes, mouths wailing and eyes streaming with tears. As the procession exited the church, it was met by a convoy of Camargue horses, small and sturdy with bone-white coats and platinum-blonde manes, steered by gardians in their traditional dress: floral shirts, fedoras and ties. The congregation filed out behind, following automatically, a hive mind in devotion to its queen.

The carnival was soon back in full swing as the procession moved through the streets of the town, accompanied by barrages of flamenco guitar, smooth ribbons of brass, and castanets which snapped like firecrackers. Food stalls had popped up along the route, selling fig cakes, snail soup, and cabbage rolls, faces gurning at every turn as they washed it all down with yet more plum brandy.

I made for the beach, keen to get a good vantage point ahead of the procession arriving. A gardian was occupying the gathered crowds by charging a few euros for rides on his Camargue horse, who he said was named Escargot – 'He's not the quickest,' he explained with a chuckle. Suddenly overcome with a pang of nostalgia for jolly old Blighty and donkey rides on the beach at Weston-super-Mare, I climbed on and allowed Escargot to plod along the sand for a few minutes. I closed my eyes and imagined myself as a Camargue cowboy, dancing with obsidian bulls in the *course camarguaise*, raising wild red rice in the wetlands, carving out a life among the flamingos and the salt in this strange place at the borderland between earth and sea.

The sound of hooves gathered on the promenade; those of us standing on the sand turned to face the approaching cavalcade, then bent down as one, rolling up our trousers, taking off our shoes and holding them in our hands as we joined the march into the water. Sara was carried until her pallbearers were chest-high in the drink, and those handsome horses gathered around her in an imperious array, pale bellies touching the ocean, their riders hoisting iron Camargue crosses, gardian tridents, and velvet standards of deep burgundy embroidered with the image of the Three Marys. On the horizon, storm clouds were coalescing, pierced by spears of sunlight; darkness and its opposite, roiling on the face of the deep. It was like an image of the Wild Hunt – a host of spectral horsemen, preparing their pursuit.

Then came the moment it had all been leading up to: the baptism in the ocean. The statue of Saint Sara was lowered from its litter into a little wooden boat and allowed to bob for a while on the surface of the sea, as its minders held it upright and gathered devotees scattered it with flower petals like confetti over a blushing bride. As Sara's boat touched the water, the humidity broke, and drops of rain began to ripple the surface all around her; threads to the heavens, joining the ocean and the sky.

I am not Romani, nor Catholic, but I have rarely felt more alive than I did that day. Riding a white horse across the sand, necking plum brandy, and running barefoot into the sea in a caravan of gypsies – these are things which make life voluptuous.

9

UTOPIA
Experiments in Society

You know what's more sustainable than staging a 'sustainable festival'? Not staging a festival at all. That's exactly the kind of negative thinking that wouldn't fly with the tech bros of Silicon Valley, who flock in their thousands each year to the dusty wastes of the Black Rock Desert, 100 miles north of Reno, Nevada, in pursuit of the world's greatest party. Burning Man, in the public imagination at least, is the transformational festival *par excellence*: a temporary city which springs up for a week each year as an experimental society unencumbered by cash or commodification, and running instead on community, artistic expression, and (their words) 'radical self-reliance'.

Burning Man takes place against the aggressively hostile backdrop of 'the playa', a long-dead lakebed whose finely powdered gypsum sand is so searingly alkaline that it can deal lasting damage to skin and internal organs. 'Burners', as alumni of the festival like to call themselves, enjoy boasting to civilians back home, with a brave limp or well-timed cough, about how long they have been laid low by this year's case of 'playa foot' or 'playa lung' – war wounds for the faint of heart.

Burning Man is the world's most famous example of what I will call utopian festivals. These events position themselves as laboratories for new ways of living: society in safe mode, where experiments in commerce, governance, and communalism can be staged in a temporary, semi-supervised setting. Participants emerge dusty and dazed, but with fresh ideas on how things should be done, and a renewed zeal with which to spread the good word to the wider world.

Among the '10 Principles' along which Burning Man proceeds are decommodification – *our community seeks to create social environments that are unmediated by commercial sponsorships, transactions, or advertising*[47] – and gifting, with any exchange of goods to be carried out in the spirit of donation and generosity. Money is worthless at Burning Man, except in the case of ice, which is on sale for $12 a bag, and, of course, entrance to Black Rock City itself, which ranges from $575 (the lowest-priced standard entry ticket) to thousands of dollars for entrance to luxurious pre-erected camps. These so-called 'plug-and-play' areas allow people to pay (often vast sums) for a place in a comfortable, catered tent, bypassing the usual requirement to help build an ordinary camp in the spirit of radical participation and self-reliance. The plug-and-play camps are not affiliated with the Burning Man authorities, but they persist despite the festival having claimed to be stamping down on them since at least 2015, when CEO Marian Goodell declared, 'We

---

47. Burningman.org

are absolutely committed to ceasing the plug and play culture.'[48]

Despite the evidence to the contrary, 'Your money's no good here' remains one of the sanctimonious sayings beloved by Burners. Ironic, considering they represent some of the wealthiest people in the United States and, by extension, the world. According to the official Black Rock City Census, 54% of festival attendees in 2023 had a personal income of more than $75,000 (the U.S. median income for the same year was $59,428), and 8% of Burners enjoyed a personal income of more than $300,000 each year.[49] High-profile Burning Man attendees in recent years have included famed anti-capitalists Elon Musk, Jeff Bezos, and Google founders Sergey Brin and Larry Page.

Another of the 10 Principles of the Burn is 'Leave No Trace', and the festival makes much of its mission to become carbon negative by 2030. Once again, though, Burning Man has long been accused of tone-deaf hypocrisy when it comes to environmental matters. As many as 3,000 private jets are estimated to ferry the most well-heeled attendees to the festival's very own Black Rock City Airport each August. Even many of the well-intentioned Burners, who stay in traditional camps and take part in the original spirit of participation and communalism, sleep in air-conditioned RVs which burn a huge amount of fuel. And who can blame them? It's one hundred degrees outside.

---

48. 'Here's What Burning Man Is Doing to End Turnkey Culture' at Burningman.org
49. Black Rock City Census 2023.

The festival's hypocrisy burns brightest in its famous fire installations. Although Burning Man has always culminated *Wicker Man*-style, with a giant wooden effigy being set ablaze, there have often been additional fire-based installations among the many giant artworks which scatter the playa and are a major part of the festival's aesthetic. In 2007, in line with that year's eco-focused 'Green Man' theme, one of the artworks, named *Crude Awakening*, involved igniting a 1,000-foot pillar of flame around a wooden oil derrick. The exhibit was positioned as a satire of the fossil fuel industry, and was, you guessed it, propelled by 3,400 litres of jet fuel and 7,600 litres of liquid propane. And this in the very same year as a self-congratulatory blog post on the Burning Man website declared, 'Burning Man's entire year-round operations went "green" in earnest [in 2007], wherein the staff upped recycling and composting efforts, and thoroughly re-thought and reduced the environmental impact of Burning Man's headquarters.'[50]

There is something delicious about the irony of the world's billionaires gathering to dance in the desert in celebration of their self-inflicted apocalypse, effigies burning in oceans of oil, the world beyond them burning, too. The deepening climate crisis is only serving to make the difficult conditions at Burning Man – which, after all, are the whole point of staging the festival in an inhospitable desert – even more extreme. In 2022, the hottest Burning Man on record, temperatures reached 103°F (39°C), prompting many Burners to do the sensible thing: pack up and go home. The following year, in 2023,

---

50. '2007 Event Archive', Burningman.org

apocalyptic floods turned the dusty playa into a gigantic mud bath, trapping festivalgoers in increasingly unpleasant conditions. Tents flooded, litter piled high, and toilets overflowed, prompting organisers to encourage attendees to urinate in plastic bottles.[51] The internet rejoiced in their misfortune, letting out a collective whoop of *schadenfreude*. Memes spread like wildfire, as did gleefully outlandish rumours about conditions on the ground – outbreaks of Ebola, and recourse to cannibalism – underpinned by the perception that the sins of climate change, and of just generally being unbearable, were coming home to roost upon Burning Man's gathered elites.

In the light of which, it would have seemed slightly hypocritical for me to have flown all the way to Nevada to attend Burning Man, only to then fly home and write a book chapter criticising them on the basis of their eco-credentials. And besides, when I tried to buy a ticket, it was sold out. And so I looked closer to home. When I set out to write a book about the festivals of the world, I did not expect my adventures to carry me not just once, but twice, to Chepstow. And yet.

With a rucksack on my back containing all a man could need for a weekend at a modern music festival – a tent, a sleeping bag, and a family pack of Imodium – I trudged through the green fields of south Wales. I was moving through a landscape populated by strange creatures. Goat-headed figures in crowns of laurel, seven feet tall

---

51. The *Independent*, 'Burning Man attendees share ordeal with urine bottles as clean-up begins after exodus'.

and dressed in shredded robes. A man in a kurta pushing a wheelbarrow full of exotic stringed instruments and skin drums, which murmured among themselves as they bobbled along the grassy ground. A woman dressed (in either protest or praise – it is often hard to tell) as a wind turbine, in a white skinsuit with a plastic propeller affixed to her forehead.

I reached a quiet hill on the edge of the campsite and dropped my bag at my feet. To one side of me was the Wye Valley gorge, a deep tear in the stone, smothered in dark forest, emanating mystery. To the other side was the Severn Estuary and the old Severn Bridge – a borderland of lugworms, rattling lorries and rotting infrastructure. I pitched my tent facing the gorge and set out to explore.

Green Gathering describes itself as the UK's original off-grid festival. It began in the early 1980s with meetings at the Green Fields, an area of Glastonbury Festival dedicated to environmental activism. Early attendees included members of the Ecology Party, which would be renamed the Green Party in 1990 and become the parliamentary face of the British environmentalism movement. Subsequent gatherings were held at various events associated with the New Age Traveller movement; nowadays, seasoned Green Gathering veterans speak with misty eyes about storied events like 1985's Battle of the Beanfield, in which Wiltshire Police violently prevented a so-called 'Peace Convoy' of campervans and foot travellers from setting up the Stonehenge Free Festival, in one of the largest mass arrests of civilians in British history.

These days, although there is a full programme of musical acts across several stages at Green Gathering, the main focus is on workshops and talks which promote environmental action, social justice causes, and left-wing politics, as well as personal pursuits like foraging, meditation, and permaculture. This was the question I was hoping to explore at Green Gathering: whether, on a personal or societal level, for better or for worse, a festival can change the world.

In some ways, I thought as I walked around the site, Green Gathering looked much the same to me as any of the hundreds of other hippyish festivals held in the fields of Great Britain all summer long: cosmopolitan in spirit, but not in flesh. The people, certainly, seemed familiar – plummy accents, purple hair, and a near-complete lack of ethnic diversity. White men in dreadlocks advertised shamanic drum workshops; white women in aprons cooked Tibetan curries and momos. Sparks flew and hammers clinked in coppersmith workshops and knife forges. Screams emanated from within a tent dedicated to the art of beekeeping, while wellness tents, alongside Swedish, deep-tissue, and hot-stone treatments, advertised 'intuitive massage' – the art of making it up as you go along.

Although the food stalls were meat- and fish-free, not all the attractions were veggie-friendly: outside an animal-skin processing workshop, deer and squirrel hides were laid out on a row of tree stumps. I asked a customer, red-faced from scraping gristle from a rabbit pelt, what there is to gain from learning how to process an animal skin. 'The way society's going, we're all gonna need to know how to do these things soon,' he said, in the kind of cheerfully doomsaying tone which often accompanies forecasts of the downfall of capitalism.

The programme explained that this section of the festival, the Craft Area, promised 'practical skills for a sustainable life'. But it does not require much critical thought to conclude that the wearing of animal skins – like the carving of wooden cutlery, or the foraging of one's own food – is not in any way scalable or sustainable. These are not egalitarian, societally minded exercises, but remain, like utopian festivals themselves, leisure activities for the chosen few. And that's fine, actually. It's clear what's really going on here: that the increasing popularity among middle-class urbanites of tactile skills like spoon-carving and pottery throwing, and bushcraft survival skills like fire-making and shelter-building, are a response to our coddled existences, where food, warmth and water come to our soft hands so easily that our brains, hardwired for struggle, need to simulate hardship in order to fill the void. I say this not to denigrate such activities, of which I am a keen proponent – but only to acknowledge that my friend, an enthusiastic homebody, may have something right when she mockingly scrutinises my decision to go camping in the wild when I have a nice warm flat I could stay in instead: 'The picture of privilege. You have to make yourself homeless just to feel something.'

It was in the Craft Area that I'd arranged to meet Kat Bennett, who works in communications for the festival. 'This was mental last year,' she said, indicating the animal-skin processing workshop. 'A group of people took exception to it, and they organised a protest, right here, during the festival.'

This pearl-clutching, performative self-examination is a feature of these kind of events, such that I had no doubt that the 'Whiteness self-repair workshop' promised on the programme would have a large and self-flagellating choir to preach to. Utopian festivals, incidentally, are generally overwhelmingly white, often in marked contrast to the wider landscapes in which they sit. Burning Man, for instance, was 78.2% non-Hispanic White in 2023, in comparison to 46.4% for the state of Nevada as a whole.[52] Chepstow, in fairness, is an overwhelmingly white town – 96.4%, according to the 2021 census[53] – and although many Green Gathering attendees are out-of-towners, this is a small festival, so it would be surprising if it were particularly cosmopolitan. But the same pattern is borne out at much larger festivals, too. In 2022, the comedian Lenny Henry, when asked about Glastonbury, commented, 'I'm always surprised by the lack of black and brown faces at festivals.' Unlike Burning Man, Glastonbury does not publish demographic information, but you only have to spend a day there to understand how overwhelmingly white and middle class it is, despite the festival having made efforts in recent years to book a more diverse lineup of performers. Part of the reason for this may be socioeconomic, with a music festival being an increasingly expensive way to spend a weekend, but it's fair to assume that there are cultural reasons for it, too. I scanned the Green Gathering programme – with its whiteness self-repair workshops and sessions on bringing down capitalism, one billboard at a time – and then looked out across the teepees and the green fields, full of smiling white faces who, in large part, do very nicely out of the status quo. And I wondered how much change could really be effected by events like this; these ivory towers built on good intentions.

---

52. Data USA: Nevada, 2023.
53. United Kingdom census, 2021.

All of which being said, there is a great deal to admire about Green Gathering. 'The whole festival is renewable,' Kat said. 'Research shows that you spend less carbon coming here than you would if you stayed at home, and over 80% of the waste produced here is recycled or composted.' Unlike events like Burning Man, which preach climate concern while leaving an Atlas-sized carbon footprint on the desert each year, Green Gathering is genuinely carbon-neutral, not using any fuel-burning generators at all and deriving all its energy from solar, wind, and (occasionally) pedal power. It has been like this since the festival's beginnings, and indeed some of the solar panels I saw powering the food-stall ovens looked like they'd not been upgraded for several decades, great battered tin-foil satellite dishes which wouldn't have looked out of place on the Clangers' moon base.

While the whole thing feels like a charmingly low-key solar-punk expo, parts of Green Gathering have the same more explicitly mock-dystopian aesthetic as themed areas at festivals like Glastonbury – stages in corrugated iron shacks hung with hand-painted signs bearing slogans like 'Decarbonising Minds'. But here the message rings a little truer, not just because of the festival's use of renewable energy, but because of the amount of genuinely useful information which it provides to punters. (Not to mention interesting facts – did you know, for instance, the average large digital billboard uses the same amount of energy per year as eleven houses?) As we walked around the site, I saw workshops on how to build off-grid water systems, and information tents telling people how to apply for green grants from the Welsh government for solar panels. Useful, actionable things among the more nebulous and esoteric offerings listed on the programme (Friday, 2.30pm, 'Taoist sexuality with Jacob').

All very admirable – but an eco-minded weekend is one thing. Are festivals like this capable of effecting lasting change, or even getting their message through to people who don't already share the same ethos? 'On behaviour change, we've been accused of preaching to the choir,' said Kat. 'But the world as it is, is really overwhelming; it's hard to know how to do everything right. What we offer is a toolbox.'

Environmental action aside, Green Gathering offers its attendees the same great gift provided by so many festivals: the chance to cut loose from society's normal conventions, to proceed temporarily along different tracks. Many modern festivals make conscious efforts to emulate the conditions which arise organically in traditional festivals, such as liminality, the carnivalesque, and connection to the landscape and to the ancient reaches of the human past. Glastonbury has its very own stone circle, a centre for shamanic drumming, druidic rites, and all manner of entheogenic rituals – built not in the Neolithic, but in 1992. Green Gathering's programme in the year of my visit exhorted revellers to 'rekindle a childlike curiosity in the liminal', and there was even a sound installation to that end, *Shrines to the Liminal*, a set of ramshackle structures in a forest clearing, fitted with chimes and old piano keys which sighed and tinkled with each breath of the wind.[54]

Nakedness was another recurring theme. 'It's very free here, very open,' said Kat, and right on cue we rounded a corner to be greeted arse-first by a naked man practising

---

54. By the artist Jessica Rost.

his best downward dog. Equally prominent, though, was masquerade, and the harking back to pre-Christian religion, both embodied by the costumed pagan gods I had seen on my arrival at the festival. We saw them again now, as we entered a grove of trees; they were a walkabout performance group from Ibiza, Kat explained, called Theatre of the Ancients. But they were off duty now, and their ragged veils and rams' heads had been lifted or placed aside to allow for the smoking of roll-up cigarettes and the sipping of coffee from paper cups.

To one side, in front of a huddle of Portakabins, a group of middle-aged men stood chatting. Kat pulled one of them aside and introduced us. Steve Muggeridge, known to all as Muggs, is a director of Green Gathering and a stalwart of the festival scene. With his long leather jacket, shoulder-length brown hair and fedora, he appeared as a kind of festival sprite; he reminded me of Tolkien's Tom Bombadil, a wise and enigmatic being who had been there since the very beginning and had seen it all.

Steve told me that his first involvement in the festival scene came at the Stonehenge Free Festivals between 1981 and 1984. 'The closest description of the Free Festivals would be "tribal gatherings" of New Age travellers, Pagans, partygoers and urban adventurers,' he said. It was these who made up the Peace Convoy, a cavalcade of colourful campervans which would travel together between festivals and political protest camps. 'With their marquees and banners, they had the feel of an encamped medieval army combined with a vintage vehicle rally,' Steve said. 'There seemed to be magic in the air at such places; one could get swept away with it, as indeed I was.

'They were great parties. But I was also intrigued by the claims from some engaged elements that alternative societies, diverging from mainstream consumerist culture, might find a contemporary framework through these events.'

What would those societies entail? 'Broadly, freedom of association in their own land; freedom of access to the land; an intuitive feeling of connection with ancient traditions, often by gathering at ancient sites; a disposition to embrace environmental sustainability, in part informed by engagement with ancient belief systems; and hopes that New Age beliefs might provide an ethical compass for alternative and progressive community,' Steve said.

Utopian festivals, however, have the capacity to turn dystopian very quickly – and not just on the whims of the weather, as in the case of Burning Man. A utopia is built on openness and trust: things easily abused by hostile agents. Steve told me a startling story about the final days of the Stonehenge Free Festival which brought to mind the tragedy at the Altamont Free Concert in 1969, when Hells Angels, hired as security, fatally stabbed 18-year-old Meredith Hunter during a performance by the Rolling Stones – an event often earmarked as the death of the utopian dream of the 1960s.

'The final Stonehenge Free Festival [in 1984] was marred by a biker gang running amok, burning some stalls and intimidating people in what was, of course, a completely lawless environment,' Steve said. 'Not all the tribes were friendly or shared the vision.'

Since that time, Steve said, more structure has been imposed on festivals of this kind, which has improved matters considerably. 'Festivals have evolved into far more focused and useful explorations of community,' he said. 'They have been and continue to be opportunities for re-figuration, offering portals for alternative pathways for people and communities. I can't tell you the number of times I or a colleague have been told that Green Gathering or [its precursor] Big Green Gathering changed their lives and started a campaign group or project.'

Steve pointed to eco-entrepreneur Dale Vince, a fellow veteran of the Free Festival days (and erstwhile Green Gathering speaker), who spent years living as a New Age traveller before founding Ecotricity, the world's first green energy company. Steve also cited activist movement Climate Camp, who set up a series of large camp-protests in the 2000s and were hailed by the *Guardian* in 2009 as the saviour of the environmental movement.[55] 'Much of their funding came from their bar concession, "The Last Chance Saloon", at the Big Green Gathering,' Steve said. He reeled off more examples: 'Road protesters from Twyford Down, Peace Camp campaigners, groups such as Ecotrip, Occupy – in fact, waves of protest groups, the ancestors of Extinction Rebellion and Just Stop Oil. No other festival has this history of support.'

I wondered at this point whether utopian festivals, which claim to strive so ardently for unity and harmony, could have the opposite potential – to sow division and strife. It's difficult to see the Battle of the Beanfield as anything other than a shameful episode of police overreach and brutality, but the legacy of other events is more muddled. The original 1969 Woodstock Music and Art Fair was the culmination of the hippy dream of the 1960s, billed as '3 Days of Music and Peace' and presaging Glastonbury (by one year) as the prototypical utopian festival. Yet its 30-year anniversary event, Woodstock

---

55. The *Guardian*, 'Climate Camp: saviour of the environmental movement?' by Tom Levitt.

1999, was a disaster: a *Lord of the Flies*-esque portrait of what can happen when 220,000 human beings are left to their own devices in a large field. Uncomfortably hot weather and frustrations over technical problems and poor sanitation turned into something apocalyptic on the festival's Sunday evening, with mass brawls breaking out, food trucks looted and burned, and many alleged incidents of sexual assault, including four alleged rapes. This is an extreme example, of course – but a striking one, given it bears the Woodstock name, and one which throws into stark relief the fact that festivals have the capacity to showcase the darkest, as well as the most optimistic, sides of human nature.

Still, for the majority who have a positive experience, festivals can feel all too fleeting. 'It's commonplace to hear people say they wished the event could be a month long, or a permanent community,' said Steve. 'They're a temporary iteration of a society or community many would prefer to live in.' A vision which reverberates, occasionally, into the real world.

I said goodbye to Steve and Kat and carried on wandering around the site. Keen to come away from the festival with some practical knowledge, I attended a 'foraging walk' led by a woman called Jo. She announced herself in unarguable style – 'I hold the record for the number of plants used in a salad in the UK. That's 325' – and proceeded to list some examples of the near-endless uses for the plants which were growing on the festival site. 'Yarrow has a liquoricey taste,' she said, holding up a fern-like leaf, 'and it stops bleeding very quickly. Soldiers would use it on the front during the Second World War.' I had my doubts that its effectiveness extended to treating shrapnel wounds, or closing holes ripped through bones by machine-gun rounds, but she went on, 'Sorrel has a lovely citrussy flavour. We can even have a nibble on some grass.' One young man, large and stooped with sad cow-like eyes, expressed an uncommon interest in this latter claim, and stayed behind picking at the ground as the rest of us stood up to follow Jo into the woods.

'As we walk over, I want you all to try fox walking,' said Jo. 'With each step, put the outside of your foot down first, and roll your weight inwards towards the ball of your foot. And as you walk, put your arms outstretched in front of you and wiggle your fingers. This activates your peripheral vision. It's a way of training yourself to notice things in the woods in a wider field of vision, which is obviously useful for hunting, but for foraging, too. We call it using "owl eyes".'

We followed her instructions and proceeded towards the woods, arms outstretched and fingers waggling, a gaggle of bare-footed, jazz-handed zombies. Once we were ensconced within the trees, Jo uttered a collection of words to make the most fearless heart turn cold: 'Partner up with the person next to you. We're going to do a trust exercise.'

My partner was an older lady called Camilla. One of us had to pretend to be a tree, and the other had to try to push them over ('to encourage rootedness'). We were spared the embarrassment, though, by a rustling in the trees, from where a toothless man emerged brandishing a rusty implement. 'I went for a poo and when I was digging my hole I found this old spoon,' he said. 'Wanna see?' His wording didn't make clear beyond reasonable doubt where exactly he'd dug out this old antique from – much less whether he'd washed his hands – so we all politely declined, and the workshop fizzled out into an early end.

Back in the main festival area, an earnest woman in an Extinction Rebellion T-shirt was trying to encourage punters to attend a workshop by saying with a smile, 'Would you like to help bring down capitalism today?' – and it was working, because in a milieu like this, it would be embarrassing to refuse. Curiously, though, the spirit of capitalist enterprise was all around us. A camper had erected a hand-painted sign outside their tent saying 'Anecdotes, £2', which had attracted what was to my mind a surprisingly long queue. A group of young lads, clutching a football, bounded up to me like Dickensian urchins, and their leader, the eldest boy, said, 'Scuse me, sir, if we do some tricks for you, would you give us a tip?' I told them I had no change. He didn't flinch. 'We have change, if you have notes.'

I half expected him to whip out a card reader. They had me cornered – and I couldn't help but be impressed by their thrusting entrepreneurship, the type which often betrays a childhood spent abandoned by ditzy bohemian parents to run amok around music festivals. They had learned from the best, after all – no one does capitalism-in-disguise like a stall at a music festival. One of the cafés nearby had a signboard outside outlining their origin myth, which included the line: 'We started out as a "guerilla café", selling home-made cakes to revellers.' Just a café, then.

But maybe I am being ungenerous. Festivals, and all the people involved in them, face an uphill battle to make ends meet. Fifty UK festivals were cancelled in the first half of 2024 alone,[56] including high-profile events like NASS,

---

56. Association of Independent Festivals.

a music and skateboarding festival held at the Bath and West Showground in Somerset. Even nearby Glastonbury, arguably the world's most famous music festival, is perennially hard-up; it makes only a slim profit each year (although it does donate millions to charity), and famously can only afford to pay its headliners a fraction of what they would receive for equivalent gigs elsewhere, blundering through instead on prestige and well-earned goodwill.

Most importantly, for all that New Age types can be inconsistent, they are also in my experience mostly kind, well-intentioned people, earnestly trying to make improvements to an uncaring or actively hostile world. They are also generous in the sharing of cider and foraged goods, and so I passed a splendid evening in the woods among new friends, howling at a crescent moon and enjoying the stylings of 'climate crisis cabaret' act Fossilheads – 'We put the "Oooh!" in existential doom!'

A golden shard of dawn lasered its way through a gap in the door of my tent, arrived at my eyelids, and blew up my head like a cantaloupe on a firing range. I jumped up, moaning, and began careening about my tent like a bat in a cave that's driven to psychosis by the camera flash of a dim-witted tourist. Eventually I found the zip and fell out into the world as if being born again, still swaddled in my sleeping bag like a large slug, scattering the dew from the roof of my tent as pegs and guy ropes flew in my wake. The world seemed a hostile place this morning; low-flying gulls screamed overhead. I wriggled out of my sleeping bag and headed towards the food stalls in pursuit of coffee, past meditating early risers, singing circles and morning *qigong* classes. I crested the top of a hill and was greeted by the sight of a bearded man going through his morning exercises outside his tent, his potbelly gyrating and pushing out his tie-dyed T-shirt with each forward thrust, revealing his bare balls. I stood for a moment, mesmerised as if by a hypnotist's pendulum – but when, with surprising agility, he flipped floorward into a wheel pose, I decided I needed a change of scene. These hippies were starting to get to me.

The Wye Valley had been calling to me ever since I'd pitched my tent: this deep, dark gorge, wreathed in oak and birch, which seemed to breathe in and out with each scattering of birds and rustling of leaves. I had spotted a gate leading into the forest while walking around the site, and I slipped through it now, the sounds of the festival being muffled almost immediately and then slipping from my consciousness entirely. The falling dew crackled in the canopy of the woods; the knotted trunks of ash and yew trees were gnarled into silent screams. Eventually I met the River Wye, where a sweet barky smell, like rooibos tea, hung over the path. Huge ferns, hung with water droplets, brushed against my legs, giving the feel of a cool rainforest. Feeling myself at one with the natural world, I decided to try and implement some of my newfound skills. I nibbled on what I thought was an innocuous leaf of wood sorrel, and felt an almost immediate compulsion to evacuate my bowels; I tried fox-walking, and fell down a ravine. It was clear that I was not yet sufficiently transformed, so I headed back to the festival, rubbing my sore elbow and consulting my programme in search of yet more delicious self-improvement.

My eye was drawn to a talk about to start in the Voices of Gaia tent, entitled 'Plant medicine & some surprising history behind remedies' and delivered by herbalist Geoff Soma. I made the short walk to the tent and sat down on the edge, by the door, should the need arise for a quick getaway. Geoff took to the stage, a middle-aged man in a bright floral shirt, to modest applause.

'Who's heard of Helen of Troy?' he asked, expectantly – most of the crowd, I'm pleased to report, put up their hands – and he held aloft a yellow flower. 'Elecampane. Helen's tears fell and these flowers sprang up, so the story goes. Now, I'm going to pass round some tea.' An attendant brought a tray round with tiny paper cups containing a clear-brown liquid. After sharing a couple of nervous smirks, my neighbours and I drank the brew – it was not unpleasant: earthy and slightly astringent.

Geoff said, 'Now, the *beaudy* of elecampane' – he spoke like Tony Blackburn – 'is that it brings up a lot of phlegm. It's what we call an expectorant. It's great for colds.' Right on cue, a man in the second row began to cough chestily. 'Look at this guy,' said Geoff, pointing with glee. 'Phlegm is liderally *ejaculading* from his mouth!'

I'm not sure if it was the hangover, the herbal tea, or the humid afternoon, but I began to drift off, strange phrases entering my waking dreams in Geoff's local-radio drawl ('We are big ring doughnuts. From your mouth to your anus – it's just one long tube, baby ...'). I came to just as Geoff was holding forth on the subject of chronic fatigue syndrome. 'Yuppie flu, people used to derisively call it. But in times gone by, people would talk about being elf-shot: falling ill after being shot by an elf's invisible arrows. And what were the symptoms of being elf-shot? Feeling fatigued, lethargic, losing your zest for life.'

A woman in the crowd took exception to the implied connection between chronic fatigue syndrome and elves –

'My sister has M.E.,' she protested – and Geoff clarified that he was being metaphorical. But then he went on, 'You know, in Iceland there's a real reverence for the unseen liddle folk. In 2013, they were building a highway from Reykjavik to the Alftanes Peninsula. They reached a village and found a rock where the locals said the liddle folk lived. They went to the big guy in Reykjavík and said, "Sorry guvnor – we godda move the road." He said, "Cor, blimey." But they moved the highway. It took 'em months, but they did it. So in Iceland they know the power of being elf-shot. This stuff can cure that,' he added, shaking a bag of dried roots.

As it happened, I had been in Iceland just a few weeks earlier, to attend another festival: the midsummer gathering of the Ásatrú religion, a heathen revival of the Norse religion of Odin, Thor, Loki and the rest. Ásatrú has been the fastest-growing religion in Iceland for the last twenty years, with membership now standing at around 7,000 – a significant number in a country whose entire population only numbers 382,000. But its increasing popularity, as I was to discover, has less to do with the worship of one-eyed gods, world trees and Valkyries, and more to do with a renewed desire to connect with the natural world, an imperative given fresh urgency in the minds of many by the mounting climate crisis.

Icelanders may have less to feel guilty about regarding environmental matters than the rest of the world, being privileged to live in a country whose seething volcanism ensures that nearly all the country's electricity is provided by sustainable geothermal power. But Iceland's unique geology, which conspires with the country's northerly latitude to create some of the world's most mind-blowing natural landscapes, also instils in its people a deep, almost mystical respect for the natural world. This manifests in part through religious expressions like Ásatrú, whose ritual activity centres around the changing seasons, with outdoor *blóts* (feasts) held in places of great natural beauty each solstice and equinox.

I had come to Iceland to experience Ásatrú's midsummer blót, held shortly after the summer solstice. But first, I was taking advantage of the comparatively mild summer weather to explore Iceland's natural landscape, which so inspires the ritual and mythological one, and to seek an answer to a question which had been bothering me, even before I encountered the bewitching oratory of Geoff Soma: do Icelanders really believe in elves?

There is an abiding stereotype that they do, and a number of surveys have been presented as proof of this – most recently in 2022, when a poll by Prósent reported that 31% of Icelanders believe in *alfá* (elves; fairies). I'd barely been in Iceland for a couple of hours when, in a park beside Reykjavík's domestic airport, I encountered an 'elf stone' just like the one Geoff Soma would later talk about. An information board explained that the rock had been known to have elven associations ever since workers tried to move it during the construction of a hotel, as a result of which, 'trouble ensued. In Iceland, it is common knowledge that elves do not like to give up their homes without a fight; usually it is humans who must instead stop their own interfering ways.'

Speak to the locals, though, and you get a more nuanced picture than from tourist-facing, Anglophone information boards. In the glacial valley of Thórsmörk, as we ate our packed lunches in a rest area, I asked a couple of Icelandic hikers for their take on the existence of the *huldufólk* (hidden people).

'It's not so much a literal thing, even though it's not uncommon for building projects to be re-routed or postponed because they cross the path of an elf rock,' said one of the hikers, a young woman called Sara. 'I think most Icelanders would obviously see elves as a metaphorical, mythological thing rather than a literal, physical thing. But lots of Icelanders have a strong sense that mythology is important. It helps people feel a connection to their Icelandic identity – to the language, the mythology, and the natural landscape.'

Culture and nature are rarely more explicitly intertwined than they are in Iceland. Thórsmörk means the Valley of Thor, the gung-ho Norse god of thunder and lightning, and similar mythological references are found in place names across the country – from the Kerlingarfjöll mountains, named for an old troll woman said to steal away naughty children, to Thórsmörk's Álfakirkja ('Elf Church'): a huge cave-rock, like a bullet hole in a crumpled wizard's hat, which yawned at us from across the valley as we munched on our sandwiches.

I suggested that this desire to cultivate a connection with cultural tradition and the natural world did not only explain the number of Icelanders who profess a belief in elves, but was also behind the rise in popularity of Ásatrú, whose midsummer feast I would be attending that evening. Sara's boyfriend, Magnús, who had been biting his tongue up until this point, shook his bag of crisps and wrinkled his nose. 'Those people are weird,' he said.

'We're not weird or anything,' said Hilmar Örn Hilmarsson, the Ásatrú high chieftain. 'The big factor behind us becoming the fastest growing religion in Iceland for the last twenty-odd years is that people have realised we're not eccentrics. People used to think we'd be jumping around in the nude around bonfires, but we don't do any of that,' he said, before pausing and breaking into a puckish grin. 'That would be impractical.'

Hilmar's association with Ásatrú has been five decades long, but it is only one facet of a richly colourful life. A gentle, white-haired man in his mid-sixties, he is well known in Iceland as a musician and producer, having collaborated with the likes of Björk and Sigur Rós over a long and varied career – although he remains modest about his many achievements. 'I am the author of some of the worst lyrics written in Icelandic,' he told me with a chuckle. 'I should be publicly shamed.'

Hilmar and I were standing in Thingvellir National Park, a rift valley half an hour's drive east of Rekjyavík which marks the point where the North American and Eurasian tectonic plates meet. This geological fault is the source of Iceland's volcanic power, as well as the only place on Earth where you can walk in between two tectonic plates – everywhere else they are found on the planet, these continental borders lie deep under the sea. 'We have Europe one way and the Americas the other way,' said Hilmar. 'We're standing on the edge.'

Thingvellir is a liminal place, a place in-between; it's no mystery that Hilmar chose it as the site for the Ásatrú midsummer feast. It has the feeling of a place of great power, a nexus of physical and spiritual energy. 'These power spots, you find them all over the place,' Hilmar said. 'There was an English geologist called Paul

McCartney, believe it or not, who found that many of the bigger stone circles and sacred places in England lie next to a major geological fault. The Rollright Stones [Neolithic stones in Oxfordshire] have very high silicate content, for example. So, there's a theory that there's some electromagnetic energy that is being let off in these places.'

Electromagnetism aside, Thingvellir is a place that can stir the soul on looks alone. Under our feet, the black volcanic earth was cracked from beneath into rippling networks of fissures and lightning forks, like optic blood vessels, or the shell of an egg ready to hatch. The evening sun cast the lava fields in a warm glow, and the purple inflorescences of lupine flowers swayed in their thousands in a gentle breeze.

Hilmar excused himself; the ritual was about to begin. He made his way through a gathered crowd to a grassy clearing at the foot of a cliff, where colourful standard flags, bearing images of dragons and Viking kings, stood flapping in the wind. Hilmar joined a group of four women, all of them in traditional Norse dress – Hilmar in a royal-blue robe, the women in flaxen tunics and headdresses. Hilmar was handed a wooden oath ring, which he held on one side; one of the women held the other side of the ring, while the other gave an impassioned reading of Old Norse poetry from a leather-bound book. Periodically, Hilmar would pour a honey-coloured liquid onto the floor from a drinking horn inscribed with Norse runes. This went on for ten minutes or so, before Hilmar dispensed the final contents of the horn onto the ground, and the ceremony was over.

The crowd dispersed to a white marquee, where barbecued meats and cans of beer had been laid out on long benches. After a young man gave another rousing rendition of Norse poetry inside the marquee, I found Hilmar, still clutching his drinking vessel. It was made of ox horn, he told me, and the liquid he had been pouring from it was mead. 'It serves the purpose of a sacrifice – we don't sacrifice animals anymore, of course,' he said, before leaning in conspiratorially to add: 'But we can't get mead in Iceland. So, I had some friends from America bring it over for me.'

For all its pomp and ceremony – the mead and the drinking horns and the Viking costumes – Ásatrú is a practical concern for Hilmar and its thousands of other adherents. Partly, it's about sustaining a connection to Norse mythology and the Old Norse language, both of which find their modern-day spiritual home in Iceland. The modern Icelandic language is considered very close to Old Norse and is deliberately preserved to remain as such. Modern inventions receive evocative compound terms made up of archaic words, such that the Icelandic word for computer is *tölva* – literally, "number prophetess". The medieval authors of the Icelandic sagas, meanwhile, are considered largely responsible for preserving Norse mythology as we know it today – particularly the poet and statesman Snorri Sturluson, who is thought to have compiled the *Prose Edda* in the thirteenth century.

'98% of what we know about Norse mythology is from Icelandic literature – we preserved it when it was wiped out everywhere else. We had the good sense to keep the stories alive,' Hilmar said. 'We learn the history and literature in school in Iceland; we're exposed to it from a very young age. It makes you feel rooted, in a good sense.'

More than anything, though, connection to nature and the changing seasons is the underpinning motivation of Ásatrú, certainly beyond theology or devotion to any higher power. Hilmar told me that Ásatrú's invocation of the Norse gods, and their associated mythology, is symbolic and metaphorical, rather than literal. 'That's sometimes difficult for other people to grasp,' he said. 'They want this to be on a par with other religions, talking about something bigger than us which is co-existing with us,' Hilmar said. 'But really that still is what we're talking about: we have a big belief in nature's spirits in Iceland, like you had in the UK, once. That's the purpose of seasonal rituals like this one: to connect people with the cycle of the year. It makes you think like a farmer, in that you move with the year and the soil.'

The optics of an Ásatrú feast may be different from Green Gathering – Viking robes instead of harem pants; flagons of mead and glistening piles of lamb hot dogs in place of jackfruit curry and kombucha. But the motivation of both festivals is the same: a rooting in and celebration of the earth, partly in the hope that festivals like these can effect positive change. Hilmar had told me that Ásatrú had been voicing environmental concerns since the 1960s, 'when no-one else would listen'.

It's not totally fair to directly compare Green Gathering or an Ásatrú blót with Burning Man, a huge festival whose stated aims are more societal than ecological. And yet, revisiting Burning Man's 10 Principles, I'm struck by how many of them could apply equally to all three of these events: radical inclusion, gifting, civic responsibility, communal effort, leaving no trace. I'll leave you to come to your own conclusions about how much these or any other festivals can be said to live up to such lofty ambitions, but it's certain that they are all propelled by the same conviction: that a festival, by hook or by crook, through the groundswell of a grass-roots movement or the proselytising power of a blazing pillar of flame, has the power to change the world.

LAST RITES
Festival, Ritual, and Death

SULAWESI, Indonesia

The highlands of Tana Toraja sped past, the landscape revealing itself in a blur of broad brushstrokes: emerald-green rice paddies, dogs snapping at dust particles suspended over sunlit lanes, and towering *tongkonan* longhouses, levitating on stilts, their roofs curved in imitation of a buffalo's horns. I was riding pillion on a rattling motorbike through rural Indonesia, my destination the funeral of a perfect stranger, my only ticket to entry a jerrycan of palm wine and a crate of clove cigarettes.

Many attempts have been made to describe the unusual shape of Sulawesi, the eleventh largest island in the world and the second largest entirely in Indonesia (after Sumatra), which reaches, many-limbed, between the seas of Celebes, Banda, Java and Flores. It has been described as a letter K, a spider, and an octopus, none of which are quite right; a more anatomically accurate comparison might be a single-amputee starfish, bracing its remaining limbs against a stiff wind or an electric fan. It's a beautiful place, in any case – and not just from space.

Tana Toraja occupies an area of about 800 square miles in the centre of Sulawesi, near the borderline where the provinces of South and West Sulawesi meet. It is the homeland of the Toraja people, who number around 450,000 here and who are notable for their elaborate death rituals, with funeral ceremonies often lasting several days and involving a veritable bloodbath of animal sacrifice which makes Eid al-Adha look like Tiggywinkles Wildlife Hospital. Torajan funerals are highly attended affairs, with guests numbering into the thousands and encompassing the family of the deceased, friends, and strangers. Which is where I came in. The more guests at a funeral, the greater the honour accorded to the deceased. The novelty provided by foreign guests is perceived to add an extra patina of glamour to proceedings, a fact not lost on the local tourism industry – such that it is now easy to turn up in the city of Rantepao and find a guide who is willing to take you to whichever funeral happens to be taking place in the vicinity. Which is exactly what I did.

Reaching a vantage point, my guide, Paulus Padang, stopped his motorbike so we could take in the view. Rice fields tumbled down the mountainsides, great green terraces which glistened in the late morning sun. Water buffalo plodded in the channels, scattering unseen ricefish in their wake. At the far side of the valley reared up cliffs of limestone, their faces pockmarked with holes and adorned with what looked from a distance like colourful flags. '*Liang batu*,' said Paulus. 'Rock tomb.'

We got moving again, along bumpy roads enclosed by grassy banks, where feral dogs and long-eared goats snuffled and grazed. As we approached our destination, petrol fumes and excitable chatter began to fill the air; the road got busier and then became so choked with people and vehicles that we could go no further. Paulus parked his bike, and we proceeded on foot, quickly coming across the cause of the congestion. A clearing had formed in the traffic around four skinny young men struggling to contain an enormous water buffalo, which they were restraining with ropes tied to its horns. The animal was frothing at the mouth, gnashing at the bit between its teeth, sputtering and hissing in terror and rage. I looked at Paulus, who smiled serenely and offered me a crisp. 'I think he knows what's coming,' he said.

Squeezing warily past the buffalo and its handlers, we crested a hill and came upon a clearing in a forest, dotted with the same horn-roofed buildings we had seen on the way. People bustled between the pavilions with pots of coffee and bundles of banana leaves; friends stood chatting in animated huddles; a toddler chased after a ragged-looking cat, grasping at its tail. Amid this scene of easy conviviality, a constant stream of young men were coming and going in double file, each pair carrying on their shoulders a pig trussed up in a bamboo frame. The men would reach a patch of dusty scrub in the centre of the clearing and then dump the pigs there by the dozen, lying them on their sides still in their bamboo prisons, wailing and coughing in the rising dust.

I can still hear their shrieking now – a banshee scream of pure terror which eventually receded beneath the babble but continued in the background all afternoon, my mind occasionally tuning into it like some demented radio station; an unsettling counterpoint to the relaxed conversation, the kindly condolences, the laughter of playing children which made up the foreground. The pigs,

Paulus explained, were donated to the family of the deceased by friends and neighbours. It's the ultimate measure of status in Tana Toraja: the higher your position in society, the more animals are sacrificed at your funeral. A man with a microphone went between the pigs one by one, announcing the name of each one's donor as if they were raffle prizes at a village fête.

Occasionally, one of the pigs was sacrificed where it lay with a carving knife to the heart – no altar or ceremony – and carried out of sight behind the pavilions, where the hairs were blowtorched off its skin and its body separated and barbecued. Pools of mud and crimson blood mingled in little troughs and valleys where the earth had been churned by passing feet. The central principle of these sacrifices is the return of blood to the earth. The same thing is symbolised by the chewing of betel nut and the spitting out of its bright red residue, splashes of which paint pavements in villages and towns across Sulawesi.

The pigs who were newest to the party wriggled and wheezed and frothed at the mouth. Those who had been lying there for longer were still and silent and resigned. The sacrifices made for unpleasant viewing, but at least the meat was being eaten – and for a carnivore like me, it is probably no bad thing to occasionally experience first-hand the violence that brings my meat to the table.

Paulus guessed that there were a thousand pigs there that day – the deceased had been a high-status man in the community. Not all the pigs would be sacrificed, Paulus explained; some would be kept by the family to be sold on or donated in turn to an upcoming funeral. The family of the deceased never sacrifice the pigs or buffalo themselves, Paulus said – a practice which would be deemed to bring them bad luck. I asked why. 'Taboo,' Paulus offered quietly – one weighty word which required no further explanation.

For all the pigs sacrificed at the average Torajan funeral, they are just a support act; the headliners, in spiritual terms, are the buffalo. Torajans believe that buffalo carry the deceased to heaven, and the more of them that are sacrificed, the quicker the journey. On the day I attended, dozens of buffalo had been dragged along, like the reluctant one we'd seen on our way in. They stood tied to posts in the middle of the clearing, not far from the poor pigs – but they were just there to watch; they would be sacrificed tomorrow, Paulus said. Buffalo are the ultimate symbol of class and wealth for Torajans. Not only are their longhouse roofs shaped to resembled bovid horns, but their entrances are marked with water buffalo skulls, the bigger the better, which hang over their front doors. The rarest morph of Torajan water buffalo – white-coated with blue eyes – sells for up to one billion Indonesian rupiah (some £50,000).

Paulus indicated that we should pay our respects to the family of the deceased. I attempted without success to avoid the blood and the filth, which caked my shoes as we crossed the clearing to the pavilion on the other side. I was welcomed warmly by the family, who seemed genuinely pleased by the presence of myself and the handful of other Western tourists. The guide industry in Rantepao, the tourist centre and largest town in Tana Toraja, is booming, but Torajans have resisted monetising the funerals themselves. The only donation expected of foreign tourists is the same as for Torajan guests: a small gift as a mark of respect to the dead – palm wine, sugar, or a brick of cigarettes. A lady in late middle age, whom I took to be the family matriarch, received my offering gratefully, and in return invited me to sit down, presenting me with a cup of coffee and a package of banana leaf, which I unfolded to find a sweet cake made from pounded cassava.

I was struck by how everyday it all seemed, despite the abattoir scene unfolding outside. I and the other tourists were watching the endless conveyor belt of pig sacrifice with a kind of slack-jawed semi-horror, but none of the Torajans in attendance seemed to be paying much attention to it at all. The screaming pigs, the dust and the blood were background furniture for most of the attendees, who sat smiling and chattering away happily. I didn't see any tears; the only wailing came from those pigs still bothering to express some resistance to their sorry fate. With Paulus acting as translator, I exchanged pleasantries with the family, who asked about my trip and laughed good-naturedly at my unwise choice of footwear – a pair of Adidas Sambas, once swan-white, now caked in mud and pig blood.

Over our coffee, my hosts asked me about my trip. I was spending two months in Indonesia, having begun in Bali and gone east to Lombok, Sumbawa and Sumba, to Flores and Komodo (where I had a close encounter with a rather corpulent dragon), and now north to Sulawesi. Paulus puffed out his cheeks in bemusement and told me he had rarely ventured outside of his homeland. He told me that Torajans don't travel much, because they would rather spend all their money on elaborate funerals. Looking out at the scores of attendees, the hundreds of doomed pigs and buffalo, the vats of palm wine and the piles of barbecued meat, I could believe it.

Everybody grieves privately in their own way, but communal mourning rituals – funerary festivals –

represent their own vibrant spectrum in cultures across the world. Often, grief is dealt with through cultural customs which can seem incomprehensible to outsiders. The Ilongot people of Luzon, Philippines, for example, were documented by the anthropologist Renato Rosaldo in 1993 as reacting to grief by embarking on a spree of decapitating rival villagers. While this may be taking venting to rather extreme lengths, Rosaldo's work with the Ilongot highlights an important facet of grief: that it is often characterised as much by rage as by sadness.[57] The Igbo people of Nigeria, meanwhile, engage in highly dramatised funeral rites known as *ikwa ozu* – literally, 'celebrating the dead'. Huge amounts of alcohol are consumed over several days, and a mock trial is held to determine who, if anybody, was responsible for the death. On the death of a married man, the widow is expected to engage in a series of strange and seemingly demeaning rituals: to drink the water that was used to wash her husband's corpse, to shave her head and sleep outdoors without a blanket for over a month, to fast for long periods, and, when she eats, only to do so with her unwashed left hand.

These are all mourning rituals – the collective cultural enactment of individual grief. The distinction between grieving and mourning is significant but subtle. Grief is a person's internal, emotional response to loss. Mourning is the outward expression of that grief. Despite the maximalist examples I have listed above, mourning rituals are often simple gestures: they're as likely to include a widow dressing in black or a family holding

---

57. Renato Rosaldo, 'Grief and a Headhunter's Rage'.

a quiet memorial service as they are to entail a whole community gathering to sacrifice hundreds of pigs and buffalo.

On first sight, the joyful aspect of the Torajan funeral-festival made me wonder if the Torajans had cracked some secret code, using festivity to overcome the sadness of grief. But it would be wrong to say that Torajans do not grieve or feel sadness when a loved one dies. The anthropologist Roxana Waterson, who has spent decades studying the Toraja, recounts in one of her papers a story of a recent widower holding his wife's corpse, weeping all night long, and asking her permission to remarry.[58] 'Of course, at first when someone dies, the family may cry, because they're not able to endure the feeling of loss,' Paulus told me. 'But we are very aware that we will all die, too. We believe that if the family cries too much, it makes it harder for the soul of the dead to travel to the hereafter.'

Waterson describes the Toraja as consciously recognising that the ritual aspects of their funerary ceremonies serve as a kind of replacement for their emotional sadness – a box in which to place their grief, which is dealt with once the animals are sacrificed. 'The sacrificing of buffaloes at funerals is described as *sonda pa' di' ki'*, "taking the place of our pain (or sorrow)",' she writes. 'I was once asked whether people in my country felt no grief at a death, since they neglected to kill any buffaloes?'[59]

Taking the place of sorrow. Whether through repression, replacement, distraction or delusion, funerary rituals are a way of dealing with something universally upsetting,

---

58. Roxana Waterson, 'Taking the Place of Sorrow: The Dynamics of Mortuary Rites among the Sa'dan Toraja'.
59. Ibid.

confusing, and, most of all, mysterious. Nobody knows what happens to us when we die, even if they think they do. The vast majority of people experience at least a small measure of doubt around this issue, whether their cultural context allows them to admit to it or not – see the atheist's panicked deathbed conversion, and the fear of death exhibited by even the most devout believer in the afterlife. But that doesn't mean that some cultures haven't divined better coping methods than others. 'It is a central paradox of any elaborate funeral that so much effort and activity on the part of the living should be expended ostensibly for the departed,' Waterson writes. Why do we do it? Because funerals are not for the dead; they are for the living left behind.

Torajans view death not as a sudden full stop, but rather as a gradual process which is only just beginning at the moment that the heart stops and brain activity is extinguished. The purpose, ostensibly, of their extravagant funerary rites is to ensure that the spirit of the deceased makes the successful journey from ancestor spirit to *mendeata*, a deity-like being believed by the Torajans to bestow good harvests. This point is central to understanding Torajan mortuary rites: they are not only framed as being for the spiritual benefit of the dead themselves, but are perceived as serving a material purpose for the living world which they have departed.

Leaving the hubbub of the funeral behind, Paulus took me to a burial ground, a peaceful clearing in a grove of trees which slanted up the side of a hill. Miniature longhouses ringed the perimeter like little shrines, wood-framed and crowned with sloped roofs of either thatch or corrugated iron. In the centre of the clearing, fingers of stone grasped upwards from the grass like stalagmites.

We approached a rock tomb carved into a great round boulder, large enough that bamboo scaffolding and ladders had been erected up its side to allow attendants to lay flowers, photographs, and little wooden crosses in recesses in the stone.

Despite the very visible upkeep of their animist funerary traditions, most Torajans are nominally Christians, converted by Dutch missionaries in the early twentieth century. That's why they have names like Paulus, and lay crucifixes on their rock tombs. (It was, in fact, the Dutch who named these people the Toraja, in 1909, from the words in Buginese – the language of Sulawesi's majority Bugis people – *to riaja*, meaning 'highland people'. Before this time, the Torajans did not perceive themselves as having a coherent identity far beyond their own village.) By that time, the Dutch had controlled Sulawesi for some 300 years, but had largely left the highlands of the interior alone, owing to a combination of the inaccessible terrain and a perceived scarcity of useful farmland or resources. Dutch Christian missionaries made their first cautious probings into the Torajan mountains in the early 1900s, and by the 1960s the vast majority of Torajans had converted to Christianity.

To complicate matters of Torajan identity even further, the Indonesian government officially recognises Torajan religion as a subset of Hinduism. Religion is a funny thing in Indonesia, the world's largest Muslim country by population. Although freedom of religion is enshrined in the constitution, there are only six legally recognised faiths – Islam, Catholicism, Protestantism, Hinduism, Buddhism, and Confucianism – and, until the option was given in 2017 to leave it blank, everybody had to pick one for their identity card. As such, many of the countless indigenous religions which do not fit into any of those six categories were shoehorned into one regardless, and in the case of Torajan religion – which the government had given the name *Aluk To Dolo*, meaning Way of the Ancestors (or, literally, Law of the Men Before) – Balinese Hinduism was chosen as its parent category.

The Dutch (and, later, the Indonesian government, whose 1950s policy of 'Indonesianization' injured many of the country's indigenous cultures by promulgating a Javanese-centric Indonesian national identity) took steps to iron out many traditional Torajan practices, including head-hunting and shamanic religious rites involving the inducement of trance states. But the Torajan funerary rites proved too strong, too vivid, too firmly entrenched to be uprooted. So, eventually, they let them be. The Dutch did have some luck suppressing one traditional element of the Torajan funeral: the cockfight. They disapproved of the gambling, rather than the cruelty. This is a sentiment shared by the modern-day Indonesian government, which has made gambling of all kinds illegal, and prohibited cockfights at all but the most high-profile Torajan funerals, for which they are granted a special licence. Illicit funerary cockfights continue regardless, however – I was invited to attend one after the funeral celebrations were over. I declined, having seen enough bloodshed for one day.

When Torajan funerals finally end after several days, the body of the deceased is laid to rest in one of the rock tombs, carved into either a boulder or the face of a cliff. For the highest members of the Torajan aristocracy, macabre wooden effigies of the dead, known as *tau tau*, are built to stand silent guard over the tombs. It was these rock tombs that I had seen from a distance when Paulus had stopped at the viewpoint earlier – festooned not with flags, it turned out on closer inspection, but with the colourful clothing of the tau tau. 'A tau tau is a statue of the dead – though we only make them for grandparents, not parents or children,' he said. 'It's a kind of photo, from a past when there were no cameras. But it's also where the soul of the dead lives temporarily, until the funeral. We usually make them from the jackfruit tree, but sometimes from bamboo, and sometimes from stone.'

The souls of recently departed Torajans are in need of these temporary dwelling places largely because their funerals are so expensive. The animals to be sacrificed, along with the money needed to stage the event itself, are donated over a period of months, sometimes years – this passing of time may also partly explain the upbeat mood at Torajan funerals – during which time the body of the deceased is embalmed and remains in the family home. 'While the dead people are still in the house, we don't think of them as dead – we call them *to makula*, or "sick person",' said Paulus. 'As long as this sick person is still in the house, we always serve them breakfast, lunch and dinner. They are positioned in the western part of the house, because the west is associated with sickness. Then, when it's nearly time for the funeral, we turn them to face to the south – the direction of death.' How do they preserve them, I wondered? 'We always used to embalm them using medicines from the forest,' Paulus said, 'but now we just go to the pharmacy. Formalin.'

Paulus opened his rucksack and pulled out a ring binder, licking his finger and proceeding to flick casually through a gallery of neatly laminated photographs which could have been taken from a behind-the-scenes shoot on *The Walking Dead*. Many of them resembled any other family portrait, with young, rosy-cheeked relatives arrayed smiling around Granny. Except that Granny was dead. Skin had taken on the look of *krupuk kulit*, an Indonesian beef-skin cracker on which I had happily been (and would no longer be) munching throughout my trip. Sunglasses sat over hollow eye-sockets, and, in many pictures, thin, lifeless lips were parted by smouldering cigarettes. In one, a man – once elderly, presumably, although it was hard to tell – had been seated in a rocking chair in a Manchester United shirt, his fingers wrapped around an old Nokia phone. 'Prize possessions,' nodded Paulus.

Even after the funerary rites have been completed, the dead are taken out of the tombs regularly, their remains cleaned up and their clothes and wraps changed. 'This ritual is called *ma' nenek*,' said Paulus. 'Depending on the region and the family, we will do it once a year, once every five, once every ten – it depends.'

Sometimes, people die too young to be considered ancestors. This eventuality is dealt with differently to the death of a family elder. In a peaceful glade, far from the screaming pigs and blood-churned earth, Paulus showed me a breadfruit tree, studded with little wooden doors like those I had seen carved into the boulder at the graveyard, only significantly smaller.

'From ancient times, it's been said that a baby without teeth is still holy and without sin. When a baby dies before it is old enough to have teeth,' Paulus said, emphasising the last word by clacking his fingernail against a canine, 'they are buried in one of these trees.' This was a breadfruit tree; karaya trees are also used. 'Both secrete a white liquid, like mothers' milk,' Paulus explained. 'They bury the baby standing up, so it can grow together with the tree. But the baby never faces home – otherwise, when it sees its mama, the baby may cry.' Only living trees are chosen, which in time will grow around the bodies, absorbing their nutrients; allowing them, in some way, to live on. 'When a bird comes to the branch of the tree then flies away, we say the baby rides the bird to heaven,' Paulus said. 'Baby Tree', read a painted wooden sign. Huge green breadfruit, ripe with life, sagged from a pregnant branch.

Roxana Waterson wrote that Torajan funerals focus on '[the] cyclical movement by which the dead are transformed into life-giving ancestors ... European funerals, by contrast, concentrate only on the sad and polluting aspect of death, and not the regenerative one.' Ultimately, this is a matter of perspective. While the Torajan narrative around the post-death journey certainly has a spiritual, metaphysical element, it also has a grounding in the physical world – the repeated contact with and tending to the bodies of the dead, for example, or the burying of children in a tree, allowing their bodies to contribute directly to new life. Making these choices does not require a literal belief in the afterlife. This kind of idea is gaining some traction in the West. We may not yet be ready to bury infant bodies inside trees, but companies are now offering 'living urns' which allow the ashes of a cremated body to be buried within the root ball of a young tree, enabling the absorption of their rich nutrients.

The upshot of all this is that Torajans appear to share little in the Western attitude towards death as an inconvenient, unsavoury and perpetually surprising matter, to be dealt with and forgotten about as quickly as possible. Rather, they stare it in the eyes: mortuary ceremonies are not just lavish and well attended, they are the primary vehicle for expressing Torajan culture. It's not that the Toraja do not experience grief and sadness, but rather that they have an ability, imparted through centuries of cultural tradition, to be intimate with the subject of death – to face it head on, to confront its consequences and physical realities. This, rather than metaphysical mythology about what happens to a person's spirit after they die, is what enables the Torajans to enjoy a healthier relationship with death than most of us endure in the West.

This would be brought home to me in sharp relief in early 2022, a few years after my trip to Sulawesi, when my father passed away after suffering from cancer for three years. In retrospect, it was obvious that he was going to die. By the time of his diagnosis, the cancer had already spread to his bones; by Christmas of 2021, he was confined to a wheelchair. By this time, he had not received treatment of any kind, beyond pain relief, for six months. Looking back, it is clear that his doctors had decided there was nothing more they could do for him. The frustration for those of us that loved him was that the doctors never saw fit to burden us with such inconvenient news. What we got instead was a constant dangling of carrots; 'If we get his blood oxygen up to a certain level, maybe we can try this or that treatment.'

It now seems obvious that these treatments were never really on the table, but at the time we believed there was a chance some of them had a prospect of being successful, partly because we weren't told otherwise, and partly because past treatments – a burst of radiotherapy, for example – had seemed to give him a new lease of life.

A friend, a former cancer nurse, told me later that medical professionals in the UK often withhold information or refrain from delivering an upsetting prognosis in favour of dropping clues so that the patient and the family can figure out the situation for themselves.

'We could look into getting a bed put in the living room,' a doctor told us to some alarm around six months from the end, when my dad was still walking around. 'Just in case he needs it – further down the line, of course.'

They knew from his test results that he would need it, and soon, but they didn't tell us in those terms. And why not? Because it's an awkward conversation to have? Some matters are more important than the brief unpleasantness of a socially awkward exchange. The upshot of it all was that when my dad began his terminal decline, we didn't realise it was happening until it became obvious, at which point he was beyond reach, unable to have the kind of conversations he should have been having with his family – unable to properly say goodbye. The one advantage of dying from a slow-acting disease should be that you are able to get your farewells and affairs in order; to reflect on your life in its totality; perhaps to impart some last words of love and wisdom. I'm sure that our lily-livered approach to death in the West means that many people are deprived of those precious things.

The consequences of that approach did not end when my father died. His death – or more accurately, my reaction to his death – has also left a legacy in my physical body. Around the time he died, my skin began to scream and weep. Angry red rashes from head to foot; blistering palms which kept me clawing at my bedsheets through wakeful nights; an itch down to the bone. The diagnosis was severe eczema, brought on by emotional stress – a textbook case, I was told, when I finally secured an audience with a dermatologist. My mind had perceived a problem between itself and the world outside, and my skin, as the barrier between those two domains, had become the battlefield. Trouble at the border between the world and me.

In the years since then, I have been prescribed steroid creams, phototherapy, and grief counselling – the latter being the most effective treatment so far, allowing me to access the emotions I was supposed to be experiencing but had numbed myself against, through shock or a lack of preparedness. Would my subconscious reaction have been different if I had been a Torajan, confronted with death from a young age, perceiving it as a transitionary phase in the circle of life rather than an abrupt full stop? Maybe.

In Sulawesi, when I had asked Paulus why the family of the deceased never sacrifice the buffalo themselves, I understood that my line of questioning had to end with his one-word answer: 'Taboo.' Cultures across the world are strewn with taboos, from prohibitions on eating pork to bestiality and bigamy. Sometimes there are obvious biological or evolutionary reasons behind something being considered taboo. More often, they are seemingly arbitrary, though this in no way affects their power. In traditional Polynesia, for example, it was deemed so taboo for a citizen to touch the shadow of a chieftain that the only way normalcy could be restored afterwards would be for the offending commoner to be put to death. Some social scientists believe taboos to be pillars of social cohesion; rules for rules' sake, the collective acceptance and observance of which helps to bind a society together. There would have been as much point in asking Paulus to justify his culture's buffalo-killing taboo as there would in asking an Englishman to explain why he will eat a cow but not a horse.

Taboos are enigmatic, but extremely powerful – and talking about death has become taboo in modern

Western culture. Where people like the Toraja make a point of ceremonially welcoming death into their lives, most cultures in the West have done the exact opposite, pushing it under the sofa, fearing it as something disgusting, polluting and taboo. About her native USA, the anthropologist Aubrey Thamann has written, 'In this culture we have compartmentalized death, banishing it to hospitals as we try to stave it off for as long as possible, and we attempt to deny an emotional reaction to the death of a loved one.'[60]

In many cultures it is considered healthy and normal to grieve for a long time; the traditional Chinese period of mourning, for instance, is three years. In Imperial China, in accordance with Confucian ideals, even the Emperor was required to take time off work when one of their parents died. In the American Psychiatric Association's Diagnostic and Statistical Manual of Mental Disorders, by contrast, grieving for more than twelve months (six months for children and adolescents) is listed as a mental illness called 'prolonged grief disorder'.

Those of us with a Western mindset conditioned by such prejudices might look upon a Torajan household, with a long-dead relative lingering stiffly in the corner, and be tempted to conclude that these people have trouble letting go. But it is in fact their willingness to deal directly with death and with the dead which enables them to live on, with death being just another natural part of life. It is *us*, thinking we are 'letting go' (read: looking away, suppressing our emotions, and distracting ourselves), who

---

60. Crossroads: Life and Death in Indiana by Aubrey Thamann, in *Beyond the Veil: Reflexive Studies of Death and Dying* (ed. Thamann, Kalliopi M Christodoulaki).

drag the dead along behind us, a ball and chain with the density of a neutron star.

There are those who are working to propel us in a more death-positive direction, however. Across the UK, there has been a rise in recent decades in 'death cafés', gatherings where people can meet to discuss grief and the end of life. The first death café was held in Neuchâtel in 2004, the brainchild of Swiss sociologist Bernad Crettaz; the first British iteration was held in London in 2011. In the years since, a bevy of books and podcasts have emerged encouraging people to talk about death and dying, and a UK-wide 'death-positive libraries' initiative was launched in 2018, with libraries in Ilford, Kirklees, Newcastle and Omagh foregrounding books about death, alongside film screenings, exhibitions and death café events.

This attitude shift is reflected in the festival calendar, too. The Good Grief Festival was established in 2020 as a series of seminars and workshops aimed towards encouraging people in the UK to speak openly and publicly about grief. On the surface, it's a far cry from a Torajan funeral – it's all online, for one thing. But it is, in an important way, similar: an example of how a communal, public event – a festival – can play a role in helping people to deal with death. Good Grief Festival was founded by Dr Lucy Selman, an associate professor at the University of Bristol.

'I've been a social scientist working in end-of-life and palliative care for around twenty years now, but the motivation for the festival really came from my personal experience,' Lucy told me over Zoom. 'My father died when I was fifteen, then a few years ago my second daughter was stillborn. The aftermath brought home how we're not good at dealing with grief in our society. You feel both the weight of people's awkwardness and not knowing how to deal with it, and also their expectations of how *you* should be acting as a bereaved person. People never know whether or not they should invite you to parties.

'I thought it would be great to have an event about love and loss which wasn't a highbrow, intellectualised version of grief, but which could really engage members of the public. We're all different, but there are commonalities in our grief, and by sharing those you can create a sense of community.'

This last point is crucial to understanding the role that communal death rituals play for people like the Toraja. For Aubrey Thamann, American society's collective cultural refusal to engage with death has led to the loss of a crucial social ingredient: our old friend, communitas. As we learned at Venice Carnival, communitas is a feeling of social connection engendered by collective experiences of liminality. It could be said that there is no more liminal state than dying – Arnold van Gennep, after all, defined liminality as the state of being at a doorway or threshold. Regardless of whether you believe in an afterlife or not, death fits that brief, both for the individual who has died and the people they have left behind. For the Toraja in the run-up to a funeral, the soul of the deceased is explicitly depicted as being in a liminal state, halfway between ancestor spirit and mendeata – a state which is resolved on the completion of their successful funeral. Given that funeral rites are the single most important expression of Torajan culture, it's fair to say that they engender feelings of communitas which play an important role in the maintenance of a healthy society.

Thamann's fieldwork centred on observing the work of funeral directors, whose role in society, as she puts it, is to 'help us to achieve communitas after a death'. When it comes to figuring out who funerals are really for, her work led her to the same conclusion that I had reached based on my experience with the Toraja. 'Every single funeral director I worked with,' she writes, 'told me that they work with the living, not the dead.'

Here in the land of the living, of course, we don't always recognise this. When we were making the arrangements for my father's funeral, we were often slowed up in our decision making by wondering what he would have wanted – classical or rock music? Ashes buried or scattered? Quiche or pizza at the wake? We often found ourselves regretting his own, repeatedly stated, opinion on how things should go down after he died: 'I don't care,' he'd say. 'I won't be there.'

By way of contrast, Lucy Selman's fieldwork involved studying how societies approach end-of-life care in India and sub-Saharan Africa, where death, as in Tana Toraja, is a visible part of life. 'In developing countries, people are not so distanced from death as we are,' she told me. 'India, for example, is well known for death and dying being integrated into everyday life in ways they're not here.'

In Varanasi, I have stood with throngs of other slack-jawed tourists on the riverside steps of the Manikarnika Ghat, gawping at bodies burning on the cremation pyres, their ashes drifting into the Ganges, embers melting into the hazy sky. Alarmingly close by, people were bathing in the river's holy waters, and, I regret to inform you, drinking it, too. ('Is it safe?' I asked my guide, Abhishek. 'Spiritually, very auspicious,' he nodded. 'Biologically, not recommended.') Hindus, of course, believe in reincarnation. Death for them is very much not the end; just the end of the latest chapter, the indestructible soul moving on to its next body in an endless carousel.

Or is it? It's tempting to draw the conclusion that members of societies with a seemingly healthier attitude towards death are simply not so bothered about it because they believe in an afterlife. The idea that belief in life after death is nothing more than a defence mechanism to offset the fear of dying comes under the umbrella of terror management theory (TMT), which was named in 2015 but has its roots in Ernest Becker's 1973 book *The Denial of Death*. TMT postulates that a cognitive dissonance resounds within the brain of every human being, caused by the co-existence of our survival instinct alongside the certain knowledge that we will inevitably die.

It's easy to see how convincing ourselves of the existence of an afterlife could be an effective balm against the terror of non-existence after death. Growing up as I did, in a godless Western milieu, I was – still am – surrounded by people who assume that all religious people believe literally in the supernatural concepts talked about in holy books and church services. And Western observers have long been tempted to draw a dichotomy between a credulous East and an increasingly rationalist, atheistic West. It doesn't take much closer examination, though, to reveal that this is reductive. A 2022 study indicated that fewer than half of the UK population (46%) now believe in some kind of life after death[61] – a precipitous decline, you might imagine, from the God-fearing past. The picture is not so different,

---

61. King's College London.

however, in India, where a 2021 survey reported that a mere 40% of Hindus, 23% of Jains, and 18% of Buddhists – all religions for which the concept of rebirth is a central tenet – believe in reincarnation.[62]

Being part of a community where people can be observed practising rituals ostensibly relating to an afterlife does not necessarily mean that everybody literally believes in its existence. This is a mistake that militant atheists often make – they assume that all religious people are as literal-minded as they are. The same is true of many expressions of terror management theory, which assume afterlife 'beliefs' to be something literal and, above all, personal, relating to one's own journey into the hereafter rather than viewing them primarily as a tool for social cohesion for the people left behind.

What's more, religious belief does not always make for smoother passage when it comes to dealing with grief; sometimes it can actually complicate things. 'Sometimes spiritual beliefs can be damaging,' Lucy told me. 'People often think being bereaved means they did something wrong or are being punished.' Believing in an afterlife does not mean that you would not grieve the loss of a loved one. It might in fact make you much more concerned for someone's eternal wellbeing, depending on their earthly conduct.

More salient than belief in an afterlife is the role played by community. In many cultures, grieving is a collective concern. In Indian, Tibetan, and Native American culture, it is the standard for families to gather together for extended

---

62. Pew Research Centre.

periods after the death of a loved one.[63] Similarly, in the societies where Lucy carried out her research, more emphasis is often placed on the collective than the individual – and this is the real point of contrast with Western culture. 'Over the last decades, maybe centuries, what we've seen in the West is the retreat into the Individual, which has become paramount,' she said. 'We've become more atomised, our families have too; less integrated into the communities around us. The concurrent rise of mental health problems is not a coincidence.'

As a result, the practice of coming together on a societal level to talk about death has been almost completely lost – to the wider detriment. 'Gathering together to discuss these things is hugely beneficial,' Lucy said. 'It's only by having events which allow everyone to share what's happened to them that people get to see their own experiences reflected back at them. If we don't give people the opportunity to come together, there's a danger of it being limited to people who can afford to pay for support or private counselling. With the Good Grief Festival, we wanted to make the knowledge available to everyone.'

In societies like the Toraja, this knowledge – the wisdom to deal with death – is implanted in everybody virtually from birth, thanks to the foregrounding of death in their society through their elaborate funeral-festivals. It's hard to imagine that events like the Good Grief Festival will lead anytime soon to death-phobic Brits exhibiting their deceased relatives in their living rooms or sacrificing pigs and buffalo by the thousand. But when it comes to the

---

63. The Conversation, 'Death and dying: how different cultures deal with grief and mourning' by John Frederick Wilson.

important stuff – easing our relationship with death and grief – it's a start.

We've seen that funerals and other mortuary rituals are just as much for the living as they are for the dead. But what if grief itself could be a tool for life? 'Grief can cause depression and anxiety – it's important to acknowledge that,' Lucy told me. 'But, as hard as it is to hear it while you're experiencing acute bereavement, grief can also be transformative; it provides you with a different perspective.' Personal grief and collective mortuary rituals both serve as memento mori – powerful and potentially life-enhancing reminders that we all must die, and therein lies the value and beauty of being alive.

'People often report the same thing on being diagnosed with a terminal illness themselves,' said Lucy. 'Any brush with death makes you reprioritise; can make you seize hold of your life. And that's what bereavement is, really, isn't it? A brush with death.'

The good news is, you don't need to suffer a bereavement or a terminal diagnosis to experience the benefits of a brush with death. Simply gathering together and addressing it – talking about it, looking it in the eye, laughing in its face, tickling its belly, whatever feels good – helps to take the fear away. Long live the funeral-festival.

II

MISCHIEF
Festivity Beyond the Grave

Lancashire, ENGLAND

'So, essentially, we're going to follow the cold hand of Death into the Underworld, where we'll meet the Dark Lord and commune with the dead. And then for afterwards, Sandra's made a chicken curry.'

I was standing in a garden shed in the Lancashire village of Ingol while Karen Higham, a Gardnerian Wiccan priestess of the second degree, tried to explain to me exactly what I'd let myself in for. Candlelight illuminated the wood-panelled walls, casting into dim relief strange ritual objects clustered around a stone altar: a broomstick propped against a corner; willow pentagrams; a black-handled blade; a statue of a hare; and two familiar-looking Venetian masks, feathered and bejewelled, hanging on the wall behind.

I asked for a second time: what would the ritual actually entail? How, exactly, would we be journeying into the Underworld? 'Oh, you know – a bit of blood sacrifice,' grinned Sandra, the High Priestess, as she wafted incense around the room.

'Probably murder a few babies!' chirped another acolyte, breezily.

'Luckily this is dry-wipe,' said Karen, prodding the vinyl floor with her toe and eliciting woops of laughter. It was all very jolly, but they still hadn't answered my question, and their vagueness was doing nothing to assuage my anxiety.

'Maybe I could just watch?' I squirmed, shamefully.

'Don't be silly,' said Sandra, kindly but firmly. 'It's not a spectator sport. You want to write about it? You have to join in.'

Death is not the end for human festivity. Elaborate funerary festivals, like those of the Toraja, help the living to mop up the sadness of death and to deal with its immediate practicalities. But the dead live on, in the minds and hearts of the living if nowhere else, and there is another entire genre of festivals dedicated to venerating the ancestors – and, sometimes, communing with them, too. I had come to Lancashire to experience one which promises both: the ancient pagan festival of Samhain.

Samhain is often described as the Gaelic precursor to Halloween. Held on 1 November, it marks the beginning of winter in the Celtic calendar, and, like Halloween, is believed to be a time when the boundary between the living world and the spirit world dissolves. Architectural clues connected to Samhain bear intriguing parallels with the megalithic temples of Malta – passage tombs, such as Ireland's Mound of the Hostages, are aligned so that the sun illuminates their inner chamber on the morning of Samhain – and further similarities with Halloween can be found in the practices of mumming and guising, going around houses in creepy costumes and singing songs in exchange for gifts of food. Far from the cartoonish, kid-friendly celebration that is modern Halloween, however, Samhain is a serious business. It remains an occasion of deep religious significance for modern Pagans, who mark it by lighting bonfires, hosting banquets, and, occasionally, communing with dark deities – or even with the dead themselves.

'Don't worry,' added Karen, sensing my anxiety. 'This is an open ritual – anyone can come along, so we don't invoke any deities or anything like that. We don't want to scare people. Just make sure that when the Dark Lord gives you a coin, you hold onto it, so you can find your way out. The Underworld is not a place you want to get lost in.'

It wouldn't be the first time I'd lost my way that day. On the drive to Ingol through the Forest of Bowland, a wild region of peat bogs and windblown fells on the western fringes of the Pennine Hills, my satnav had gone into a tailspin, as if disturbed by a mysterious electromagnetic energy. I pulled into a layby and blinked helplessly at the blue arrow spinning madly on my phone screen like a broomstick in a whirlwind, before deciding to turn around and head in the direction of a sign bearing the only name I recognised hereabouts: the village of Newchurch-in-Pendle.

Newchurch is notorious as one of the settings of the Pendle Witch Trials, a strange and terrible series of events in 1612 which resulted in ten people being hanged for the crime of maleficium – causing harm by sorcery or witchcraft. The drama started with a young woman called Alizon Device being accused of bewitching a passing pedlar who had refused to sell her some metal pins. The pedlar fell lame shortly afterwards, possibly suffering a stroke, which was presented as evidence of her guilt; Alizon later confessed, falling on her knees and weeping in court that she had sold her soul to the Devil. The events in Pendle set one particularly horrifying precedent for later witch trials: allowing a child to take the stand as a witness in a murder trial. Nine-year-old Jennet Device was at the centre of the Pendle trial, giving testimony which resulted in her entire immediate family being killed as witches.

Modern interpretations tend to portray the Pendle witches as 'cunning folk' who made a living as simple herbalists and healers and became innocent victims of a particular brand of hysterical religious extremism, fired by Puritanical zeal and tinged with the unmistakable stench of misogyny. Several of the accused protested their innocence to the end, and at least one of them, Alice Nutter – to whom a poignant statue now stands in the village of Roughlee, two miles from Newchurch – may have never had nothing to do with witchcraft at all, being caught up in the accusations instead for following another then-illicit spiritual path: that of Roman Catholicism. Some of the accused did confess fully to their supposed crimes, appearing to believe in their own powers, although torture was likely involved in the extraction of their confessions.

To this day, a heaviness hangs over this part of England. Pendle Hill dominates views from Newchurch and the surrounding villages, and is one of those natural features which seems to emanate a malevolent agency – a crouched hunchback of a hill which threatens to rise up from the earth at any moment, shaking from its back the burial mounds, farmsteads and drystone walls scattered here by humans over numberless centuries. I wandered through the graveyard of St. Mary's Church, whose tower bears an unusual feature around two-thirds of the way up: a sunken oval known as the Eye of God, built for unknown purposes but reputed to protect villagers from evil spirits.

It recalled to me the Eye of Sauron, and I wondered if it may have been an inspiration for J.R.R. Tolkien, who is known to have written much of *The Lord of the Rings* at nearby Stonyhurst College, where his son was a teacher, and to have wandered often in the surrounding villages and countryside.

It's a curiously paganistic feature to find on a church, and a measure of this place, shaped by centuries of the intermingling of heathenry and Christianity. This was the atmosphere in which the hysteria of 1612 was brewed. The writer Rachel Hasted wrote that Lancashire in the late sixteenth and early seventeenth centuries was 'an area fabled for theft, violence, and sexual laxity'. Moreover, she wrote, it was a place 'where the church was honoured without much understanding of its doctrines by the common people'.

Nowadays, the legacy of the tragic events of Pendle's past is mainly expressed in the form of jaunty consumerism. Carved above the door of the Witches Galore gift shop on Newchurch's high street is an exhortation in antique Lancastrian English, half sales pitch, half memento mori: 'Gerrit spent. They don't pupockits i shrahds [Get it spent. They don't put pockets in shrouds].' On sale inside are stuffed toy witches, tarot cards, fridge magnets, and other such tat, apparently more worthy of your hard-earned lucre than, say, an inheritance pot for your children.

It was 1 November on the day of my impromptu visit to Newchurch. The commercialist dregs of last night's Halloween celebrations lay draped on doorsteps and wheelie bins: bedsheets cut with eyeholes and stained with fake blood; plastic skeletons slouched louchely on porch benches; carved pumpkins, gutted of their innards, their Chelsea grins beginning to distort horribly as they collapsed under their own weight. For those of a Pagan persuasion, though, this time of year is about much more than jack-o'-lanterns and horror movies. Samhain is one of the four most important points on the calendar for many Pagans: a time to mark the coming of the dark half of the year, when the veil between this world and the next is at its thinnest. A time for journeying into the Underworld.

We walked out of the shed-temple, past the hot tub and across the patio, into Sandra's house. On entering through the conservatory, I was immediately leapt upon and enclosed into a warm embrace by Sandra's jet-black Newfoundland, Blossom – six-feet-plus on her hind legs, and as slobbery and lovely a hellhound as you could ever hope to meet.

We proceeded to the living room, where the rest of tonight's attendees had gathered while I was being shown around the temple. There was a spread of snacks and drinks on the table. I had been running late on the drive over and suddenly realised I hadn't contributed anything to the party, despite Karen having told me there would be food and drinks after the ritual. I stopped at a petrol station and made for the snacks. Crisps were too informal, I decided; pretzels too pretentious. Unthinkingly, I grabbed a couple of boxes of 'reduced to clear' cake slices, pasted with Halloween-orange icing and cartoonishly demonic faces.

It only occurred to me afterwards that anything overtly Halloweenish might represent something of a faux pas at a Samhain gathering – like bringing coronation chicken sandwiches to a Fourth of July barbecue. On arrival at the house, I had proffered my pumpkin fancies, which were laid with the Twiglets and the party rings. They were politely received, but I still felt I had put my foot in it somewhat.

There were twelve people here in all. Most were middle-aged and nearly all were women, many of them in elegant witchy attire, all flowing hair, shawls and black lace – like a parade of Stevie Nicks impersonators, if you can imagine such a thing existing in suburban Lancashire. Everyone was very friendly. I exchanged introductions, learning that among their number were travellers on every walk of life: NHS therapists, accountants, pest controllers.

A couple of the others, like me, were first-timers, unknown to the group and drawn to this open ritual by sheer curiosity. Most of them, though, were members of the same coven: Gardnerian Wiccans who gathered here regularly to practise magic and invoke their chosen deities. This is how Samhain was being celebrated tonight, by groups like this across Britain, Ireland, America and beyond, in sacred groves, stone circles, and garden sheds.

Gardnerian Wicca is named for its founder, Gerald Gardner, a civil servant, writer, amateur anthropologist and nudist who is now recognised as the 'Father of Wicca'. In the first decades of the twentieth century, Gardner worked in Ceylon (now Sri Lanka), Borneo, and Malaya (now Malaysia), spending his spare time studying the traditional folklore and practices of the local inhabitants. He returned to Britain in 1927 and began exploring occultism, spiritualism, and Rosicrucianism (as well as naturism, an interest which was to stick with him throughout his life), eventually coalescing his influences into a religion of witchcraft which he practised with a small group of followers in the Hertfordshire village of Bricket Wood.

Gardner claimed that he learned the principles of what would become Wicca from a coven of witches in the New Forest, who practised the same ancient witchcraft religion as the Pendle witches – a tradition, stretching back unbroken since pre-Christian times, which had been continuing to operate in the shadows since the suppression of the witch trials. This was in keeping with the theories of various academics, most prominently British Egyptologist and folklorist Margaret Murray, whose 1921 book *The Witch-Cult in Western Europe* did much to popularise the idea. This theory – known as the witch-cult hypothesis – has since been discredited, however, with the consensus now being that there was no continuous British witchcraft cult, and that even the Pendle witches and their contemporaries were isolated practitioners rather than members of an organised religion. This probably means that Gardner either invented the New Forest coven, or that they really existed but had themselves only been formed in the early twentieth century, in response to the witch-cult theories, and as an attempt to revive or take part in an ancient witchcraft tradition.

Today, Wicca is an umbrella term encompassing diverse modern witchcraft traditions, with Gardnerian Wiccans possibly representing the closest thing to an orthodoxy, following most closely the original precepts and practices laid out by Gardner and his acolytes in the 1940s and '50s. Even for these relative traditionalists, though, Wicca is defined by syncretism and eclecticism. There are two major deities: a Triple Goddess, split into the aspects of the Mother, the Maiden and the Crone; and a male Horned God, whose death and resurrection are plotted throughout the annual cycle known as the Wheel of the Year.

Many Wiccans, though, freely choose deities to worship from various pantheons, with the Norse and Greco-Roman gods particularly popular. Karen had told me about a coastal ceremony she had recently attended, honouring both the Wiccan Triple Goddess and Poseidon, Greek god of the seas. At first, this brazen cherry-picking from different religions can seem slightly maddening. But I've come to admire it. They are only being open about the same process of co-option and adaptation which propels the evolution of all religious traditions.

Wicca is a mystery religion, based on secret initiation rites, the details of which Karen and Sandra steadfastly refused to reveal to me. Karen must have seen me eyeing up the ceremonial blade (known as an athame) lying on the altar, though, quick as she was to reassure me: 'There's no spilling of blood involved. My deities aren't interested in that. And even if they were, it would only be my own they'd want, not anyone else's.'

Sandra gathered us on the sofas and explained in a little more detail about what tonight's ritual would entail. 'We're going to form a circle outside around the firepit, and then, one by one, Death, represented by the figure of the Hag, will come and tap you on the shoulder, and lead you into the temple. There you'll meet the Dark Lord – that's my husband, John' – John gave a cheery wave and a 'Hello!' from the corner of the room – 'whom you can greet as you wish: by bowing or just standing before him. Everyone does it differently. The main thing is to concentrate on the people you've lost, who you might like to commune with. Samhain is about remembering and getting in touch with our ancestors.'

Samhain is spoken of as the time of year when the borderline between the natural and the supernatural is blurred, spirits and fairies roam our earthly realm, and the souls of the dead revisit their former homes. Karen told me about the Samhain practice of a dumb supper, where a black table is laid with black plates and lit with black candles, with a place set aside for a recently deceased loved one. Food is eaten in silence, in order to better tune in to the occasion and commune with the attendant spirit. Here in northern England, as a further example of how pagan and Christian traditions appropriate from and fold back into one another, a common feature at a dumb supper is the soul cake, a shortbread-like biscuit which was introduced into Christian celebrations of All Souls' Day in the Middle Ages to commemorate the dead. Dishes are also often served backwards, beginning with dessert and ending with the starter, as a reflection of the concept of the Otherworld as a mirror image of our own, separated by a veil. There again is Bakhtin's description of the carnivalesque – 'the world upside down'. Karen doesn't like dump suppers, though, she told me. 'I can't keep quiet for that long!'

Experiencing the dead after they are gone seems to be a cross-cultural phenomenon. Many people could swear they had fleetingly locked eyes with a lost friend on a busy train platform or felt a grandparent's comforting hand on their shoulder during a time of quiet crisis. The Hopi people of the southwestern United States experience 'mourning hallucinations', wherein they report direct experience of the recently deceased; I dream often about my father, allowing me to recalibrate my memories of him, back to how he was before he was ill.

Connection with our ancestors is universal, but as ever, the ways in which perennial truths are expressed in the festival mode vary colourfully across the world.

The Malagasy people of Madagascar engage in a jolly rite known as *famadihana* ('the turning of the bones'), which sees corpses disinterred every few years, wrapped in straw mats and then given new burial shrouds, while their descendants dance around them. In the mountains of northern Thailand, spirit mediums whip themselves into a trance, carry the spirits of the ancestors on their shoulders, and dance with members of the family and wider community in a practice known as *faun phi* – Spirit Dance.

As striking as the differences, though, are the similarities. The parallels between Halloween and Mexico's Día de los Muertos – the playfulness with images of skeletons and death, the fixation on sweet treats, and so on – are, as discussed earlier in the book, likely superficial, and can probably be explained by the influence of colonial Christianity. A more salient similarity is the shared element of offering. In Mexico, gifts of *pan dulce* (sweet bread), pulque, sugar skulls and other treats are laid for the ancestors at graves and home altars. The trick-or-treating of modern Halloween (also practised in Mexico) has its origins in 'souling', the practice of going door-to-door to beg for soul cakes and other foods, these offerings said to appease the spirits of the wandering dead.

It is probably no coincidence that many festivals of the dead occur at the same time of year, between late August and early November – this often marks a time of harvest, even in places where it does not herald the beginning of winter or a darker time of year.

This is true across Asia, where ancestor worship is the focus of several events throughout the calendar, the height of activity being Ghost Month, the seventh lunar month of the year, and in particular the Ghost Festival, held on the fifteenth day of that month. This is a cognate of Samhain and Halloween – a time when the realms of heaven and hell are opened, and the spirits therein are able to roam the earth (it also coincides, similarly to Samhain and Halloween, with the autumn harvest).

Many people believe this to have real-world consequences, which they take very seriously. It is deemed terrible luck, for instance, to undergo surgery, buy a house, get married, or risk confronting any other major life event during Ghost Month, in case the wandering spirits see fit to interfere. This has tangible consequences for, among other things, the property market, with house prices tending to slump during Ghost Month even in Singapore, the kind of place where you wouldn't expect superstition to get in the way of good business. Perhaps this shouldn't be a surprise, though; a common observance at the Ghost Festival is the burning of 'hell money' – votive joss paper in the form of fake banknotes, believed to alleviate the financial concerns encountered by the dead in the afterlife.

This time of year is when festivals of liminality burn at their brightest. In Wales, 31 October was traditionally known as Ysbrydnos (Spirit Night), believed to be a time when spirits and ghosts ran free. Revellers would dance around a bonfire, being sure to hasten home before the embers died out, lest they be eaten by fearsome ghouls: a tailless black sow and a headless white lady. People would avoid crossroads, graveyards, gates and stiles at this time of year – liminal points, places of the threshold – because it was here that spirits were believed to gather.

The carnivalesque suspension of society's normal rules is also in evidence at this time of year. At no other point in the calendar is a blind eye turned so readily to the indiscriminate toilet papering of trees, egging of houses, and other such rapscallionism. In the foul swamp in which I was reared – the rural south-west England of the 1990s – such larks were confined to the wheelhouse of trick-or-treaters and limited to Halloween night itself. Often, however, it has been 30 October, the night before Halloween, when individuals across the Western world have felt emboldened to engage in transgressive acts ranging from light-hearted practical jokery to enthusiastically mindless violence.

Residents on the Canadian side of Niagara Falls know this occasion as 'Cabbage Night', named for the practice of scrumping rotten cabbages from neighbourhood gardens and delightedly hurling them through the night in a community-wide brassica fight. Across the border in Quebec, the tradition of stealing door mats led to 30 October being known as 'Mat Night', while down in Detroit the more ominously named 'Devil's Night' came to be associated in the late twentieth century with increasingly serious incidents of arson and violence. Increased policing and the introduction of community outreach programmes had the effect of diminishing these incidents around Halloween; Detroit's arsonists subsequently decided to save their energies for 4 July instead, which saw a corresponding increase in crime.

For four years between 2014 and 2018, so-called Mischief Night in New Orleans (also held on 30 October) turned political, with organised parades of activists voicing their discontent around issues like police brutality, racism, and controversial building projects like the Bayou Bridge crude oil pipeline. The spirit was one of wilfully violent protest. A report by anarchist website *It's Going Down* quoted participants boasting about their extreme brand of vigilante justice, which included brandishing bottles at police for trying to arrest people, and setting fire to a car whose driver was deemed to be driving recklessly. 'There's always been a push and pull between popular ways of celebrating and ways that established powers would like us to party and parade,' said one interviewee. 'Our Carnival traditions are those that actually want to "turn the world upside down".'[64] Whether you agree with their methods or not, these were not mindless thugs; they were thugs well versed in the meaning and power of the carnivalesque.

Here in Lancashire, 30 October is also known as Mischief Night. The timing has changed over the centuries, but the gist remains the same: an evening of carnivalesque abandonment of the status quo, when people are allowed to get away with things they normally would not. Back in 1897, Mischief Night was celebrated on the other side of the Wheel of the Year, on the night before May Day. According to a contemporary compendium of folk traditions:

> The evening before May Day is termed Mischief Night by the young people of Burnley and the surrounding district. All kinds of mischief are then perpetrated. Formerly shopkeepers' signboards were exchanged; 'John Smith, grocer' finding his name and vocation changed by the sign over his door to 'Thomas Jones, tailor' and vice versa; but the police have put an end to these practical jokes. Young men and women, however, still continue to play each other tricks, by placing branches of trees shrubs or flowers under each other's windows, or before their doors. All these have a symbolical meaning … Thus 'a thorn' implies 'scorn',

---

64. It's Going Down, 'New Orleans Mischief Night: An Interview with Revelers'.

'wicken' (the mountain ash) 'my dear chicken', a 'bramble' for one who likes to 'ramble', &c. Much ill feeling is at times engendered by this custom.[65]

All pretty tame, then. The modern-day inhabitants of north-west England, by contrast, take craven criminality to new heights each Mischief Night, to the extent that the *Liverpool Echo* was compelled in 2023 to describe it as 'perhaps the most dreaded night on the calendar for families across Merseyside'. 'Mizzy Night', as it is known locally, sees a yearly upsurge in vandalism and violent crime, with windows bricked through, emergency workers attacked, and wheelie bins set ablaze. The damage was so bad in 2019 that it compelled then-mayor Joe Anderson to publicly decry the 'feral kids' who he claimed were behind the damage. Perhaps, I would put to him, there were other forces at play – the impish sprites of the festival world, pulling the perpetrators' strings through that night's thin veil. Ultimately, though, Mayor Anderson chose to blame the parents.

The commenters on a 2023 online *Liverpool Echo* article entitled 'Should Mischief Night be banned?' were not so sympathetic. 'I shall have bleach in water guns waiting for the first rat to try annoy our street [smiley face emoji shrouded by love hearts],' read a comment from one user with the pen name 'Stop being nasty'. Someone else had made a more insightful point: 'Maybe if it [Mischief Night] hadn't ... been given a name in the first place,' they wrote, 'then the youth of today wouldn't think it was the

---

65. *Lancashire Folklore*, compiled and edited by John Harland and TT Wilkinson.

norm to do it.'[66] This latter observation betrays an insight not normally associated with online comment sections – it illustrates the power, for better or worse, bestowed by giving a festival a name. The moniker 'Mischief Night' codifies and legitimises the mischief, and the more sinister behaviours carried out under its guise.

Perhaps, though, festivals like this serve a purpose. Samhain is a hole in the veil between two worlds, through which the Otherfolk squeeze out of their shadow realm and into our land of the light. That they are able to do so for one night only ensures our safety for the rest of the year. Halloween, similarly, is a tear in the Christian calendar through which sprites, ghouls and goblins are allowed to stick their claws for a limited period of time – perhaps a concession on the part of the Church to allow people to get their pagan proclivities out of their systems for the rest of the year. Maybe the same logic is at play in the tolerance of Mischief Night, trick-or-treating, and other such behaviour, usually considered transgressive but socially accepted on this one night of the year. It acts like a pressure valve, allowing people to cut loose in the hope they will be more likely to behave themselves the rest of the time.

Similar forces are certainly at play at Venice Carnival, at Up Helly Aa, and during the climactic violence of the Romería de El Rocío. They also explain why the police turn a blind eye to behaviours like open drug taking at music festivals, and why the authorities suspend their persecution of Romani people for the duration of the Pèlerinage Gitan. This phenomenon – festival as pressure

---

66. *Liverpool Echo*, 'Should Mischief Night be Banned?' by Remy Greasle.

valve – can also be observed in Japan each summer. I first learned about the Abare Festival from a guide at a museum on the remote Noto Peninsula, who was showing me a collection of magnificent ceremonial paper lanterns. They were beautiful – 40 feet tall, with pine-wood frames stretching windows of rice paper on which were rendered colourful scenes from Japanese mythology. These lanterns are painstakingly assembled throughout the year, with the exquisite blend of craft and artistry which characterises so much of Japanese culture – only to be enthusiastically ripped to shreds during the first weekend of July. 'It's kind of a … how would you say it? A violence festival,' the guide explained with an apologetic smile.

Also known as the Fire & Violence Festival and literally translating as 'Rampage Festival', this event turns the usually unassuming town of Ushitsu into an arena of chaos. A parade of twelve topless local men carry the paper lanterns to the town pier. Already well sozzled on sake before they begin, they have yet more booze poured into their mouths by onlookers throughout their procession, during which it is incumbent upon the lantern-bearers to inflict as much damage on their cargo as possible, smashing the lanterns against walls, lampposts, and the road beneath their feet before the remains are eventually burnt on huge bonfires at the pier. The charred and battered lanterns are then taken into the town's main shrine, where they are blessed by priests. The violence at this festival is considered an act of prayer, dedicated, as is the whole event, to the destructive deity Susanoo.

And this in Japan – a place stereotyped for its politeness, where saving face is paramount and a public outburst is a shameful act. Exactly the kind of place, perhaps, which needs festivals like this the most.

'It sometimes happens nowadays,' wrote Friedrich Nietzsche, 'that a gentle, sober, retiring man becomes suddenly mad, smashes plates, upturns the table, shrieks, raves, insults the whole world …'[67]

And well he might. We all must, once in a while.

On the table in the middle of the room was a large bag of dried herbs. Karen picked it up and carried it into the kitchen, emerging a few minutes later with a tray of small paper cups, filled with a yellow-brown tea. 'It's mugwort,' she explained to me. 'It's very mild – it just helps some people see and feel things a bit better.'

'We promise it's not Kool-Aid!' someone piped up to a smattering of laughter, having sensed my hesitancy. It was too late for me now anyway, I thought – in for a penny, in for a pound, and I knocked it back. It tasted earthy and sweet.

We stepped back outside and stood in a circle around a smouldering firepit. Mist wreathed a gibbous moon. Dry leaves were passed around with a Sharpie, with people invited to write the names of dead loved ones on them and let them be either carried off by the wind or consumed by the fire. A symbol of letting go, Karen explained.

Soon we would be entering the temple, but not before a number of important ritual objects were located. An assistant came out of the shed looking flustered, saying to Sandra in a low and panicked voice, 'I can't find the stones and coins!'

---

67. Friedrich Nietzsche, *Beyond Good and Evil*

'By the cauldron – in the owl bag!' Sandra hissed back, before heading inside to help find them.

One or two of the group began chanting – wordless one-note drones at first, which then morphed into Samhain songs, with a cadence like nursery rhymes. 'Samhain, Samhain, let the ritual begin / We call upon our sacred ancestors to come in,' went one. 'Oh, blessed are we, the Taker of Souls we shall see / On Samhain Eve,' sang another. Then came silence.

'I can't remember any more,' said someone nervously.

'We could do "Summer is a-Comin' In",' someone else suggested.

'We *cannot* do "Summer is a-Comin' In",' admonished Karen. 'That's a Beltane song.'

'I just thought we could change it to "Winter is a-Comin' In",' came the timid reply.

There was a rustling at the temple door. A hunched figure emerged and started shuffling towards the group – the Hag! I hadn't been sure what to expect, but was still slightly thrown to see that 'the Hag' was in fact Sandra, wearing a velvet cape and a Halloween mask which would have been rejected by the costume department of *The Witches* for being too on the nose.

There was no way of knowing who the Hag would choose first, Sandra had warned us, just as there is no way to predict when Death will step in to shuffle us off this mortal coil. But in this instance, the Hag seemed to choose people in order of who was standing closest to the temple door, which was not only efficient but also had the added health and safety benefit of making sure she didn't have to sweep her velvet cape over the firepit.

As she hobbled up to each person, the Hag sniffed around their shoulders. 'She's smelling their proximity to death,' whispered Karen. When the Hag had made her mind up, she took her chosen person by the hand, clasping between her fingers and theirs a glowing blue artefact, which separated like a starfish into many limbs.

'What's that she's holding?' I asked Karen.

'You'll just have to wait and see,' she replied, in the same annoyingly enigmatic way she had been speaking earlier.

The Hag came for my companions one by one, until I was the only one left, trying to will myself warm from the dying embers of the fire and wondering what they were all doing in there without me. Preparing a sacrificial altar? Raising the wicker man?

My dark fantasy was shattered by that familiar shuffling of the Hag outside the temple door – it was my turn. She approached me, sniffing around my shoulders. I avoided contact with her rubber mask's googly eyes, which stared dementedly like those of an aye-aye at some indeterminate point above my head. I shuddered as the warty rubber nose brushed against my neck. She lifted her hand to mine. The bright blue 'starfish' I had seen earlier was in fact a glow-in-the-dark ice pack in the shape of a hand – a rather literal representation of the 'cold hand of Death'. I had wondered what John had been referring to earlier when I heard him reminding Sandra to 'get the things out of the freezer'.

I won't lie: it felt silly. But it also helped put me at ease, which may have been the point – Karen later told me that things get a lot more serious at events confined to their coven, when outsiders aren't present. I lifted a black lace veil to enter the temple, into a fog of incense smoke and a chorus of wordless chanting. A stone was pressed into my right hand. In the centre of the room, in front of the altar, stood the Dark Lord (John), his grey fleece covered by a black cape and his balding head shrouded by a black horned helmet. I placed my stone in the basket at his feet, and he replaced it in my hand with a small coin. The coin is analogous to the obol in Greek mythology, given by Charon the ferryman to visitors who cross the River Styx into Hades. In this understanding, the Dark Lord is a psychopomp – one who guides souls to the Underworld. For the ancient Egyptians, this role was taken up by the jackal-headed god Anubis; for the Norse, by the Valkyries, who guide the dead to Valhalla.

Two of the other people taking part in the ceremony had recently lost loved ones. They were crying and softly rocking at the side of the room, clearly deeply moved by an experience of connection with those who had passed on. I was grieving, too, but I neglected the chance to properly engage with the ritual, refusing to think, as I had been invited to do, of individual people I had lost while I was standing before the Dark Lord. The way I justified this to myself at the time was that this wasn't my religion, I was here to observe, it would be unprofessional or disrespectful in some way to pretend to be a real participant. Deep down, though, I didn't allow myself to engage with it for fear that there was something in it – that dalliances with Dark Lords and portals to the Underworld could have grave metaphysical consequences for me or, worse, for the souls of my loved ones themselves. Particularly if, as was likely, I did something wrong – dropped my stone, lost my coin, stepped on the Dark Lord (John)'s cape, or similar.

So, when my turn came, I just stared at the Dark Lord's feet and thought instead about how I'd embarrassed myself with the Halloween pumpkin cakes. Eventually, I raised my eyes towards Karen, who gave me an encouraging nod which I took as my cue to sit down.

Virtually as soon as I did, the Dark Lord removed his helmet and cape and then he was just John again, standing there in his bare feet and his Boden fleece. The others began filing out of the door. The ritual was over. Curry time.

'Remember to hold onto your coins,' said Sandra, 'or you'll get trapped in my shed!' It struck me that Sandra's shed was a kind of limbo: a place in between; an arena of liminality. ('Limbo' and 'liminal' have similar roots: the Latin words limbus (hem, border) and limen (threshold).) The shed suddenly appeared to me like the Black Lodge in *Twin Peaks*: an extra-dimensional place, peopled with strange characters – dwellers on the threshold – which acts as a portal to a world beyond. Such special spaces hold great significance in the festival world: holies of holies, places where the magic happens, into which only certain participants can encroach, and only at certain times. I thought of the rogue masong in Phuket, swinging enragedly with a stick at the schoolchildren who had trespassed onto the firewalking arena; I thought of the Baby Tree in Sulawesi, sagging with huge breadfruit, its insides nourished by infant bodies.

The specific role played tonight by the shed – that of portal to the Underworld – has many analogues in cultural traditions around the world. The slopes of Ming Mountain in the Chinese municipality of Chongqing, for instance, are home to Fengdu Ghost City, a centuries-old complex of temples, shrines and monasteries combining elements of Taoism, Buddhism and Confucianism, their walls covered in frescoes depicting people being tortured in baroque and imaginative ways for their various earthly sins. The third day of each third lunar month sees the Ghost Town Temple Fair, when a mock sacrifice is carried out by the king and queen of the Underworld. Nowadays, not unlike my Samhain ritual experience, costumed actors depicting Underworld deities meet tourists arriving at the complex and lead them across the threshold with some ceremony. (Choice advice from the Chongqing Tourism website: 'Do not hit the actors or actresses even if you are frightened.')

Many liminal ceremonies are held in a special place, set apart for the purpose. R. Gordon Wasson wrote of his magic mushroom experience taking place in a 'thatched hut, some distance away from the village'. Victor Turner, meanwhile, wrote of the Ndembu people of the Congo constructing special huts for the purpose of rituals involving liminality: 'This hut is known as kafu or kafwi, a term Ndembu derive from ku-fwa, "to die," for it is here that the chief-elect dies from his commoner state,' he wrote in *Liminality and Communitas*.

Like the Ndembu chief-elect, like the mushroom eaters of Mexico, and like the whirling dervishes during their sema, John underwent a kind of identity death when he entered the shed to assume the guise of the Dark Lord. Masking and costumery, as they do at so many festivals, had allowed him to travel into another identity. John had assumed a slightly frightening aspect during the ceremony, but now, as he plated me up some chicken bhuna and Bombay potatoes, he couldn't have been more convivial.

We sat down with our food and I asked John what it was that had drawn him to Paganism. Like Karen and Sandra, he's a Gardnerian Wiccan, and has been practising for around twenty years. 'For me, it's about connection,' he said. 'With the seasons, with nature, and with other people.' This last point is key to differentiating the power of religious festivals, such as Samhain, from private, solitary practice. 'Time is the most precious gift you can give,' he said. 'So, the very act of deciding to set time aside to spend with other people in any kind of shared experience – that's a powerful thing.'

For John, festivals like Samhain also serve another profound purpose: allowing us to confront and become comfortable with the dark side of life. 'The dark is not a place to be afraid of. In fact, it's somewhere we need, a place to retreat to from the glare when life's moving at 100 miles per hour,' he said. 'There's no experience of light without darkness – that's the whole idea of the Wheel of the Year, of grounding ourselves in the changing seasons.'

My affectionate ribbing in this chapter of the more cartoonish elements of that night's ceremony may well be a defence mechanism, aimed at softening the scarier aspects of a ritual involving travels to the Underworld and meetings with a Dark Lord. I'm not a Wiccan or a member of any other religion, so it would have been logical for me to have approached the ritual completely coldly, secure in the knowledge that it was all a load of claptrap. But that's not what I felt at all. While I wouldn't say I bought into it, I can tell you that I clutched my coin as if my life depended on it, keen to avoid even the admittedly remote possibility of an eternity spent wandering adrift in the Underworld (or, indeed, Sandra's shed). Many of us have these feelings more often than we would care to admit. It's the same reason I have never dabbled with a Ouija board; I don't believe in ghosts, but I'm afraid of them all the same. My fears were not based in rational thought, but in feeling. Once again, I had been swept along by a festival's ocean of meaning.

For the first time since leaving the darkness of the temple, I took the coin out of my pocket and looked at it. It wasn't one I'd seen before – it was shaped like a modern British pound coin, but was revealed on closer inspection to be a 3-pence piece from 1954. I offered it back to John, who raised a palm in refusal.

'Keep it,' he said. 'One day you might be going through a dark period, and you'll come across it. It will remind you that we all go to the Underworld, but then we come back. Back to the light.'

ACKNOWLEDGEMENTS

First and foremost, my thanks go out to all those people who welcomed me into their festival worlds while I was researching this book. A handful of them are named in these pages, but many more are not; of those, I would particularly like to thank Viveka Velupillai, Hélène Salvadori, Agustín Morilla, and Dr Josh De Giorgio. Elsewhere, I'd like to thank Lucie Grace and Professor Alan Williams for their invaluable introductions, Shafik Meghji for his guidance and encouragement, and my editors, in particular Andy Turner, Ellie Cobb, Amanda Canning and Lorna Parkes. Huge thanks also go out to my agent, Tom Cull, and the team at Icon Books for giving me such a welcoming and supportive home as a first-time author. Most of all, I would like to thank my family and my friends – who know who they are.